Praise for t

FROM MILWAUKEE

"When the wanderlust strikes, this comprehensive guide is just the tool Milwaukee-area travelers need to happily head out for the day with confidence. Touring, shopping, sampling local chow—*Day Trips® from Milwaukee* is a perfect pleasure-trip planner. Just don't forget to come home!"

—Kathy Buenger, editor, *Northshore Lifestyle*

"From the small village to the large city, this book offers a variety of trips to satisfy any 'adventurer.'"

—Judy Jepson, editor, *Exclusively Yours* magazine

Help Us Keep This Guide Up to Date

Every effort has been made by the authors and editors to make this guide as accurate and useful as possible. Many things, however, can change after a guide is published—establishments close, phone numbers change, facilities come under new management, etc.

We would love to hear from you concerning your experiences with this guide and how you feel it could be made better and be kept up to date. While we may not be able to respond to all comments and suggestions, we'll take them to heart and we'll make certain to share them with the authors. Please send your comments and suggestions to the following address:

The Globe Pequot Press
Reader Response/Editorial Department
P.O. Box 480
Guilford, CT 06437

Or you may e-mail us at:
editorial@globe-pequot.com

Thanks for your input, and happy travels!

Day Trips® Series

GETAWAYS LESS THAN TWO HOURS AWAY

DAY TRIPS®
FROM MILWAUKEE

Second Edition

Martin Hintz
and
Daniel Hintz

The Globe Pequot Press

GUILFORD, CONNECTICUT

Day Trips is a registered trademark.
Maps by William L. Nelson and M. A. Dubé

ISBN 0-7627-2490-0
ISSN 1541-8960

Manufactured in the United States of America
Second edition/First printing

 **To all the travelers**

Contents

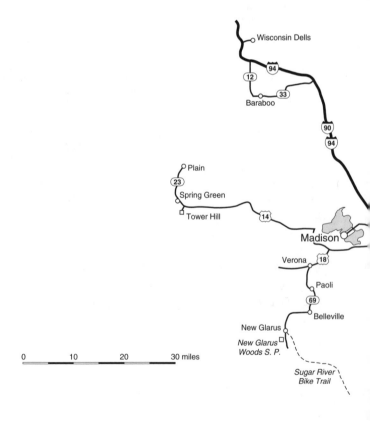

Wisconsin Dells

94

12

33

Baraboo

90

94

Plain

23

Spring Green

Tower Hill

14

Madison

Verona 18

Paoli

69

Belleville

New Glarus

New Glarus
Woods S. P.

Sugar River
Bike Trail

0   10   20   30 miles

ACKNOWLEDGMENTS

The authors wish to thank all those who contributed their thoughts, suggestions, and tips for this book: the travel professionals, friends, folks on the street, the butchers, bakers, and candlestick makers who ensure that road trips around Wisconsin are really something special. And special thanks to Simona Aldressi and Cynthia Tomik for their assistance.

INTRODUCTION

Lakes and loons, ballet and baseball, state parks and pretty nice folks. That's Wisconsin in a traveler's nutshell.

Milwaukee may be tucked into the far southeastern corner of Wisconsin. But it has easy access to all of the above . . . and more. The state's largest city is within a hop and a jump to a plethora of communities offering fantastic attractions, galleries, museums, river walkways, fishing, great restaurants, and festivals of all kinds. And let's not forget the comfortable pillows awaiting the tired traveler at the end of a day of exploring.

Day-trippers have a wealth of hidden and not-so-hidden getaways that are within a two-hour drive from downtown Milwaukee. This book provides a peek at a few favorite locales we've discovered and explored over the years. Each trip offers a special something for every type of traveler. The prize might be seeing the fabulous architecture of Frank Lloyd Wright in Spring Green or observing the annual migration of thousands of honking Canada geese to Horicon Marsh. Several of these excursions are as fun as touring the world. You can visit Belgium, sail across Lake Geneva, and watch that Swiss fella from New Glarus shoot an apple off his son's head.

Even the time traveler has fun. Take part in a temperance rally or speak your opinions at a town hall meeting in Old World Wisconsin, a state historical site that showcases nineteenth-century rural life. Thrill to fifes and drums prior to a battle reenactment around the Wade House, a former stagecoach stop and marshaling center for Civil War troops. Then move ahead to contemporary Wisconsin. Go stargazing at the Elkhart Lake auto races; maybe actor Paul Newman will stroll past on the way to his super-powered formula car. Then day-trip to Madison to spot politicians flocking around the State Capitol before meandering down nearby State Street to the University of Wisconsin campus.

You don't want to rush on any of these adventures. Part of the fun is keeping an open schedule and exploring a site in all its rich detail. And we encourage you to get out of your car and walk around a bit. This not only enhances circulation but also allows you to experience firsthand all the fun and excitement we've experienced in several decades of poking around the Badger State. To expand on what we've provided in this book, ask the locals what else there is to see and do in their town. Wisconsinites are proud to show off what they have in their own backyards, both literally and figuratively. Maybe you'll find a hidden rock garden or a neat coffeehouse down the street. You'll most certainly discover many new things on your own.

Of course, we'd be lax if we didn't point the way to great grub. Really, there's plenty for every taste. Wisconsin hasn't earned the title as the Dairy State for nothin', after all. So drop by Babcock Hall, part of the ag science department at the University of Wisconsin, for freshly made ice cream. It's got a butterfat content soaring somewhere in the zillionth percentile. You can munch bratwurst at the Sheboygan Brat Fest, sip a rare vintage in Fond du Lac, sample something superbly fishy at a dockside restaurant in Port Washington, and satisfy a sweet tooth at the Honey of Museum in Ashippun.

You certainly don't need to be quiet on a day trip out of Milwaukee. In fact, we encourage you to let loose by cheering for the Packers at Green Bay's Lambeau Field or oooohing and aaahing at the antics of water-skiers on Janesville's Rock River. After all, a good day-trip experience involves all the senses.

Whether you tumble back to Milwaukee after a full day of exploration or decide to spend the evening at a quiet, comfortable bed-and-breakfast or historic hotel, Wisconsin has more than enough to fill a great weekend or midweek getaway. Heck, if you don't see it all on one trip, that means you'll simply have to take another jaunt!

Additional information on travel attractions around Wisconsin can be obtained from the Wisconsin Division of Tourism, 201 West Washington Avenue, Box 7976, Madison, WI 53707; (608) 266–2161 or (800) 432–8747. The Web site is www.travelwisconsin.com.

Order free travel guides from the division to round out your day-trip getaway files. Among the publications are the *Official Wisconsin Travel Guide, Wisconsin Adventure Vacations, Wisconsin Heritage Traveler, Wisconsin Lodging Directory, Wisconsin Bed & Breakfast Directory, Wisconsin Multi-Cultural Guides, Native Wisconsin, Wisconsin State Parks Visitors' Guide, Wisconsin Snowmobile Guide & Trails Map,* and *Wisconsin Attractions Guide and Highway Map.*

We'll see you on the road.

USING THIS BOOK

Restaurants: Restaurant prices are designated as $$$ (Expensive: $15.00 and more per person), $$ (Moderate: $5.00 to $15.00 per person), or $ (Inexpensive: $5.00 and less per person).

Accommodations: Designated $$$ (Expensive: $100 and more per night), $$ (Moderate: $50 to $100 per night), or $ (Inexpensive: $50 and less per night). Rates often change seasonally, so call first to confirm prices.

Credit Cards: Designated ☐ for restaurants and lodging; there won't be such a marker if the establishment does not take credit cards.

Highways: Designated I for interstates, U.S. for federal highways, and the number for state routes. County roads are designated as such.

Hours: Hours are listed where available, but remember that times do change. Phone numbers are provided so you can call ahead.

The prices and rates listed in this guidebook were set as of press time. It is wise, however, to call restaurants, stores, attractions, and lodging establishments to ensure you have the most up-to-date information.

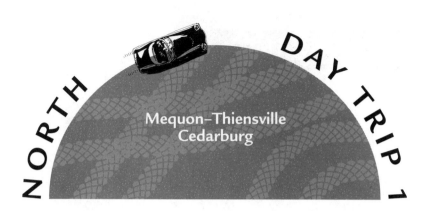

Large, oak-shaded homes and vast, landscaped lawns—with all the appropriate bayberry and rosebush adornment—generally mark this area, which is barely a twenty-minute drive north of downtown Milwaukee via I-43. Out here you certainly know you are in the other-worldly 'burbs. Even some birdbaths appear to be Olympicsize whirlpool hot tubs, complete with verandas.

Preferring to skip the rush of the interstate, you can also take any of a number of surface streets and country trunk routes into the city's near-northern hinterland. State highways 181, 57, and 167 are other major routes through the region. Subsequently, this part of Ozaukee County is easy to reach for the avid day-tripper seeking new adventures. The proximity of Mequon-Thiensville and Cedarburg makes it a logical choice for a first stop on a leisurely drive north of Milwaukee.

Of course, if you travel too far to the east, bring flippers. The rolling, green waters of Lake Michigan lap against Mequon's cliff-side eastern border.

MEQUON-THIENSVILLE

The Mequon town name comes from an Ojibway word, *Miguan*, meaning "ladle." Apparently, a bend here in the Milwaukee River resembled this useful tool. The land was first plotted in 1833 for G. South Hubbard, who later built the Range Line Inn on his

North Day Trip 1

property. The long, low building is still a popular dining spot. Religious dissidents from Pomerania and East Prussia made up the bulk of the area's original farming community, drawn by the fish-rich river and the area's amazingly fertile soil. The town of Mequon was part of Washington County until 1853, when county boundaries were readjusted and it was incorporated into Ozaukee County.

A flour mill was constructed in 1842, becoming the center of the growing community of Mequon, which was classified as a city by 1957. At 48 square miles, it is now Wisconsin's fourth-largest city in land area. The vicinity around the old mill eventually came to be called Thiensville, which was incorporated as a 1-mile-square village in 1910. Mequon now surrounds Thiensville, with their boundaries virtually indistinguishable, as suburban sprawl gobbles up what's left of the once pastoral scenery. Despite the malls, gas stations, and fast-food outlets along the main thoroughfares such as Port Washington and Mequon Roads just off I-45, there remains plenty to see and do in the area. Several produce farms survive, with their roadside stands overflowing with fresh vegetables and fruit in summer and autumn. Look for them on the western edge of Thiensville, especially in the vicinity of State Highway 60 and side roads such as Ozaukee County Highway Y, Pioneer Road, and the rustic Hawthorne Road. But look fast. Multilevel homes are springing up here faster than mushrooms after a rain, edging out the pumpkin patches and cabbage plots.

The area sports three private country clubs and one public golf course and fifteen parks and nature preserves. It is also home to Concordia University (theater office, 262-243-4444), Milwaukee Area Technical College/North Campus (262-238-2200), and the Wisconsin Lutheran Seminary (262-242-8100), with their attendant cultural and sports activities.

WHERE TO GO

Pommerntag. Mequon City Park, 11333 North Cedarburg Road, Mequon. Usually held on the last Sunday in June, this outdoor German festival hearkens back to the days when German farmers used to bring their vegetables into the villages for sale. Brass bands, ethnic food, cultural and genealogy displays, and dancing make for loads of fun. Free admission and free parking. For details contact the *Pommerscher Verin Freistadt,* a local German-American club, in nearby Germantown; (262) 376-7641 or (262) 242-0653. Try the Web site at www.execpc.com/~pommern.

Family Fun before the Fourth. Main Street, Thiensville. Parades, fireworks, and a street festival highlight the activities traditionally held on the Saturday before the Fourth of July. Much of the fun spills over into Thiensville Park, which nestles on the banks of the Milwaukee River. Call the chamber of commerce, (262) 512-9358.

Interurban Railroad. Hike or bike this stretch of reclaimed railroad right-of-way between County Line Road (just west of State Highway 57) to Highland Road, on the southern perimeter of the Mee-Kwon Park Golf Course. The trail roughly parallels Cedarburg Road, for a quiet getaway in rural suburbia. The trail is only about a fifteen-minute drive from downtown Milwaukee. Ozaukee County has other bike routes, as well, that make for good riding. Contact the Mequon-Thiensville Chamber of Commerce for a map (262-512-9358) or write 250 South Main Street, Mequon, WI 53092.

WHERE TO EAT

Howard's Pub & Grille. 5208 West County Line Road, Mequon (½ mile west of Green Bay Road/State Highway 57). "Eat In" or "Carry Out." Those are watchwords at Howard's, which offers a broad range of daily lunch and dinner specials, plus a good fish fry. Lunch hours are 11:00 A.M. to 2:00 P.M. Monday through Thursday and until 2:30 P.M. on Friday; dinners run from 5:00 to 10:00 P.M. Monday through Thursday and until 10:30 P.M. Friday through Sunday. Call (262) 238-9881. $$; ☐

Range Line Inn. 2635 West Mequon Road, Mequon. While the area around the inn has been surrounded by subdivisions for years, its cozy comfort carries diners back generations to the era when this was a stagecoach stop. Great for steaks. Hours vary, so call (262) 242-0530. $$$; ☐

WHERE TO STAY

American Country Farm. 11211 North Wauwatosa Road, Mequon. The stone cottage, now a bed-and-breakfast, was built in 1844. It overlooks an overgrown apple orchard where deer like to browse. The building has a private patio, with a choice of twin beds or a king-size bed. Fireplace, kitchen, and bathroom with a shower are part of the layout. Continental breakfast provided. Call (262) 242-0194. $$; ☐

Chalet Motel. 10401 North Port Washington Road, Mequon. Proprietors Lindsay Walsh and Bob Briese run a clean, comfortable motel, regularly used by out-of-town guests coming to weddings and other family functions. Call (262) 241-5542 or (800) 343-4510. $; ☐

Sybaris Pool Suites. 10240 North Cedarburg Road, Mequon. For a romantic spot to take your main squeeze, the Sybaris pulls out all the candlelight stops. Be ready to snuggle. It's only minutes from home! Call (262) 242-8000 or check its Web site at www.sybaris.com. $$; ☐

CEDARBURG

The economic potential of Cedar Creek drew the first settlers to this settlement about a twenty-minute drive north of Milwaukee. Of course in the 1840s, it took a couple of hours by horse and wagon to traverse that distance. But today, as it was then, a trip to Cedarburg is a great day in the country and a fine getaway for Milwaukee folks. In the old days visitors picnicked and played ball games along the banks of the smoothly flowing creek, a picturesque stream that eventually runs into the muscular Milwaukee River. Several user-friendly parks in Cedarburg still attract day-trippers from the Big City. Now picnic baskets are usually packed with Brie, white grapes, and fine wine rather than the beer, blood sausage, and pickled pigs' feet of the late 1800s and early 1900s.

German and Irish pioneers carved out their homesteads from the surrounding forests and built five dams along the creek to service several gristmills they also constructed. Although the village's main street, Washington Avenue, was then only a dirt track, merchants and traders from Milwaukee regularly called on the Cedarburg mills to order products. When the first railroad came to town in 1870, Cedarburg subsequently prospered. Two nearby quarries provided quality Niagara limestone for the grand houses that eventually replaced the first log cabins and many of the early frame homes. The stone was augmented by lovely cream city brick. As a result, the town is one that certainly will not easily be blown away. A *Walk Through Yesteryear* brochure, describing the town's older buildings, is available from the visitor center.

But the day-tripper can be "blown away" by all the things going on in this quaint little burg. For information swing by the Cedarburg Chamber of Commerce & Visitors Center at the corner of Washington and Spring Streets and peruse the racks of information. Hours are 10:00 A.M. to 4:00 P.M. Monday through Friday, 10:00 A.M. to 4:00 P.M. Saturday, and 11:00 A.M. to 3:00 P.M. Sunday. Or call (262) 377-9620 or (800) CDR-BURG.

WHERE TO GO

Cedarburg Cultural Center. W62 N546 Washington Avenue, Cedarburg. Stroll through the center's halls to study displays on Cedarburg's history and heritage. An extensive exhibit of photos and memorabilia give the town story in a lighthearted and easily understood way. The facility also hosts many weekend arts and musical events such as jazz concerts featuring such major performers as Ron DeVillers and the Jack Carr Big Band. In autumn the center holds a Blues in the 'Burg series. Center admission is free, except for the special programs and concerts. Call to check ticket prices and times. Hours are 10:00 A.M. to 5:00 P.M. Tuesday through Saturday and 1:00 to 5:00 P.M. Sunday. Call (262) 375-3676.

The Family Farm. 328 Port Washington Road, Grafton. The farm is southeastern Wisconsin's largest farm zoo, with plenty of sheep, goats, and other critters to feed and pet. Take a ride in a wagon pulled by draft horses or walk along the farm's nature trail. Admission is charged. The farm is open 9:00 A.M. to 4:00 P.M. Wednesday through Saturday and 11:00 A.M. to 4:00 P.M. Sunday through October. Since hours vary, call (262) 377-6161.

Covered Bridge Park. Covered Bridge Road (north of Cedarburg). Walk across the last remaining covered bridge in Wisconsin. And be sure to bring a full picnic basket for some outdoor munching and relaxation in the oak-shaded park along Cedar Creek. Drive west on State Highway 60 from I-43 or north on Washington Avenue out of Cedarburg to Five Corners (just beyond the Firemen's Park, the Ozaukee County Fairgrounds, and the Cedarburg Community

Pool). Then go north on Covered Bridge Road. Canoeists love putting in at Covered Bridge Park and paddling downstream the 5.5 miles to Boy Scout Park in Cedarburg.

Christmas in the Country. N70 W6340 Bridge Road, Cedarburg. When out driving on a pre-holiday day trip, take in this art show, featuring seventy-five juried artists. The show is held annually in the Cedarburg Winery area of the Cedar Creek Settlement. The shows have been presented since the late 1970s, featuring noted painters and designers from around the region. The program is usually held the first weekend in December. Hours are 10:00 A.M. to 5:00 P.M. Friday, 10:00 A.M. to 8:00 P.M. Saturday, and 11:00 A.M. to 5:00 P.M. Sunday. Call (262) 377-9116 for the correct weekend.

Cedarburg General Store Museum. W61 N480 Washington Avenue, Cedarburg. The wooden frame building, which dates from the 1860s, now houses an array of art, antique advertising, and Depression-era memorabilia. The Cedarburg Visitors Center and Chamber of Commerce are located here, as well, so this can be a first stop on a tour of Cedarburg's downtown. Although the museum is free, donations are accepted. Guided group tours are available by appointment if there is a day-tripper motorcade. Hours are 10:00 A.M. to 4:00 P.M. Monday through Friday, 10:00 A.M. to 3:00 P.M. Saturday, and 11:00 A.M. to 3:00 P.M. Sunday. Call (262) 377-9620 or (800) CDR-BURG.

Ozaukee Arts Center/Brewery Works Arts Complex. W62 N718-730 Riveredge Drive, Cedarburg (1 block west of Washington Avenue; take Bridge Road east 1 block to Riveredge and then turn north/left 1 block). Cedarburg's fine-arts complex is home to traveling and permanent exhibitions of major state and regional artists. Workshops are a regular component of the center's regime. Check out the *objets d'art* in the retail shop, located in an old brewery. Parking is available behind the stables. Call (262) 377-8230 for hours and programs.

Ozaukee County Pioneer Village. 4880 Ozaukee County Highway I (10 miles north of Cedarburg in Saukville). Seventeen buildings dating from between the 1840s and early 1900s make up a re-created living-history village. Craftworkers demonstrate a range of activities from spinning to blacksmithing. Check the village's calendar to see if there is a Revolutionary or Civil War encampment and battle reenactment on any particular summer weekend. The complex is open from noon to 5:00 P.M. Wednesday, Saturday, and Sunday from Memorial Day weekend (closed Memorial Day Monday) to Labor Day weekend. Also open Saturday and Sunday until the second Sunday in October. Admission. Call (262) 377-4510.

WHERE TO SHOP

Cedar Creek Settlement. N70 W6340 Bridge Road, Cedarburg. The settlement, listed on the National Register of Historic Places, is one of the town's original mills. A warren of shops has been laid out inside the old structure and its outbuildings. Antiques, fine arts, furniture, jewelry, clothing, and gifts can be found throughout the mill, which has retained its weathered beams and some of its long-quiet machinery. One shop, the Cedar Creek Winery, offers regular tastings and helps host special events such as the Wine & Harvest Festival (held the third full weekend in September) and a Winery Open House the third full weekend in March.

Other activities at the settlement include a Winter Festival on the first full weekend in February and a Strawberry Festival on the fourth full weekend in June. Hours for the settlement complex are 10:00 A.M. to 5:00 P.M. Monday through Saturday, 11:00 A.M. to 5:00 P.M. Sunday, and 10:00 A.M. to 9:00 P.M. on the Five Festival Fridays before Christmas. Winery hours are 10:00 A.M. to 5:00 P.M. Monday through Saturday and 11:00 A.M. to 5:00 P.M. Sunday. Call (262) 377-8020 or (800) 827-8020.

Bernsten's Candy. W61 N520 Washington Avenue (located in the Stagecoach Inn), Cedarburg. Bernsten's candy has been made here the same wonderful way over the past three generations. The aroma of fresh chocolate emanating from the shop interior is enough to draw candy-holics from miles away. Hours are 10:00 A.M. to 6:00 P.M. Monday through Saturday and noon to 4:00 P.M. Sunday. Call (262) 377-0660.

Amy's Candy Kitchen. W62 N579 Washington Avenue, Cedarburg. What's with all this great candy in Cedarburg! Handmade Belgian chocolate is the specialty of this house, which has also won four blue ribbons at the Wisconsin State Fair for its fudge. *Milwaukee Magazine* has voted Amy's caramel apples the best in the greater Milwaukee area. And if that's not enough, try the toffee, fairy food, turtles, and a host of other delicious wonders. Hours are 10:00 A.M. to 9:00 P.M. Monday through Saturday and noon to 8:00 P.M. Sunday. Call (262) 376–0884 or (800) 513–8889. Or check the Web site, www.amyscandykitchen.com.

The Irish Trader. W63 N674 Washington Avenue, Cedarburg. No leprechauns lurk in The Irish Trader, but you'll find fine art, jewelry, delicious food items, wonderful music, and comfortable, classy clothes. Brand names include Chary Ltd., Branigan Weavers, Mullingar Pewter, and other top products from the Auld Sod. Hours are 11:00 A.M. to 5:00 P.M. Monday through Thursday, 11:00 A.M. to 8:00 P.M. Friday and Saturday, and noon to 5:00 P.M. Sunday. Call (262) 375–7474 or (888) 474–7474.

WHERE TO EAT

C. Wiesler's Saloon & Eatery. W61 N493 Washington Avenue, Cedarburg. The landmark old building has an outdoor deck for brew sipping and pub grub that is perfect for steamy summer nights. It's the only deck in town, by the way. Then take in C. Wiesler's Walleye Fridays for the traditional fish fry. Hours are from 11:30 A.M. daily to bar closing. Call (262) 377–8833. $

Cedarburg Coffee Pot Family Restaurant. N61 N514 Washington Avenue, Cedarburg. Breakfast is served all day in this casually friendly downtown eatery. Homemade daily specials call to mind all the great comfort foods of home. The desserts call out from their cases, so be careful. Daily hours are 5:00 A.M. to 9:00 P.M. Call (262) 377–1202. $; ☐

The Chocolate Factory Subs & Ice Cream. W62 N577 Washington Avenue, Cedarburg. Tucked in a neat old building on Cedarburg's main drag, this old-fashioned ice-cream parlor and sandwich shop is perfect for quick drop-ins on a hot summer day . . . or a frosty winter one, as well. After all, hot fudge tastes wonderfully delicious regardless of the season. Hours are 11:00 A.M. to 9:00 P.M. Sunday through Thursday and 11:00 A.M. to 10:00 P.M. Friday through Saturday. Call (262) 377–8877. $; ☐

Cream & Crêpe Cafe. N70 W6340 Bridge Road, Cedarburg. Just like the early pioneers to Cedarburg (well, kinda), day-trippers can dine on crepes overlooking Cedar Creek. But today's snug comfort is much appreciated. Open 10:00 A.M. to 5:00 P.M. Monday, 10:00 A.M.

to 8:00 P.M. Tuesday through Saturday, and 11:00 A.M. to 5:00 P.M. Sunday. Call (262) 377-0900. $$; ☐

Cream City Coffee. W62 N605 Washington Avenue, Cedarburg. This is one of the coziest places in town, with its perfume of freshly baked goodies and steaming espresso. Juices, bulk coffee, and fresh soup are available. Hours are 6:00 A.M. to 8:00 P.M. Monday through Thursday, 6:30 A.M. to 10:00 P.M. Friday and Saturday, and 7:00 A.M. to 8:00 P.M. Sunday. Call (262) 376-1366. $; ☐

WHERE TO STAY

The Stagecoach Inn. W61 N520 Washington Avenue, Cedarburg. This historic old inn was built in 1853 of local stone. It features twelve rooms with whirlpools, fireplaces, and an extensive array of antique furniture. The inn is in downtown Cedarburg, making for easy access to shops, restaurants, and pubs. Call (262) 375-0208 or (888) 375-0208. $$

The Washington House Inn. W62 N573 Washington Avenue, Cedarburg. There's nothing equal to the down comforters on the beds in the Washington House. They are pleasure max, especially on a frosty winter getaway. Room rates include a late-afternoon social hour and a homemade continental breakfast. Call (262) 375-3550 or (800) 554-4717. $$-$$$

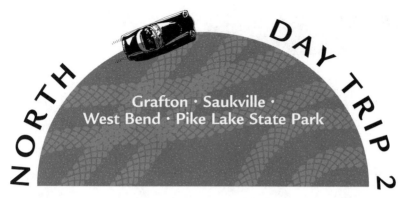

For a fast getaway to a relatively rural area close to Milwaukee, this road trip can be done in a day or served up in delightfully delicious morsels. A drive around this part of Wisconsin, barely an hour north and northwest of Milwaukee, is especially fantastic during autumn, when all the oaks and maples show their colorful stuff. While there's the unfortunate blight of creeping ranch homes, you can still enjoy the rustic get-out-of-town ambience that permeates the area. If you take the time to enjoy a day trip here, your heart and spirit will be amply rewarded.

GRAFTON

Grafton is a city of 10,000 folks in the center of Ozaukee County, about a twenty-minute drive north of Milwaukee and situated at the edge of the hills and woods of the Kettle Moraine forest land. The town limits abut those of Cedarburg (North Day Trip 1). The Grafton area was explored by two French priests from Green Bay who reported that the local Native Americans, especially the Potawatomi, were friendly and that trade possibilities were excellent. In 1839 Timothy Wooden and Jacob Eichler and their families were the first white settlers to hack out fields from the woods, build homes, and set up housekeeping. The area became a center for wheat growing, with local mills grinding flour hauled to nearby Milwaukee for shipment via the Great Lakes to outside markets. The Milwaukee River, which flows through town, is great for canoeing and fishing. Golfing is available at the Edgewater Golf Course (262–377–1230),

1762 Cedar Creek Road, which is on the north side of Grafton, and at the Country Club of Wisconsin (262-375-2444), 2241 Ozaukee County Highway West, adjacent to I-94.

For more information contact the chamber of commerce office, located at 1624 Wisconsin Avenue, Box 132, Grafton. Hours are 9:00 A.M. to 3:00 P.M. Monday through Thursday and 9:00 A.M. to noon Friday; closed on Saturday and Sunday. Call (262) 377-1650.

WHERE TO GO

The Family Farm. 328 Port Washington Road, Grafton. The farm is southeastern Wisconsin's largest farm zoo, with plenty of sheep, goats, and other critters to feed and pet. Take a ride in a wagon pulled by draft horses or walk along the farm's nature trail. Admission is charged. The farm is open 9:00 A.M. to 4:00 P.M. Wednesday through Saturday and 11:00 A.M. to 4:00 P.M. Sunday. Open by appointment December through January. Call (262) 377-6161.

WHERE TO SHOP

Seth's Antiques. 1233 Twelfth Avenue, Grafton. Furniture, glass, and pottery are big sellers for owners Vijay and Barb Seth, who specialize in Victorian-era antiques. Hours are 10:00 A.M. to 5:00 P.M. Monday through Saturday and noon to 5:00 P.M. Sunday. Call (262) 376-1862.

Grafton Ski & Cyclery. 1208 Twelfth Avenue, Grafton. If you need a new bike for trekking the Kettle Moraine Forest, stop by and talk with Bill or Sally Pence. They have Trek, Klein, Giant, Diamondback, GT, and other brands. And if you need a quick repair, they can help, as well. Hours are 10:00 A.M. to 8:00 P.M. Monday and Friday, 10:00 A.M. to 6:00 P.M. Tuesday and Thursday, 9:00 A.M. to 4:00 P.M. Saturday, and 11:00 A.M. to 4:00 P.M. Sunday; closed on Wednesday. Call (262) 377-5220.

WHERE TO EAT

Grafton Family Restaurant. 1305 Wisconsin Avenue, Grafton. Mark and Betsy Kranich ensure that their guests have plenty of reasonably priced comfort food such as a taco salad special on

Wednesday, spaghetti on Thursday, and beer-batter fish on Friday. Hours are 7:00 A.M. to 2:00 P.M. Monday, 6:00 A.M. to 7:00 P.M. Tuesday and Wednesday, 6:00 A.M. to 7:00 P.M. Thursday and Friday, 6:00 A.M. to 8:00 P.M. Saturday, and 6:00 A.M. to 2:00 P.M. Sunday. Call (262) 377-7690. $$; ☐

Ghost Town Tavern & Restaurant. 990 Ulao Road, Grafton. Chicken, seafood, steak, and burgers make this a Grafton hot spot. Hours are 11:00 A.M. to 2:00 P.M. for lunch and 5:00 to 9:00 P.M. for dinner Monday through Saturday. Sunday dinner is from 4:30 to 10:00 P.M. Call (262) 376-9003. $; ☐

Big Apple Bagels. 1961 Wisconsin Avenue (Oak Street Commons Center), Grafton. Hours are 6:30 A.M. to 7:00 P.M. Monday through Friday, 7:00 A.M. to 6:00 P.M. Saturday, and 7:00 A.M. to 5:00 P.M. Sunday. Call (262) 376-9920. $; ☐

Ferrante's Grafton Hotel. 1312 Wisconsin Avenue, Grafton. Amy Ferrante-Gollwitzer and Lori Moran-Ehr have been operating the restaurant in this century-old building since 1997. While emphasizing Italian-American food such as pizza and pasta, the Sunday prime rib special is also popular. Lunch hours are 11:30 A.M. to 2:30 P.M. Monday through Friday, with dinner from 5:00 to 9:00 P.M. Monday through Friday and 5:00 to 10:00 P.M. Friday and Saturday. Sunday hours are 4:00 to 8:00 P.M. Call (262) 376-9290. $$; ☐

SAUKVILLE

Saukville, as with most early Wisconsin communities, sprang up along a waterway. This friendly little town on the banks of the Milwaukee River is about a half-hour drive north of Milwaukee and only 4 miles west of Lake Michigan. The first white landowner was William Payne, who purchased his property in a government sale in 1835. His home was at the intersection of two Native American trails and near a large Menominee and Sauk village. He built a hotel there to capitalize on the crossroads traffic. The trails eventually became military routes linking Green Bay and Fort Dearborn (Chicago), which ensured that Payne's hotel would do a thriving business. His building still stands and can be seen at the corner of East Green Bay

Avenue and Ulao Road. The east-west military road is now State Highway 33 (Dekora Street).

In 1836 Payne sold some land to Solomon Juneau, one of the founders of the city of Milwaukee. Juneau was an Indian agent for the American government and needed a base at Saukville from which to conduct his business. Saukville's first church was built in 1858. By 1870 the Milwaukee and Northern Railroad laid a track through town, and a new wooden bridge was built over the Milwaukee River. To protect the town a fire department was established in 1886. The village was incorporated in 1915. It is now primarily a Milwaukee bedroom community, although there is some light industry. Saukville now has seven parks totaling 109 acres, with a range of recreational activities from softball to picnicking. A bandstand in Veterans Park is the site for summertime concerts and near where the original Native American pathways converged (now at the intersection of East Green Bay Avenue and East Dekora Street).

The Saukville Chamber of Commerce can be reached at (262) 268-1970.

WHERE TO GO

Crossroads Rendezvous. The annual rendezvous, held the third weekend in May, in Peninsular, marks the village heritage as a link between Native American and early settlement. Sponsored by the Saukville Area Historical Society, participants dressed as buckskinners, Native Americans, fur traders, and soldiers demonstrate life as it was on the early frontier. Admission is charged. Call (262) 284-3271.

Oktoberfest. Saukville celebrates its German heritage in a mid-September ethnic blowout held in Grady and Triangle Parks. Music, food, dancing, an arts-and-crafts fair, and a beer garden are among the attractions. Call the chamber of commerce at (262) 268-1970 for the particulars.

Oscar Grady Library. 151 South Main Street, Saukville. The library is an old, two-room schoolhouse that was used from 1925 to 1957 and was converted to the library in the 1980s. The building was renovated in 1997 and has a lot of material on old Saukville if history is a day-tripper's hobby. Hours are 10:00 A.M. to 8:00 P.M.

Monday through Thursday, 10:00 A.M. to 5:00 P.M. Friday, and 10:00 A.M. to 1:00 P.M. Saturday. Call (262) 284-6022.

Walking Tour. A brochure outlining some of the historic buildings in downtown Saukville is available from the Saukville Chamber of Commerce, Box 238, Saukville, WI 53080. Start a stroll in Peninsula Park, the site of a Menominee village when the first settlers moved into the neighborhood. The park is along a pleasant bend in the Milwaukee River. Nearby is the Queen Anne–style Kempf Hotel and Tavern (201 East Green Bay Avenue), built in 1897. The building remains in use as a pub. Adjacent to the Kempf is the Schanen Gardens Tavern, 311/313/317 East Green Bay Avenue. This site was originally a general store when built in 1865. It was later turned into a tavern with an outside beer garden popular with the local German residents of town. Two small frame houses, at 343 and 345 East Green Bay Avenue, were built in the 1850s.

There are several other buildings of note in town. The old Saukville State Bank, 234 East Dekora Street, was in operation until the 1930s, when it closed. After going through many owners, it is now home to the Mesina II restaurant. The brick firehouse, 200 North Mill Street, served as the town fire station until 1962.

WEST BEND

There are several ways to reach West Bend, the Washington County Seat. From Saukville drive west on State Highway 33 (the old military road) to West Bend. The ride is about only 14 miles, so it shouldn't take long. From Grafton take State Highway 143 to Washington County Highway G and turn north. G will take you into West Bend's south side.

West Bend is midway between Milwaukee and Fond du Lac (Northwest Day Trip 3). Subsequently, if coming directly from Milwaukee, take I-45/41 and exit on I-45 North, getting off on State Highway 33 West (yes, you'll drive through Saukville). But if you miss the I-45 split from I-41, continue on I-41 to State Highway 144 East. This drive will take you past Big and Little Cedar Lakes and Silver Lake before hitting West Bend's southwest side. The city is 35 miles from the northern border of Milwaukee and 19 miles west of

Port Washington on Lake Michigan (North Day Trip 3).

The city is one of the fastest growing in the state, due to its convenient location and accessibility to larger urban areas to the north and south. This has its economic benefits, but the once-rustic Kettle Moraine countryside that surrounds West Bend is gradually evolving into a subdivision/shopping mall nightmare.

The region was once populated by the Potawatomi and Menominee nations. The first settlers hunkered in along the banks of the Milwaukee River in the early 1840s, using the rapids for their mills. The Milwaukee–Fond du Lac road running through West Bend was heavily traveled by freight wagons and stages, making the community a regular stopover. This helped West Bend become a trading center.

The railroad arrived in 1873, ensuring even more growth. West Bend was incorporated in 1885, and the population doubled over the next few years. In the 1960s the city annexed surrounding areas to bring the population to more than 15,000. At present more than 28,000 residents call West Bend their home. The city is also home to the West Bend campus of the Moraine Park Technical College (one of three state schools in the tech system) and the University of Wisconsin Center–Washington County (UWCWC).

The university center has an excellent fine-art series that attracts national and regional talent, contributing to the cultural image of West Bend. There are also several community performance groups that attract Milwaukee-area day-trippers who appreciate talent. Among the organizations are the Theater on the Hill, Musical Masquers, Moraine Chorus, River City Irregulars, Moraine Symphony Orchestra, Spotlight Productions, and the Stagedoor Players.

On the business front the corporate headquarters of West Bend Mutual cover 160 acres and include a 150,000-square-foot office building at 1900 South Eighteenth Avenue. This landscaped spread is a far cry from the insurance company's original storefront operation of the nineteenth century. Only group tours are offered through the site, but you might be able to link up with one of these if you call the company in advance (262-334-6442) and find out who has made a reservation.

The city is noted for its park system, which incorporates 825 acres, as well as being recognized for its proximity to the Kettle Moraine State Forest (Northwest Day Trip 1). Both the urban parks

and the state forest provide loads of outdoor recreational oppor-
tunity. For details on camping, canoeing, hiking, boating, and fishing,
contact the Washington County Parks Department, (262) 335-4445.
For more information on the community in general, contact the
West Bend Area Chamber of Commerce, 735 South Main Street,
West Bend, WI 53095-0522, or call (262) 338-2666. Hours are 8:30
A.M. to 5:00 P.M. Monday through Friday. Check the town Web site at
info@wbchamber.org.

WHERE TO GO

Washington County Historical Society Museum. 320 South Fifth
Avenue and 340 South Fifth Avenue, West Bend. The museum on
Courthouse Square is located in the 1889 county courthouse and the
old county jail, dating from 1886. The complex opened in 1997,
holding artifacts and memorabilia of the county's past. The courthouse is on the National Register of Historic Places. Viewing the
renovated circuit courtroom and the jail cells makes for an interesting stopover. Hours are 10:00 A.M. to 4:00 P.M. Wednesday through
Friday and 1:00 to 4:00 P.M. Sunday. The third floor of the courthouse holds the historical society's research department, including
an extensive photo collection of more than 5,000 images. Details on
the museum and appointments for delving into the society's volumi-
nous files can be made by calling (262) 335-4678.

West Bend Art Museum. 300 South Sixth Avenue, West Bend.
The museum holds the world's largest collection of paintings by
Carl von Marr, a noted nineteenth-century artist who came from
Munich to live in Milwaukee. The facility also houses an extensive
display of works by Wisconsin artists. Hours are 10:00 A.M. to 4:30
P.M. Wednesday through Saturday and 1:00 to 4:30 P.M. Sunday. No
admission is charged, but donations are welcome. Call (262)
334-9638.

Riverfront Parkway City of Sculptures Art Walk. West Bend.
The walkway takes visitors along the banks of the Milwaukee River,
weaving through residential neighborhoods and the downtown.
Among the sculptures seen on the way are the *Tableau in Steel,* by
David Genszler and a limestone piece entitled *Fluvio,* by Paul Trappe.
One of the most fun is *Musical Frog Trio,* by Charles and Beau Smith
of Atland. Look for this whimsical statue of frogs playing a guitar,

fiddle, and trumpet outside the West Bend Art Museum. New sculptures are added yearly, purchased by corporate and individual donations. But you should also view the pre-history bird-effigy mounds dating from about A.D. 300. Look for them along the Milwaukee River near Quaas Creek near Riverside Park between River Road and East Decorah Road.

WHERE TO SHOP

Amity/Rolf Outlet Store. State Highway 33 at Rolfs Road, West Bend. Many leather products produced by Amity are sold here, along with an excellent line of Rolf wallets. For hours call (262) 338-6506 or (262) 334-6951.

West Bend Company Outlet Store/Museum. 400 Washington Street, West Bend. The outlet sells factory-direct products, with all sorts of utensils and appliances that are perfect for the household. Bring a large van to load up on all the good deals. Hours are 9:00 A.M. to 5:00 P.M. Monday through Saturday; closed Sunday and holidays. Wednesday is Senior Citizen Day, with even better bargains. Call (262) 334-6951.

WHERE TO EAT

Omicron Restaurant. 1505 South Main Street, West Bend. Full menus throughout the day, with wine and beer served, as well. Hours are 6:00 A.M. to 10:00 P.M. daily. Call (262) 335-0777. $$; ☐

Barth's Linden Inn. State Highway 144, 1 mile north of West Bend on I-41. Dinner and cocktails are served daily from 4:00 P.M. to closing. Thursday is prime rib night, with a great fish buffet on Friday. A champagne brunch is offered from 10:00 A.M. to 2:00 P.M. Sunday. Closed Monday. Call (262) 644-6953, or (414) 344-5432 for Milwaukee callers. $$; ☐

WHERE TO STAY

West Bend Inn. 2530 West Washington Street (between I-41 and I-45), West Bend. Indoor and outdoor pools make for a clean day-tripper overnight getaway, at least. Call (800) 727-9727. $$; ☐

Cedar Valley Center. 5349 Washington County Highway D, West Bend. The center is located amid one hundred acres of hills and ponds, with walking trails. While it is usually used as a conference center, guest rooms are available. One log house sleeps eleven, so a day-tripper can bring a large family if seeking an overnight. Call (262) 629–9202. $$; ☐

Americinn Motel. 2424 West Washington Street, West Bend. The motel offers whirlpool suites and an indoor swimming pool. Call (262) 334–0307. $$; ☐

PIKE LAKE STATE PARK

Pike Lake State Park is one of the prettiest locales in this part of Wisconsin, tucked in the heart of the Kettle Moraine. The region's glaciated hills and valleys were formed during the last great Ice Age that crushed Wisconsin between 10,000 and 15,000 years ago. The lake itself covers 678 acres, with the 1,350-foot-high Powder Hill offering a great panorama of the surrounding countryside. In geology parlance the hill is officially called a kame, formed when an ice sheet starts to melt and crack. Meltwater on the surface flows down through the several thousand feet of ice to deposit tons of rubble. When the glacier completely melts, a cone-shaped hill of debris is left—hence, Powder Hill. The park has several miles of trails that wind around the woods and fields near the lake. A self-guided ¾-mile nature trail is in the northeast section of the park. The Ice Age Trail, part of the 1,000-mile-long path that traces the rim of the ancient glaciers, also runs through the park. Bikes cannot be ridden on park trails, except for the marked path that leads to the Hartford Bike Trail on the north end of the lake.

Though there are no boat launches in the park itself, several private launches are found nearby. A map of the sites can be picked up in the park office, 3340 Kettle Moraine Road, (262) 670–3400. A designated swimming area is marked with buoys between Memorial Day and Labor Day; however, no lifeguards are on duty. A grassy slope leading to the beach is a great picnic area, with grills, play-ground, shelters, and bathrooms.

Even in winter the lake can be used. Fans of ice fishing flock here from Milwaukee, setting up their windbreaks and drilling holes in the ice. Panfish are plentiful, with the occasional bass or another larger fish being plucked from the dark, deep lake waters. Remember, though, that this is one lake on which vehicles are prohibited in winter, regardless of the ice thickness.

Speaking of winter, the cross-country ski trails at Pike Lake are superb. There's an adequate mix of easy and tough challenges for all ranges of skiers. Some trails are groomed but not on a regular basis.

The park also has thirty-two campsites, but none have electrical or sewer hookups. One site is reserved for the physically challenged. Camping permits are required, which can be purchased at the park office. A state park sticker is also required to visit any part of the park.

The fields and woods in the park are a bird-watcher's paradise. Look for nuthatches, jays, owls, juncos, chickadees, cardinals, woodpeckers, and dozens of other species. They flit from limb to limb and soar overhead, lending their calls, chirps, and cries to a natural symphony. A keen-eyed hiker can also spot white-tailed deer, the largest animal in the park. Foxes, badgers, woodchucks, squirrels, and rabbits are among the other critters that call the park their home. Sit on a log somewhere and watch what goes on around you. It's surprising the amount of hustle, rustle, and bustle there is amid the leaves, grasses, and ferns as the animals go about their business.

The state park is reached via U.S. 45/41 northwest from Milwaukee. Exit on State Highway 60 and drive west toward Hartford. The park is on the south side of the highway, about a forty-five-minute drive from Milwaukee.

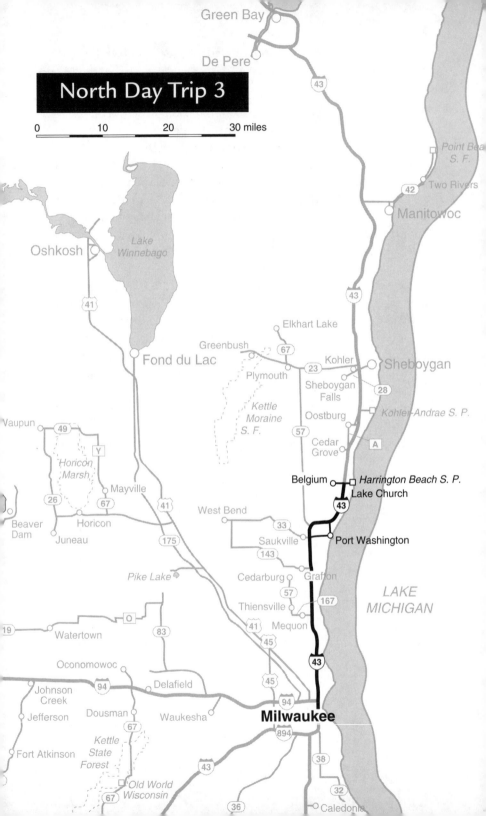

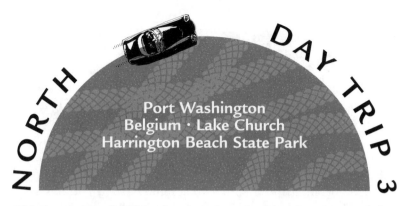

Port Washington
Belgium · Lake Church
Harrington Beach State Park

This jaunt out of Milwaukee is a short, quick drive to several fun places just north of the city via U.S. 43/W-32. Within a forty-five-minute drive, you combine a peek into small-town life with vistas of Lake Michigan, with a touch of history and some outdoor leg-stretching. What a great combination. There's almost too much to cram into one day, especially if you want to spend time exploring. But since you are so close to Milwaukee, you can always make a quick run to your home base and return another day.

PORT WASHINGTON

There are two ways to reach Port Washington, only 25 miles north of Milwaukee. You can go up one route and return the other. The choice is yours.

The first option is along I-43/State Highway 32, where you take the Highway 32 exit (number 93) north and drive east about 7 miles, aiming for the twin smokestacks of the Wisconsin Electric Power Company. You know if you've gone too far if suddenly you are swimming in Lake Michigan.

The second, more picturesque, route is rural Ozaukee County Highway C, reached by exiting the freeway at Pioneer Road in Mequon. Cross the Northwestern Road tracks and turn north at the lake, where C becomes Ulao Parkway. At County T, turn east and go about 1 mile to pick up Lake Shore Road. Simply follow that road past the farms and new houses that are starting to spring up like mushrooms where corn once grew. Lake Shore Road will rejoin C after about 3 miles. To the right are the rolling green-blue waters of the vast lake with its ever-changing face. C will take you right into downtown Port Washington through its residential south side.

Founded in 1835, thirteen years before Wisconsin became a state, the city is now the county seat of Ozaukee County with a population (2000) of 10,467. In 1870 the federal government authorized dredging of an artificial harbor to accommodate the town's shipping and fishing industries. It was the first such man-made harbor in the country. Other harbor improvements were made over the years, including a lighthouse on the north end of the breakwater in the 1930s. A new marina was added in 1997, along with a beach, lakefront walkway, and park. When the commercial industry began dying out in the 1950s and 1960s, charter sportfishing slowly expanded. At present you can reserve chartered half-day and day trips out of Port Washington to try your angling skills for coho salmon or German brown trout. A fish-cleaning station at the marina is a busy place during the summer season.

St. Mary's Church presides over Port Washington from its perch on a high hill overlooking the houses, stores, and harbor below. The structure, dedicated in 1884, is at the corner of Johnson and Van Buren Streets. A view from the churchyard offers a great view of Lake Michigan. For another fantastic vista perch on one of the benches in Upper Lake Park on Lake Street and look to the watery horizon to the east. The state of Michigan is somewhere over beyond the waves, about a 70-mile sail. This park is great for picnics. To reach Upper Lake Park, drive through Veterans Memorial Park, scene of the World's Largest Smelt Fry, which is usually held annually in early April. Smelts are tiny, silvery fish that call the lake their home. The park's band shell has a painted backdrop of a huge American flag.

For additional details on Port Washington, contact the chamber of commerce. Call (262) 284–0900 or (800) 719–4881. The chamber's Web site is www.discoverusa.com/wi/ptwash.

WHERE TO GO

The Pebble House. 126 East Grand Avenue, Port Washington. Home of the Port Washington Chamber of Commerce and its visitor information center, the building was a gatehouse for

Wisconsin Electric's Port Washington Power Plant from 1935 to 1985. Its origin, however, goes back to 1848, when Edward Dodge, a local blacksmith, built the structure. He and his wife spent weeks gathering stones from the nearby Lake Michigan shore and used them for the facade of their home. Architectural historians say the stone design was used in New York state by English émigrés and that it is similar to sixteenth- and seventeenth-century English flintwork. In 1975 the house was placed on the National Register of Historic Places. It was moved to its current location in 1985. The building is open all year from 10:00 A.M. to 4:00 P.M. Monday through Friday and from 10:00 A.M. to 1:00 P.M. on weekends from April through October. Call (262) 284–0900 or (800) 719–4881.

WHERE TO SHOP

Bernie's Fine Meats. 119 North Franklin Street, Port Washington. The store opened in the 1940s, with current owners John and Jan Salchert as owners since 1974. The store is known for its summer sausage, hanging in chunky one- and two-pound links from hooks behind the glistening glass display cases. Bernie's sells upward of 8,000 pounds of the sausage around Christmas, much of which is shipped around the country by die-hard fans wishing to curry favor with friends, relatives, and business acquaintances. Homemade bacon is another top seller, with more than 1,000 pounds a week flying from the store.

Gift boxes are big for the holidays, several containing cheese, jam, and coffees as well as mettwurst, liver sausage, and smoked chicken, in addition to the summer sausage. Hours are 8:00 A.M. to 5:30 P.M. Tuesday through Thursday, 8:00 A.M. to 6:00 P.M. Friday, and 8:00 A.M. to 3:00 P.M. Saturday. Call (262) 284–4511 or (800) 363–5919. You can also fax your order to (262) 284–4145.

Oma's Breads. 477 West Grand Avenue, Port Washington. Out-of-the-ordinary breads at Oma's range from biscotti to scones and on to mini–cream puffs. The regular breads are just as wonderful: sourdough, boules, baguettes, ficelles, foccacia, cheddar rolls, and an additional five special breads a day. Hours are 6:00 A.M. to 6:00 P.M. Wednesday through Friday, 6:00 A.M. to 3:00 P.M. Saturday, and 8:00 A.M. to 3:00 P.M. Sunday. Call (262) 284–4246 or e-mail to omas@execpc.com. The store's Web site is www.execpc.com–ugrounds/omas.htm.

Serendipity Cards & Gifts. 221 North Franklin Street, Port Washington. For souvenirs, educational games, puzzles, candles, collectibles, and giftware, drop into Serendipity. If collecting miniature lighthouses is your hobby, the store has lighthouse replicas, books, prints, and buoy bells, plus ship and steamboat artwork and models. Open year-round except for Sunday from January through April. Hours vary seasonally. In summer the store is open from 10:00 A.M. to 6:00 P.M. Monday through Thursday, 10:00 A.M. to 8:00 P.M. Friday, 10:00 A.M. to 5:00 P.M. Saturday, and 10:00 A.M. to 4:00 P.M. Sunday. Around Christmas Serendipity is open until 9:00 P.M. on Friday. Call (262) 284-0075.

Port Antiques. 314 North Franklin Street, Port Washington. Of course, Port Washington has antiques shops. Port Antiques specializes in furniture, with a wide range of items that will certainly grab the attention of anyone looking for that special something. Daily hours are 10:00 A.M. to 5:00 P.M. Call (262) 284-5520.

WHERE TO EAT

Sweetheart Cakes. 620 West Grand Avenue, Port Washington. This is the place to be when cookie cravings hit. Baker Hans Van Vorshelen comes in at 7:00 P.M. each night to prepare his pastries and breads for the next day's offerings. Chocolate chip cookies are the top seller, at 35 cents apiece and $3.95 per dozen, according to longtime clerk Laverne Redig. Long johns bursting with Bavarian cream and apple cinnamon donuts (each 85 cents) are morning favorites. Hours are from 7:00 A.M. to 1:00 P.M. Tuesday through Thursday, 7:00 A.M. to 3:00 P.M., Friday and Saturday, and 4:00 A.M. to 1:00 P.M. Sunday. Closed on holidays. Call (262) 284-6221. $

Harry's Restaurant. 128 North Franklin Street, Port Washington. For down-home comfort food, from breakfast eggs to broasted chicken dinners, you can't beat Harry's. The restaurant, strategically located in downtown Port Washington (and only 1 block west of the harbor), opened in 1936 and has been a staple of the town's eat-and-meet scene ever since. Plunk down at the counter or plop into one of the booths. Hosts Bertie and Dale Mahal make sure that everyone is comfortable, that conversations remain amiable (even when talking politics), and that coffee cups stay filled. Open from 5:30 A.M. to 7:30 P.M. Sunday through Thursday and Saturday, and from 5:30 A.M. to 8:00 P.M. Friday. Call (262) 284-2861. $; □

Buchel's Colonial House. 1000 South Spring Street, Port Washington. Chef Walter Buchel, his wife, Irmgaard, and their son, Joseph, present fine Old World dining the way Wisconsinites like their meals away from home. After all, it's in the family tradition. Walter's father was personal chef to Franz Joseph II, prince of Liechtenstein. And several other Buchel brothers operate restaurants elsewhere in Wisconsin. Call (262) 375-1180. Reservations are strongly suggested. $$$; ☐

Smith Brothers Fish Shanty Restaurant. 100 North Franklin Street, Port Washington. The restaurant has been a community landmark since it opened in 1934. The Smith family, however, had been fishing on Lake Michigan since the mid-1800s. While their menfolk plied the water, two of the Smith women—Evelyn and Hope—began selling fried fish on Fridays. They added some chairs and a table, and thus the restaurant was born. Today, still true to its name, Smith Brothers serves a grand Great Lakes Sampler of broiled whitefish, sautéed walleye, and deep-fried perch. Shrimp, calamari, lobster tail, snow crab, and Atlantic salmon are also on the menu. For the nonfish eaters, there's pasta and—okay, okay—even fillets. Hours are 11:00 A.M. to 10:00 P.M. on Friday through Sunday and 11:00 A.M. to 9:00 P.M. the remainder of the week. $$; ☐

Smith Brothers also has take-out service to accommodate at-home diners, as well as a fish market adjacent to the restaurant. For a fine, finny feature on the dinner table, Smith Brothers has walleye, perch, and more exotic species such as black shark. The market is open 10:00 A.M. to 7:00 P.M. Saturday through Thursday, and 10:00 A.M. to 9:00 P.M. Friday.

For all the latest at Smith Brothers, call (262) 284-5090.

WHERE TO STAY

Best Western Harborside Motor Inn. 135 East Grand Avenue, Port Washington. The inn is across the street from the Smith Brothers Fish Shanty Restaurant, making for easy access. The south side of the building fronts part of the harbor. Located in downtown Port Washington, the motor inn is convenient to all the shopping and outdoor activities that the city offers. Call (262) 284-9461. $$-$$$; ☐

There are also several fine bed-and-breakfast inns in the city. They include the **Port Washington Inn**, 308 West Washington Street, (262) 284–5583. Each emphasizes coziness and comfort in grand style. $$–$$$; ☐

BELGIUM AND LAKE CHURCH

From Port Washington return to U.S. 43/State Highway 32, drive about ten minutes north, and exit at the Belgium off-ramp (exit 107) on Ozaukee County Highway D. Immediately to the west of the freeway is the village of Belgium, population 1,678. The community is about halfway between Chicago and Wisconsin's Door County tourism mecca. The bright green hearts on the village's welcome signs indicate the residents' Luxembourg heritage, which dates from the mid-nineteenth century. The Grand Duchy of Luxembourg is known as the "Green Heart of Europe," hence the heart symbol. The town's motto is *"Mir bleiwen wat mir sinn!"* That is the local lingo for "We remain what we are!"

Some two dozen easily identified stone homes dating from the eighteenth century are sprinkled throughout the town; however, a sprawl of modern ranch houses on both sides of Main Street (which is also County Highway D) spreads out from the heart of the old village. Each second Sunday in August, Belgium hosts its Luxembourg fest, with a parade, dancing, and plenty of great eating. On the preceding Sunday is an Antique Farm Tractor Parade. Visit Belgium's Web site at www.dataplusnet.com/~belgium for more details.

In addition to Belgium and Port Washington, other Luxembourgers settled in nearby villages such as Fredonia, Holy Cross, and Dacada. Another crossroads Luxembourg community, Lake Church, is on the eastern side of exit 107 off I-43—2 miles east of Belgium on County Highway D. The cemetery behind St. Mary's Church in Lake Church is the last resting place of many of the neighborhood's early settlers. The church was built in 1856. The church is on the way to Harrington Beach State Park.

WHERE TO EAT

Hobo's Korner Kitchen. 100 East Main Street, Belgium. Since its opening in May 1987, Hobo's has been a major truck stop/eatery on the I-43 route between Milwaukee and Green Bay. As such, you can be sure you'll get plenty of down-home country cooking. Comfort food ranges from a standard one-half-pounder burger through patty melts. For trucker-size appetites, there are center-cut pork chops, broasted chicken, and malts thick enough to hold up an eighteen-wheel semitrailer. Breakfast is served anytime, and carryouts are available. Call (262) 285-3417. Open Friday and Saturday from 6:00 A.M. to 10:00 P.M. and Sunday through Thursday twenty-four hours a day. $$; □

HARRINGTON BEACH STATE PARK

From Lake Church continue driving east on County Highway D. The park is 10 miles north of Port Washington. Guests are greeted at the Adolph and Answay Welcome Center in the lower parking area.

During the first twenty years of the twentieth century, the park was a limestone quarry. Now it has a 50-foot-deep, 26-acre lake where the rock was removed. A company town was built for the workmen, many of whom were Italian stonecutters. Foundations of their houses and stores can still be spotted in the undergrowth. After the quarry was closed in 1925, the land went through a succession of owners. The National Park Service pegged the site as park potential in 1958 because it was one of the few undeveloped stretches along Lake Michigan. In 1968 the park was established by the state and named after the late E. L. Harrington, a former superintendent of the Wisconsin Conservation Commission.

Plenty of picnic tables rim the wide expanse of grass alongside nearby Lake Michigan. Easily walked hiking trails meander in and out of the white cedar groves. Leopard frogs croak in the background, and rabbits bound across the wood-chip paths. Plank boardwalks traverse marshy areas. Along one trail near the lake is the 3,000-pound anchor salvaged from the wreck of the *Niagara*, a ship that burned and sank about only 60 feet offshore from the site. It is estimated that 169 persons, many of whom were immigrants from Luxembourg and The Netherlands, died in the 1852 disaster.

The same path takes hikers to a spit of land where the remains of a pier can be spotted. The old structure once reached 700 feet out into the lake, allowing rock to be hauled from the quarry and loaded onto freighters anchored beyond the surf.

The current 637-acre park is also a wildlife refuge, where visitors can spot white-tailed deer and loads of other animal life in the woods and meadows fronting the lake. The park has 127 campsites, 59 of which have electricity. There is an indoor group camp for eighteen and an outdoor group camp for fifty, both of which require reservations. For information contact the Superintendent, Harrington Beach State Park, 531 County Highway D, Belgium, WI 53004; (262) 285–3015. Hours are 6:00 A.M. to 11:00 P.M. for the park and 8:00 A.M. to 7:00 P.M. for the office. State park stickers are required.

If motorists don't wish to enter the park, they can pass the park entrance and continue along County Highway D to where it dead-ends at Lake Michigan. There is a small lot here where vehicles can be left for a few hours, but parking is not allowed from 11:00 P.M. to 5:00 A.M. A closed private beach lies to the north, but the area to the south is open to swimmers and beach lovers. Be warned, however, that there are no lifeguards on this stretch of sand.

WHERE TO STAY

Camping is available in Harrington Beach State Park (see above).

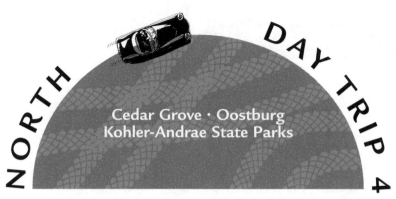

After leaving Harrington Beach State Park, drive north along Sauk Trail Road and cross from Ozaukee County into Sheboygan County. This is Dutch country, with neat farms, fat cows, and well-tended fields attesting to pride of ownership. After all, many of these Sheboygan County farmers are fourth- or fifth-generation landowners. The first non–Native American to see this territory was French explorer Jean Nicolet, who canoed along the Lake Michigan shoreline in 1635. Although assorted other adventurers and missionaries meandered through the neighborhood in the ensuing years, the first European to settle here permanently was William Farnsworth in 1814.

Only 227 people lived in the county in 1842, but by 1850 the number had grown to 8,836. The new arrivals were mostly Germans and Dutch, with a sprinkling of Irish. Rural roads with names such as Walvoord, Hoftiener, Smies, Risseeuw, and Weedmans attest to the Dutch influence.

CEDAR GROVE

Turn west on Amsterdam Road from Sauk Trail Road and drive about 1.5 miles to Sheboygan County Highway LL, which leads to Cedar Grove. The town was settled by pioneers from Zeeland, who were used to building dikes and clearing land. Since their town site was on high, flat land, they loved it. Immediately upon arrival, the pioneers cleared the trees and then plowed, planted, and harvested. It wasn't long before this stretch of Wisconsin was one of the most profitable farming areas in the state. Lush grass, moistened by the

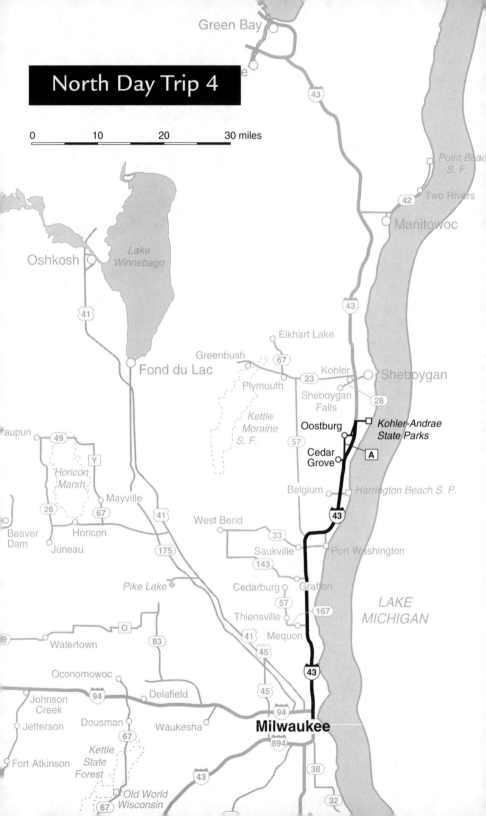

thick lake fog even in summer, meant contented cows. And there's nothing like a happy Holstein to produce fantastic dairy products.

WHERE TO GO

Holland Fest. Held on the last Friday and Saturday of July, a bell-ringing town crier announces holiday activities in the village. Folks celebrate their heritage with parades, street scrubbing, wooden shoe races for kids, Dutch films, and plenty of food. For details call (920) 668-6523.

Llamas of Bohn Creek. N1021 Sauk Trail Road, Cedar Grove. Since the late 1980s, Mark and Brigitte DeMaster and their family have been raising llamas on their farm. The parking area behind their home is reached up a slight hill along a gravel road off Sauk Trail Road. The farm has been in the family for five generations, and it shows. Trim barns, well-painted outbuildings, and sky-grabbing silos attest to all the hard work over the years. The DeMasters currently have twenty-two of the gentle, fuzzy South American creatures on their property. While DeMaster tends to his dairy cows, Mrs. DeMaster, a native of Gladbeck near Essen, Germany, spins wool that she knits and sells. Their four teenage children—Jonathan, Nicholas, Kari, and Daniel—belong to 4-H and the Alpaca-Llama Show Association, presenting their llamas at the Sheboygan County Fair and more far-reaching exhibitions. Petting of the animals is certainly allowed, when one or more of the llamas are brought out into the backyard from their pens. Admission is free; however, there is a small fee for groups of five or more. Hours are 1:00 to 5:00 P.M., but we suggest you call ahead; (920) 668-6417.

OOSTBURG

From Cedar Grove drive north on Sheboygan County Highway LL to A. Turn east and travel about 2 miles to Oostburg. The town is the abode of the "Flying Dutchmen," a nickname for the local high-school kids. Oostburg was founded in 1840, named for a village in The Netherlands that was the home of most of the original settlers. Oostburg's first site was 2 miles to the southeast, but most of the buildings were moved in 1873 to its current locale in the hopes of attracting a railroad. To add frosting to Oostburg's bid to be on the rail line, local business leader Pieter Daane built and donated a depot to the Milwaukee Lake Shore & Western Railroad.

The rail barons accepted the offer and built the line through the new town. In three years Oostburg became a thriving community. It had a mill, two general stores, a telegraph office, churches, and a hotel. Present-day Oostburg retains its small-town charm, serving primarily as a bedroom community for Sheboygan, about 6 miles to the north, and Milwaukee, some 40 miles to the south.

For answers to any questions about Oostburg and its history, town clerk Kim Simmelink is on duty at the community center, 215 North Eighth Street, from 8:30 A.M. to 4:30 P.M. Monday. Call (920) 564-3214. Or drop by the adjacent library and chat with librarian Trixine Tahtinen.

WHERE TO SHOP

Oostburg Bakery. 16 North Tenth Street, Oostburg. Baker Greg Gallenberger is the archetypical muffin man. He's up all night preparing breads and sweet pastries for morning shoppers who want to hit the road early. Simply stepping into the bakery and enjoying the perfume of freshly baked goodies is a guaranteed high. Hours are 5:00 A.M. to 5:30 P.M. Monday through Thursday, 5:00 A.M. to 8:00 P.M. Friday, and 6:00 A.M. to 2:00 P.M. Saturday. Call (920) 564-2221.

WHERE TO EAT

Bugsy's. 2 North Tenth Street, Oostburg. Owner Howard Buggs serves up great comfort food, especially soups and marvelous chili. The latter is considered among the best in Sheboygan County. Hours are 10:00 A.M. to 2:00 P.M. Monday through Saturday. Call (920) 564-6877. $.

KOHLER-ANDRAE STATE PARKS

From Oostburg venture east a half mile on Sheboygan County Highway AA to pick up Sauk Trail Road again. The road angles to the northeast and quickly parallels I-43. Within 3 miles you will hit

Sheboygan County Highway KK. Then turn east and cross the freeway. Take KK directly to Old Park Road, the entrance of Kohler-Andrae State Parks. The adjoining parks probably have the best air-conditioning in the Wisconsin outdoors. Located along Lake Michigan, the parks' maples, pines, and birches are continually breeze-ruffled. The topography here is a mix of sand, marsh, and hardwood forest. Most of the landscape was finalized during the last Ice Age, a refrigerator time only some 10,000 years ago. From that time on, the earth has continually been shaped by wind, weather, and the lake waters. About 9,000 years ago most of the present-day parkland was under prehistoric Lake Algonquin, the forerunner of Lake Michigan.

Six thousand years ago, the lake level dropped when the glaciers retreated. This long-ago shoreline can be seen along the northeast corner of Kohler-Andrae, about 14 feet above the current beach. Ancient mound builders built numerous effigies throughout the area, generations before "modern" Native Americans such as the Ottawa, Menominees, Ho-Chunk, Sauk, and others moved into the region.

French explorers poked around in the late 1600s and early 1700s. Farmers tried their luck along the shore as early as 1840. In 1927 one of the local property owners donated 122 acres of pine dunes to the state to be called Terry Andrae State Park in honor of her husband. In 1966 a 280-acre parcel was added as a memorial to Sheboygan industrialist John Michael Kohler.

The state has since purchased another 600 acres, making the combined parks about 1,000 acres, administered by the Department of Natural Resources. There are twenty-eight campsites, with Area 14 reserved for guests with physical challenges. An enclosed picnic shelter is located across from the showers. Both parks are open year-round, from 6:00 A.M. to 11:00 P.M.; the office from 8:00 A.M. to 11:00 P.M. State park stickers are required whether for a day visit or overnight. Single-visit and annual passes can be purchased at the park information office and entrance gate. Call (920) 451–4080.

WHERE TO GO

Kohler Dunes Cordwalk. An easy two-hour hike will take the determined walker about 2.5 miles up the Lake Michigan shoreline, along a vantage point atop the dunes. Eye protection is suggested on windy days because of the blowing sand. Stay on the cordwalk. Stomping around the dunes damages even hardy plants such as the endangered dune thistle, and it causes erosion as well. As another reminder, there is little shade along the way, so bring a cool beverage to sip on hot summer days.

Park at the main lot directly after the entrance near the visitor information center. The trail starts north of the lot. Other entry points can be accessed from the group campsite or behind the park office. There are two lookout points along the way, where gulls can be spotted swirling and twirling high in the updrafts over the lake. Watch for deer and skunk tracks, a testimony to the vibrant life that goes on behind the scenes of this natural, non-Disney setting. A great return trip is along the water-packed beach, where there are plenty of shells and mysterious objects washed ashore.

Woodland Dunes Nature Trail. For a shorter trip—one lasting about forty-five minutes—take this 1.5-mile hike through a heavily forested section of Kohler-Andrae. The sounds of the nearby surf blend into a pleasant composition, melding with the soughing of pine boughs overhead.

The trail begins just south of the campground area. After coming into the park, take a right turn by the campsites and look for the trail signs. The hike is along a wood-chip path, so be sure to have comfortable walking shoes. Just off the beach Native American fishermen used to stand waist-deep in the lake to net and spear whitefish and other delicious species of water life. Sometimes hooks, stone weights, and harpoons left behind by those ancients can be found. In summer use bug spray to keep the skeeters at bay.

Black River Wildlife Reserve. Trails here are about 1.5 miles north of Kohler-Andrae State Parks along the east side of Sheboygan County Highway V. On the eastern side of the pathway is the Black River, which separates the reserve from the privately held Kohler Company Wildlife Refuge. The 2.5-mile trail system weaves through a cathedral-like pine plantation and across several wide meadows. The site is open to horses, hikers, and mountain bikers, as well as cross-country skiers in winter. Call the Sheboygan County Convention and Visitors Center for more information, (920) 457-9495.

Sanderling Nature Center. 1520 Old Park Road. The center is staffed by volunteers and park employees who have a wealth of knowledge about the floral and fauna of the region. Outside the center is the keel beam of the schooner *Challenge*, a 90-foot lake freighter that burned and sank in 1916. Parts of the vessel washed ashore in 1982. The ship is one of more than fifty over the past century and a half that foundered in the rough waters off this stretch of the coast.

Inside the nature center are exhibits on plant life, animals, and fish and how they have been impacted by human presence. More than 400 plant species are found in Kohler-Andrae, fifty of which are different types of trees. Bird-watchers can also get background at the center about the 150 species that live in the park or use it on their migration routes. The center is open only during summer, with a naturalist on duty from Memorial Day to Labor Day. Hours are from 12:30 to 4:30 P.M. Wednesday through Sunday and from 1:00 to 3:00 P.M. Monday and Tuesday. Call (920) 451-4080.

North Day Trip 5

0   10   20   30 miles

Green Bay

De Pere

43

42

Two

Manitowc

Oshkosh

Lake
Winnebago

41

43

Elkhart Lake

Greenbush

67

Kohler

Sheboygan

Fond du Lac

23

28

Plymouth

Sheboygan
Falls

Kohler-Andrae S.

Kettle
Moraine
S. F.

Oostburg

A

Waupun

49

57

Cedar
Grove

Horicon
Marsh

Y

Belgium

Harrington Beach S.

26

67

Mayville

41

West Bend

43

Beaver
Dam

Horicon

175

33

T

Juneau

Saukville

Port Washington

143

Pike Lake

Cedarburg

Grafton

LAKE
MICHIGAN

57

167

19

O

83

Thiensville

41

Mequon

Watertown

45

94

45

Oconomowoc

Delafield

94

ls

134

Johnson
Creek

Dousman

67

Waukesha

43

Milwaukee

18

Jefferson

894

e

Kettle
State
Forest

38

Fort Atkinson

26

Old World
Wisconsin

32

67

36

Cal

SHEBOYGAN

Sheboygan is 52 miles north of Milwaukee via I-43, or along Sheboygan County Highway V from Kohler-Andrae State Parks. A former Great Lakes fishing port, the city of 51,000 residents lies at the mouth of the slow-moving Sheboygan River. With this traditional connection to water, it is no wonder that Sheboyganites still love to sail and toss out a baited line in the offshore waters of Lake Michigan.

As a reminder of that lake heritage, the wreck of the *Lottie Cooper* is a major attraction. Built in 1876, the three-masted schooner capsized and sank in 1894 off the Sheboygan harbor, one of sixty-two ships lost near the city over the past 150 years. The remains of the *Lottie Cooper* were discovered while surveyors were plotting the harbor bottom, prior to constructing the city marina. The ship's pieces were brought to the surface and reassembled. They are currently exhibited in Deland Park on Broughton Drive.

For the historical record Sheboygan was incorporated as a village in 1846 and chartered as a city in 1853. It is a town that prides itself on its medical facilities, schools, renovated downtown, industry, and cultural events. That image is not simply local hoo-ha. *Reader's Digest* magazine has called Sheboygan the No. 1 City in America to raise a family. To learn more about this dad-mom-kid-friendly community, contact the Sheboygan County Convention and Visitors Bureau, 712 Riverfront Drive, Suite 101, Sheboygan, WI 53081. Call (920) 457-9495.

WHERE TO GO

Indian Mound Park. 5000 South Ninth Street, Sheboygan. If driving up V (which merges into Sheboygan County Highway KK at the junction with Koene Court) from the Kohler-Andrae State Parks, look for the signs to the park. The park is 2 blocks east off KK on the southern outskirts of town. The secluded wooded lot has eighteen effigy mounds in the shapes of deer, lizards, panthers, and bears, each calling to mind the long-ago people who lived here between A.D. 500 and 1000. The area was almost developed for homes, but a concerted effort by the Sheboygan Area Garden Club saved the fifteen acres that the park now comprises. In 1927 many of the mounds were excavated by the Milwaukee Public Museum, and the artifacts found inside were taken to Milwaukee. One mound has a glass sheet over its exposed top, showing off a re-created burial complete with skeleton, pots, and other items. A trail leads past each haunting earthen construction. The cathedral-like canopy of trees ensures a reverent atmosphere. Call (920) 459-3444.

The Riverfront Boardwalk. Riverfront Drive, Sheboygan. This great walk takes casual strollers, or the dedicated runner, from the Rotary Riverview Park harbor overlook to the Eighth Street Bridge. Along the way shop or grab a bite to eat from one in a row of weathered shanties (now renovated and spruced up). The "shacks" at one time housed equipment for commercial fishermen who called Sheboygan their home port. Reminiscent of those days, charter fishing boats now dock along the boardwalk. The captains offer half-day and full-day fishing excursions for lake trout and salmon. Call (920) 457-9495.

Lakefront Promenade. Broughton Drive, Sheboygan. This pathway is great for quiet summer evenings. From this vantage point walkers admire the stars glittering over Lake Michigan's rolling waters. Take in the area between the boat launches in the Sheboygan harbor to the north breakwater, a distance of only a few blocks. Compare the look of the sailboats and that of the power-boats berthed in the Harbor Centre Marina. If you want to continue trekking, the promenade continues onto a paved trail that leads from downtown to the North Point overlook. Call (920) 457-9495.

Harbor Centre Trolley. The battery-operated trolleys putter throughout the Harbor Centre into downtown, along the riverfront, and into the marina areas. The circuit runs during daylight hours from late May through early September. A fee is charged. For rates, hours, and fares, call Sheboygan Transit, (920) 457-9495.

Festivals. Held in parks around the city, a full calendar of events runs throughout the year. Bratwurst Day, Wings and Wheels, Silver Dollar Picnic, Chicken and All That Jazz, Downtown Night, Kiwanis Lakefest, Brotz Regatta, Museum Day, JMKAC Outdoor Arts Festival, Mill Street Fest, Festival of Trees, and related events combine parades, music, and food. The Sheboygan CVB (920-457-9495) can provide dates.

John Michael Kohler Arts Center. 608 New York Avenue, Sheboygan. In 1999 the center completed a construction project that increased its size from 30,000 square feet to 100,000 square feet. Exhibits at the center focus on contemporary American art, emphasizing crafts and self-taught artists. Eleven different spaces feature solo, group, and changing displays. One gallery highlights work by the international artists-in-residence who work on their dramatic pieces at the sprawling Kohler Company plant in nearby Kohler. An education department presents an array of classes, from ballet to painting. There is even an arts-based preschool. Hours are 10:00 A.M. to 5:00 P.M. Monday, Wednesday, and Friday, 10:00 A.M. to 8:00 P.M. Tuesday and Thursday, and 10:00 A.M. to 4:00 P.M. Saturday and Sunday. Call (920) 458-6144.

Sheboygan County Museum. 3110 Erie Street, Sheboygan. The museum, the former home of an old-time judge, is located in a large brick building dating from the 1850s and includes several outbuildings. Construction projects have added more exhibit space for displays on Native Americans, the circus, ice harvesting, sports, and other local touches. Adjacent to the house is a pioneer log cabin built in 1864 and a barn housing antique farm implements. Also in the museum complex is the Bodenstab Cheese Factory, which displays dairy-related artifacts. The facility is closed Monday. Admission charged. Hours are 10:00 A.M. to 5:00 P.M. Tuesday through Saturday and 1:00 to 5:00 P.M. Sunday. Call (920) 438-1103.

Harbor Centre Marina. 821 Broughton Drive, Sheboygan. Sheboygan's marina can accommodate 281 vessels, which berth from ports all around the Great Lakes. The marina building has a lounge, grocery store, showers, and rest-room facilities. The panorama out the marina windows is great, especially when there is a storm and the viewer is snug inside rather than out on the waves. Boaters can even swim in the marina pool and use the whirlpool, a far cry from the rough-and-ready, long-ago days of life on the Bounding Main. Sailors who want to stay aboard their cabin cruisers can even hook up to cable television on the docks. Near the marina are other waterfront facilities, including Deland Park, a cheery, open space that hosts several summer festivals, a beach and bathhouse, public boat-launching ramps, the Sheboygan Yacht Club, and the Youth Sailing Center. Call (920) 458-6665.

WHERE TO SHOP

City Streets Antiques & Bears, Etc. 701 South Eighth Street, Sheboygan The shop has two floors of antiques, including beer steins, advertising artifacts, oil lamps, and old-time clothing. A Teddy Bear Den features dozens of the fuzzy little toys. Hours are 10:00 A.M. to 5:00 P.M. Tuesday through Saturday. Call (920) 803-9000.

Victorian Chocolate Shoppe. 519 South Eighth Street, Sheboygan. Thirty-five varieties of creams and truffles lure the candy fan. And how about the caramel apples, chocolate-covered strawberries and bananas, and fudge. The shop also offers sugar-free chocolates. But there are chocolate pizzas, raisin clusters, toffee bark, jelly beans, and tons of other delights. Hours are 10:00 A.M. to 5:30 P.M. Monday through Saturday. Call (920) 208-3511.

Schwarz Retail Fish Market. 828 Riverfront Drive, Sheboygan. The market, from its prime location downtown on the riverfront, presents fried, fresh, and smoked fish. Give a ring ahead for a carry-out. Hours are 8:00 A.M. to 6:00 P.M. Monday through Thursday, 8:00 A.M. to 8:00 P.M. Friday, and 9:00 A.M. to 4:30 P.M. Saturday. Call (920) 452-0576.

WHERE TO EAT

Fountain Park Family Restaurant. 922 North Eighth Street, Sheboygan. Good, down-home cooking, from burgers to blue-plate specials. Open daily from 6:00 A.M. to 9:00 P.M. and until 10:00 P.M. on Friday and Saturday. Call (920) 452-3009. $; ☐

CityStreets Riverside. 712 Riverfront Drive, Sheboygan. Located in a former fish shanty (greatly expanded), the restaurant specializes in steaks and seafood. Lunch is available from 11:00 A.M. to 2:00 P.M. Monday through Thursday, with dinner from 5:00 to 9:00 P.M. Evening hours are from 5:00 to 10:00 P.M. on Friday and Saturday. Call (920) 457-9050. $$; ☐

Trattoria Stefano. 522 South Eighth Street, Sheboygan. Chef Stefano Viglietti is a third-generation restaurateur whose family originally hailed from Liguria in northern Italy. So Viglietti comes from a long tradition of making sure that his guests push back satisfied from the table. The restaurant is open Monday through Thursday from 5:00 to 9:00 P.M. and Friday and Saturday from 5:00 to 9:30 P.M. Call (920) 452-8455. $$; ☐

Whistling Straits Restaurant. N8501 Sheboygan County Highway LS. Tucked into the Irish manor-style building at the Pete Dye–designed golf course, hearty American food is served up with loads of flair. The restaurant closes when the course shuts down in early November and reopens when weather permits in spring. During the golf season breakfast is served from 6:00 to 11:00 A.M., lunch from 11:00 A.M. to 5:00 P.M., and dinner from 5:00 to 10:00 P.M. daily. Call to confirm opening, (920) 565-6080. $$$; ☐

WHERE TO STAY

Brownstown Inn. 1227 North Seventh Street, Sheboygan. Located downtown, the inn was originally a home built in 1907. Five rooms ensure privacy, with their whirlpool baths and fireplaces. What's special about the inn is the short stroll to Lake Michigan, city shopping, and restaurants. A continental breakfast is served each morning for those who wish to wake up and start a day. It's a tough bonus because hunkering under the quilts in those four-poster beds makes it hard to crawl out and face the day. Call (920) 451-0644. $$$; ☐

SHEBOYGAN FALLS

Sheboygan Falls is primarily a bedroom community for its larger neighbor because of its proximity on State Highway 28. "The Falls" is only 2 miles southwest of Sheboygan.

WHERE TO STAY AND EAT

The Rochester Inn. 504 Water Street, Sheboygan Falls. An inn since it was built in 1848, the Rochester has come a long way over the years. Stagecoach passengers years ago would be amazed at today's whirlpool tubs, breakfast in bed, wet bar, and cable television. What's different about the Rochester are the two-level suites, with a parlor on the first floor and bedroom on the second story. Call (800) 421–4667 or log on to www.classicinns.com.

Falls Firehouse Pizza. 109 Maple Street, Sheboygan Falls. Not only is perfect pizza prepared here, but the surroundings are neat, as well. This is a restored fire station, complete with artifacts honoring the days when the building's smoke eaters answered the alarm. Naturally, some of the pizza names play off the firehouse theme, with the likes of The Barn Burner and Appetite Extinguisher. Sandwiches and homemade soup are also available. Free delivery is offered around Sheboygan Falls and to nearby Kohler. Hours are 11:00 A.M. to 2:00 P.M. Monday, Wednesday, Thursday, and Friday for lunch. Dinner is served Sunday and Monday 4:00 to 9:00 P.M., Wednesday and Thursday, 4:00 to 10:00 P.M., and Friday and Saturday 4:00 to 11:00 P.M. Closed Tuesday. Call (920) 467–8333. $; ☐

Ella's Dela. 607 Eastern Avenue, Sheboygan Falls. Pick and choose from numerous sandwich styles and edible accessories, with Ella's 8- and 10-inch subs popular with all ages of hungry folks. Hours are 9:00 A.M. to 6:00 P.M. Monday through Thursday, 9:00 A.M. to 7:00 P.M. Friday, 9:00 A.M. to 3:00 P.M. Saturday, and 10:00 A.M. to 2:00 P.M. Sunday. Call (920) 893–3022. $; ☐

KOHLER

Kohler is a planned community dating from the late 1800s, focusing around the Kohler Company plant, home for the country's leading plumbing manufacturer. The privately held company was founded in 1873 and moved to the Kohler site in 1900. To find the neat little village, incorporated in 1913, drive west ⅗-mile on State Highway 23 from Sheboygan and exit at the Kohler off-ramp (Sheboygan County

Highway Y). If driving up from Milwaukee (only an hour to the south), exit I-43 on State Highway 23 and get off on Y.

The focal point of Kohler is The American Club, built as a workers' dormitory in 1918 and now the Midwest's only Five-Diamond hotel-resort. The property is always on the Top Ten lists of facilities in North America, ranked by *Condé-Nast Traveler* and numerous other publications. The American Club wins for its service, location, atmosphere, restaurants, and rooms. Each guest room is equipped with modern Kohler bathroom fixtures. The facility sponsors several theme programs throughout the year, including a calorie-dangerous Chocolate Festival on the Thursday preceding Thanksgiving.

A member of the Historic Hotels of America, The American Club is the centerpiece of a complex that includes Blackwolf Run championship golf course, home to several national tournaments. In addition, the resort presents River Wildlife, a 500-acre private nature preserve used for hunting, fishing, trapshooting, canoeing, and related outdoor adventures. The Sports Core, an 85,000-square-foot health and fitness center, can keep a guest in shape. Numerous conferences on health and fitness are hosted at the Sports Core, including several geared toward women's issues. For information call (800) 344-2838 or (920) 457-8000. Check the Web site at www.americanclub.com.

WHERE TO GO

Kohler Company Factory Tours. Highland Drive, Kohler. Take a look at how the country's leading manufacturer of plumbing products operates. Tours are available for visitors fourteen years and older at 8:30 A.M. Monday through Friday. Reservations are necessary twenty-four hours in advance. Craftworkers in many disciplines can be seen plying their trades. The company also sponsors artists-in-residence, who work alongside the blue-collar crowd in creating metalwork, fired clay sculptures, and other pieces. The sharing of ideas has led to many interesting art pieces scattered around the factory. One sculptor fashioned a wall of faces along one factory wall, each face depicting a workman. Another was casting a deer figure, when its back caved in during the final production process. Instead of throwing out the damaged deer, the artist turned the statue into a fanciful barbecue grill, much to the amusement of the foundry workers. The tour takes about two and a half hours, so wear comfortable walking shoes. Call (920) 457–3699.

Kohler Design Center. Highland Drive, Kohler. Everything anyone wanted to know about deluxe plumbing fixtures can be had at the center. This the greatest showroom for showers since the Great Flood of Noah's day. Sample bathrooms are regularly changed, designed by North America's top interior designers. For a whimsical touch, The Great Wall of China features dozens of colorful toilet bowls, which are arranged on a wall at the far end of the display area. A museum on the company history is in the basement. Hours are from 9:00 A.M. to 5:00 P.M. Monday through Friday and from 10:00 A.M. to 4:00 P.M. weekends. Call (920) 457–3699.

The Waeldhaus. 1100 West Riverside Drive, Kohler. "The House in the Woods," about a five-minute drive past The American Club, reminds world travelers of the Bregenzerwald district in Austria—of course it does. The building was designed and built in 1931 by Austrian architect Kaspar Albrecht, who also sculpted much of the iron and pewter work found inside. And it was from that very village that John Michael Kohler, founder of the Kohler Company, came as a youngster to Wisconsin. The Waeldhaus, which sits on a bluff above the Sheboygan River, is sometimes used for private company functions, but it is open to the public daily, except holidays. Free tours are conducted at 2:00, 3:00, and 4:00 P.M. Call (920) 452–4079.

WHERE TO SHOP

The Shops at Woodlake. Woodlake Road, Kohler. After looking over options for a tub, toilet, and washbasin at the nearby Kohler Design Center, meander over to the twenty-five retail outlets at Woodlake, also part of the Kohler complex. The stores peddle a rainbow of home-accessory features, from floor tile to furniture. They accommodate shoppers who want one-stop interior design help. One of the most interesting is Artspace, a gallery of the John Michael Kohler Arts Center in Sheboygan. A variety of contemporary paintings, sculpture, jewelry, glass, painted silk, and wood objects can be checked out. Bring a shopping cart for all the buys. The shops are open 10:00 A.M. to 6:00 P.M. Monday through Friday, 10:00 A.M. to 5:00 P.M. Saturday, and noon to 5:00 P.M. Sunday. The

Woodlake Market offers a supermarket-size space for gourmet food items, plus a deli service. The market is open daily from 6:00 A.M. to 9:00 P.M. Call (920) 459-1713.

WHERE TO EAT

Blackwolf Run Restaurant. 1111 West Riverside Drive, Kohler. Dining in this log-pole-style clubhouse at the Blackwolf Run golf course always makes for a special occasion. Outdoor dining is possible, weather permitting, during golf season. Winter hours are 11:00 A.M. to 8:00 P.M. Monday through Saturday. Summer hours are 6:00 A.M. to 9:30 P.M. Monday through Saturday. Call (920) 457-4448. $$$; ☐

Horse & Plow. The American Club, Kohler. Richly appointed in dark woods, brass, and stained glass, this country tavern serves monster sandwiches and salads. It is a great ending to a day of golf, hiking, or cross-country skiing. The Horse & Plow also offers ninety brands of bottled beers for the dedicated drinker. A dance floor was added during a remodeling project in 2000. Hours are 11:00 A.M. to 11:00 P.M. Monday through Thursday and 11:00 A.M. to midnight Friday and Saturday. Call (920) 457-8888. $$; ☐

The Immigrant Restaurant & Winery. The American Club, Kohler. Fine wine makes the day at The Immigrant, noted for its continental foods and exotic American fare, such as venison and pheasant. It is a consistently named one of the best high-end restaurants in North America by food critics. Jackets required for men. Open daily. Call for hours and reservations, (920) 457-8888. $$$; ☐

The Wisconsin Room. The American Club, Kohler. The American Bounty buffet on Friday and the fantastic, table-groaning brunch on Sunday are hallmarks of this elegant wood-paneled eatery. Loads of white linen, an army of solicitous wait staff, and plenty of food make dining here a fantastic pleasure. Breakfast is served from 6:30 to 11:00 A.M. Monday through Friday and from 6:30 to 11:30 A.M. on weekends. Dinner is served daily from 6:00 to 9:00 P.M. Call (920) 457-8888. $$$; ☐

From Sheboygan drive north on I-43 only 27 miles to Manitowoc, the next stop on a day-tripper's guide for fun near Milwaukee. The freeway parallels the shore of Lake Michigan, although for some of the drive, farmlands and forest to the east will block the view. But when the lake does appear, its multifaceted complexion is delightfully varied: from stormy gray to smooth blue-green. Whenever a fog or mist hangs low over the trees fronting the shore, an element of mystery shrouds this side of Manitowoc County. You can feel the spirits of long-ago Native Americans who had traversed this landscape.

To get the real spiritual touch that this land offers, skip the freeway and drive north on Sheboygan County LS. This rustic rural road will become Manitowoc County LS (Lakeshore Road, meandering through the crossroads village of Cleveland and just to the east of Newton along Manitowoc County U). County LS enters the south side of the city of Manitowoc near the University of Wisconsin Center. Manitowoc is 79 miles north of Milwaukee, a drive by freeway of about ninety minutes or so. Taking the "road less traveled" (County LS) naturally adds as much time as you wish to poke along.

MANITOWOC

Numerous Native American nations lived in the vicinity of Manitowoc for generations before the arrival of the first white explorers.

Potawatomi, Ojibway, Ho-Chunk, and others fished in Lake Michigan, grew crops inland, and hunted in the forests. Tradition indicates that the name Manitowoc came from the Indian word *Mundedoo-owk*, meaning "Home of the Good Spirit."

French trappers moved into the Manitowoc area in 1673, using the natural harbor as a beaching point for their long birch canoes. But it wasn't until 1795 that a permanent settlement was established here by the Northwest Fur Company. After the French came a flood of Irish, Germans, Poles, and Bohemians who arrived via sailing ship from across Lake Michigan or overland by wagon from the port of Milwaukee to the south. The city was incorporated in 1836. In 1839 the Manitowoc County government was organized, with Manitowoc as the county seat. The city's location along the Manitowoc River and the lake helped it grow to be an economic powerhouse, especially in the shipbuilding industry. In 1847 the first dockyards began constructing wooden vessels. Schooners, clippers, fishing boats, and pleasure craft have been produced in the city over the years. During World War II the industry switched to tankers, submarines, and landing craft. Some of the world's richest personalities still have their yachts custom-built here.

Currently, Manitowoc remains the home port of the SS *Badger* passenger/car ferry. The ferry sails daily to Ludington, Michigan, from June through September. It leaves from Manitowoc in the spring and fall at 2:30 P.M., and in the summer at 1:15 P.M. and 12:30 A.M. A trip across the 80-mile-wide lake takes four hours. Call for reservations at (888) 947–3377 or use the line's Web site at www.ssbadger.com.

Lake Michigan's ferry history extends back to 1875 when the Flint and Pere Marquette Railway initiated cross-lake service from Ludington to Sheboygan, Wisconsin. The first ferry was the 175-foot *John Sherman*. In 1890 ferry service was expanded to include routes to Manistee, Michigan, and to Manitowoc. Over the ensuing years, more routes were developed and additional vessels added to the watery run. In 1992 the SS *Badger* began its illustrious adventures back and forth across this Inland Pond. The vessel was built in 1952 by the Christy Corporation of Sturgeon Bay, Wisconsin.

Today's *Badger* accommodates 620 passengers, 180 automobiles, tour buses, trucks, and RVs. It weighs 4,244 gross tons; is 410 feet, 6 inches long; and is 59 feet, 6 inches wide. The *Badger* stands four stories tall and is one-and-a-half-times longer than a football field. So take a break in one of the forty-eight staterooms. The trip, which cruises along at 18 miles per hour, will seem completed in a hurry. Among the famous passengers have been entertainers Jack Benny and The Who, as well as the tennis star Pancho Gonzales and the Angolan Olympic basketball team.

For the best way to know what's happening in the city, stop at the Manitowoc Visitor Information Center, located at I-43 on State Highway 151, exit 149. The center is open year-round, with a twenty-four-hour vehicle servicing. The facility has an RV and bus pull-through, free courtesy phone, and a short nature trail if you want to stretch your legs. There are plenty of maps, flyers, and assorted other promo literature available, as well. The volunteers and staff at the center wear easily noticed red vests. While at the center, be sure to pick up an Anchor Pass Savings Card for discounts at Manitowoc area stores and attractions. A logo with an anchor is posted in participating stores. The center's summer hours (Memorial Day through mid-October) are 8:00 A.M. to 6:00 P.M. Monday through Thursday and Sunday and 8:00 A.M. to 8:00 P.M. Friday and Saturday. Winter hours are from 8:00 A.M. to 4:30 P.M. Monday through Saturday. Call (920) 683-4388 or (800) 627-4896. Check the center's Web site at www.manitowoc.org/tourism.htm.

The center suggests this day-trip itinerary after a stop at its facility to pick up flyers. At 9:00 A.M. tour the Wisconsin Maritime Museum. At 11:00 A.M. move to the Natural Ovens for a bakery tour, followed by an hour lunch. At 1:00 P.M. visit the Rahr-West Museum and move on by 2:00 P.M. for a shopping stroll downtown. At 3:00 P.M. walk through the Pinecrest Historical Village. Have supper at 5:00 P.M. and be on the road home by 6:30 P.M. Or, if you want to stay overnight, you can take a stroll along the lakewalk, visit the zoo, or enjoy a summer concert in Washington Park.

The Manitowoc area is also a major stopover on the Wisconsin Ethnic Settlement Trail (W.E.S.T.), a 154-mile-long north-south route used by settlers arriving in the city and in other Lake Michigan ports. The road was first surveyed in 1834, using the route taken by Native Americans and French and English trappers. The roadway, which skips along from highway to rural lanes, generally runs along the lake. Just look for the W.E.S.T. signage.

WHERE TO GO

Capitol Civic Center. 913 South Eighth Street, Manitowoc. The 1920s-era building is home to ten local performing-arts groups. Over the years it had hosted vaudeville shows, internationally known musicians and dance programs and is now enjoying a breath of new life. Tours of the fabulous old building can be made by appointment. Maybe there's even a phantom to be found in the upper catwalks. Box office hours are 10:00 A.M. to 6:00 P.M. Monday through Friday and 10:00 A.M. to 4:00 P.M. Tuesday through Thursday. For a calendar of events, call (920) 683–2184.

Lincoln Park Zoo. 1215 North Eighth Street, Manitowoc. A Noah's Ark of beasts roam the zoo compounds scattered through a wooded park, which also has private and public picnic areas. A children's playground keeps the kids doubly happy. Daily summer hours are from 9:00 A.M. to 5:00 P.M.. Winter hours are 9:00 A.M. to 4:00 P.M. daily. Call (920) 683–4685.

Rahr-West Art Museum. 610 North Eighth Street, Manitowoc. Built in 1891 by businessman Joseph Vilas, the home was given to the city in 1941 for use as a civic center. The museum inside, with its rich woodwork and beautiful windows, hosts permanent and temporary exhibits of contemporary American art executed by the likes of Georgia O'Keeffe, David Hockney, Stuart Davis, and Jasper Johns. A selection of dolls, antique furniture, and Chinese ivory carvings round out the collection. Special exhibits are held seasonally, such as the annual Art of Tablesettings in February, a Youth Art Month display in March, and a Christmas at the Mansion in December. The building is listed on the National Register of Historic Places. Free admission. Hours are 10:00 A.M. to 4:00 P.M. Monday, Tuesday, Thursday, and Friday; 10:00 A.M. to 8:00 P.M. Wednesday; and 11:00 A.M. to 4:00 P.M. Saturday and Sunday. Call (920) 683–4501.

Manitowoc County Heritage Center. 1701 Michigan Avenue, Manitowoc. Originally the Manitowoc County Teachers College built in 1922, the building was renovated and opened in early 1999. Displays concentrate on local history. A research center, an auditorium, and a gift shop are open to the public. To confirm hours call (920) 684–4445.

Pinecrest Historical Village. Three miles west of I–43 (exit 152) on Manitowoc County Highway JJ. Turn your mind back more than a century and amble through the village, a project of the Manitowoc County Historical Society. The center features twenty-five historically important buildings brought to the site from around the county. The buildings, showing off Norwegian, German, and Bohemian architectural styles, were rebuilt as if in a real town. The oldest structures date from the 1840s. Stroll on your own through a general store, an 1890s cheese factory, and an old farmhouse. The village hosts a number of fun events, perfect for kids. They include a German festival, a Fall Harvest Fest, and a Christmas program. There is admission, but parking is free. *A reminder:* Access to persons with physical challenges is limited due to the terrain and design of the old buildings. Daily hours are 9:00 A.M. to 4:00 P.M. May through June, 9:00 A.M. to 5:00 P.M. July 1 through Labor Day, and 10:00 A.M. to 4:00 P.M. early September to mid-October and December 14 and 15. Call (920) 684-5110.

Natural Ovens of Manitowoc. 4300 County Trunk CR, Manitowoc. Hardly anything is a better perfume than that of fresh bread baking. Use all your senses when stopping by for a visit. To ensure freshness, wheat flour is delivered to the bakery three times a week, just hours after it is milled. Visitors can watch the dough being kneaded, pounded, and plumped before going into the company hearth, a monster oven that is 106 feet long and will bake 3,000 loaves per hour.

After touring the production line, take a look at the Farm & Food Museum adjacent to the plant and then purchase a few loaves from the company store to take home. The acreage where the bakery is located, about ninety minutes north of Milwaukee adjacent to I–43, also has a petting zoo with lambs, goats, and Belgian horses, a collection of antique tractors, and a wheat-harvesting museum. The company was founded in 1976 by biochemist Paul Stitt, who saw a need for fresh, preservative-free whole-grain food.

Free bakery tours are given at 9:00, 10:00, and 11:00 A.M. Monday, Wednesday, Thursday, and Friday (except for some holidays). Call (920) 758-2500 or (800) 558-3535. The Farm & Food Museum is open from 9:00 A.M. to 3:00 P.M. May through October, Monday through Saturday. Animal feeding time is 10:30 A.M. daily.

Wisconsin Maritime Museum. 75 Maritime Road, Manitowoc. A tour of the USS *Cobia*, similar to the dozens of submarines built in Manitowoc during World War II, takes guests deep into the interior of this sleek undersea hunter. Watch your head—the overhead pipes are low. Kids love peering through the periscope and spotting landlubbers on shore. The low-slung *Cobia*, a National Historic Landmark, is tethered in the Manitowoc River outside the maritime museum. Inside the museum a re-created wharf depicting a Great Lakes harbor town shows how goods were loaded aboard freighters of a century ago. Anyone interested in model ships will also enjoy the gallery featuring these miniatures. Regularly changing exhibits focus on Wisconsin shipbuilders or other shows relating to Lake Michigan. Admission is charged. Museum hours are 9:00 A.M. to 6:00 P.M. from Memorial Day to Labor Day and from 9:00 A.M. to 5:00 P.M. Monday through Saturday and 11:00 A.M. to 5:00 P.M. during winter. Call (920) 684–0218 or use the Web site of www. maritimemuseum.org.

Zunker's Antique Car Museum. 3717 MacArthur Drive Z (near the Fleet Farm store), Manitowoc. More than forty cars are displayed in Norman Zunker's stroller-friendly showroom. Oh, it would be swell to get behind the wheel of that 1941 Studebaker pickup and rev up for a run down the street! A row of old Fords dating from 1915 to 1937 is quite a sight, as is the 1928 Overland Whippet with its rumble seat. Admission. Hours are 10:00 A.M. to 5:00 P.M. May through September and by appointment the rest of the year. Call (920) 684–4005.

Manitowoc County Ice Center. Expo Grounds, Manitowoc. Glide gracefully around the rink at the Ice Center and then toss in a few intricate Olympic twirls. Call (920) 682–2098 for public skating hours on weekdays and weekends from October through March.

Boating. Almost everyone in Manitowoc has a boat or knows someone who does. There are many options for getting out on the water, whether for sailing, fishing, or powerboating. The city encourages water fans of all kinds to visit and take advantage of the local services. The Manitowoc Marina (425 Maritime Drive, 920–682–5117) is a full-service site with 250 slips, many of which are occupied by Milwaukee-area boaters. The *Chicago Tribune* has called the facility the finest marina on Lake Michigan. Proud Mary Charters (619 South Twenty-eighth Street, 920–683–3376) or any of the other guide services in Manitowoc can help reel in the big ones.

WHERE TO SHOP

Ecology Outfitters. 712 Chicago Street, Manitowoc. Top-quality gear for outdoor recreational use is found here, including Wigwam, Duofold, and Woolrich. The company also services and rents bikes and skis. Hours are 10:00 A.M. to 8:00 P.M. Monday through Friday and 9:00 A.M. to 4:00 P.M. Saturday. Call (920) 684-4061.

Golden Ring Music and Folklore Center. 1003 Washington Street, Manitowoc. Thousands of music books, plus all kinds of instruments from pianos to guitars to dulcimers, are for sale. Golden Ring also has a huge selection of bluegrass, country, blues, and Irish CDs and tapes. Hours are noon to 8:00 P.M. Monday and Friday, noon to 6:00 P.M. Tuesday through Thursday, and 11:00 A.M. to 3:00 P.M. Saturday. Call (920) 684-5242.

Pine River Dairy. 10115 English Lake Road, Manitowoc. More than 130 varieties of cheese pack the display cases. Fresh cheese curds are favorite choices of many day-trippers. Sausage, butter, gift boxes, and Wisconsin collectibles are also available. Watch the cheese being made by peering through a large observation window. It's a real bonus on the stop. Hours are 8:00 A.M. to 4:00 P.M. Monday through Wednesday, 8:00 A.M. to 5:00 P.M. Thursday and Friday, and 8:00 A.M. to 1:00 P.M. Saturday. Call (920) 758-2233.

Cook's Corner. 836 South Eighth Street, Manitowoc. More than 10,000 square feet of glittering kitchen utensils, pots, and pans is really awe-inspiring. It's hard to imagine so much cookware in one place. Even folks who can barely boil water should find a gadget here to help them improve their culinary skills. Brand names include Nesco, WearEver, West Bend, Mirro, and Krups. Owners Pete and Cathy Burback will also quickly ship items to a desperate cook anywhere in the world. A sandwich counter, with a great coffee and pastry selection, is on the right side of the front door, guarded outside by a tall statue of—what else?—a chef. Hours are 9:00 A.M. to 8:00 P.M. Monday through Friday, 9:00 A.M. to 5:00 P.M. Saturday, and 11:00 A.M. to 5:00 P.M. Sunday. Call (800) 236-CHEF. The store Web site is www.cookscorner.com.

Welnetz Studio & Art Gallery. 3501 Custer Street, Manitowoc. Sidelines in this photography studio include the sale of gemstones, jewelry, and collector prints by Norman Rockwell and Terry Redlin. Charming Santa figurines by Wisconsin artist Denise Calla are also offered. Hours are noon to 7:00 P.M. Monday, 10:00 A.M. to 5:00 P.M. Tuesday through Thursday, 10:00 A.M. to 7:00 P.M. Friday, and 9:00 A.M. to noon Saturday. Call (920) 682-4102.

WHERE TO EAT

Beernsten's Confectionery. 108 North Eighth Street, Manitowoc. Settle into a back booth for a sandwich and malt and then purchase some hand-dipped candy on the way out. Beernsten's has been a traditional stop in Manitowoc for several generations. Its old-time feel has been retained with original rich woodwork and etched window glass. Hours are 10:00 A.M. to 10:00 P.M. daily. Call (920) 684-9616. $; □

Wall Street Grill. Corner of Ninth and Buffalo Streets, Manitowoc. Start with some stuffed clams and deep-fried ravioli, move to a pound of snow-crab legs, and finish up with a piece of wonderful pie. The grill also has fifty-four varieties of beer, in case a guest is thirsty. Hours are 11:00 A.M. to 10:00 P.M. Monday through Friday and 4:00 to 10:00 P.M. Saturday. Call (920) 683-1125. $; □

Luigi's Italian Restaurant. 6124 State Highway 151, Manitowoc. Veal sautéed with green peppers or steak a la Siciliana are among the many favorites. Cold and hot sandwiches are also available. Don't forget a cannoli or tiramisù for dessert. Hours are 11:00 A.M. to 10:00 P.M. Tuesday through Thursday, 11:00 A.M. to 11:00 P.M. Friday and Saturday, and 11:00 A.M. to 10:00 P.M. Sunday. Call (290) 684-4200. $$; □

Courthouse Pub. 1001 South Eighth Street, Manitowoc. This historic brew pub and restaurant is actually a rebuilt structure replacing the burned-out original building across from the Manitowoc County Courthouse . . . hence the name. The large barroom serves up a mind-boggling array of beers, plus the usual rail drinks. Fish and steak are the calling cards, with desserts to almost die for. Hours are 11:00 A.M. to 9:00 P.M. Monday through Saturday. Call (920) 686-1166. $$; □

WHERE TO STAY

Inn on Maritime Bay. 101 Maritime Drive, Manitowoc. The city's only lakefront hotel sports 107 rooms, along with indoor pool, sauna, and whirlpool. Weekend packages are popular with Milwaukeean day-trippers who appreciate a comfortable getaway. Call (920) 682-7000 or (800) 654-5353. $$

Birch Creek Inn. 4626 Calumet Avenue, Manitowoc. Look out for the bear by the fireplace (actually the stuffed critter is only there for show). The Graunkes, who operate the cozy little B&B, make sure that guests have the chance to relax, bruin notwithstanding. Call (920) 684-3374 or (800) 424-6126. $-$$ (per couple)

TWO RIVERS

A sister city to Manitowoc, distanced by only 5 miles, Two Rivers is bounded by Lake Michigan and the two branches of the Twin River that empty into the lake. Early Ojibway called the area *Neshotah*, which means "junction of two rivers." Because of the lake and the rivers, Two Rivers capitalizes on water recreation, with boating and fishing major area sports. The Kiwanis Fishing Derby each July brings in anglers from around the country, ready to accept the tournament challenge. An annual Ethnic Fest, held in mid-September, celebrates the town's French-Canadian, Polish, Irish, Belgian, Scandinavian, and Bohemian heritages.

The Two Rivers Information Center, 1622 Jefferson Street, is open daily from 9:00 A.M. to 9:00 P.M. Call (920) 793-2490 or check the travel Web site at 207.170.38.168.

WHERE TO GO

Historic Washington House. 1622 Jefferson Street, Two Rivers. Built in 1850, this historic hotel and saloon is now a museum. Ascend the great staircase to get a better look at the murals and artwork in the second-floor ballroom. One display features an old-time ice-cream parlor and soda fountain that commemorates the invention of the ice-cream sundae in 1891 by Ed Berners, a local druggist. All the exhibit needs is someone behind the counter serving hot fudge sundaes. Free. Hours are 9:00 A.M. to 9:00 P.M., May through October, and 9:00 A.M. to 5:00 P.M. November through April. Open every day. Call (920) 793-2490.

Two Rivers History Museum. 1810 Jefferson Street, Two Rivers. An old convent has been transformed into a three-story museum focusing on the social and ethnic history of Two Rivers, as well as exhibiting artworks by regional and national painters. Free admission. Hours are 9:00 A.M. to 5:00 P.M. daily May through October and from 10:00 A.M. to 4:00 P.M. November through April.

Hamilton Museum of Wood Type. 1315 Seventeenth Street, Two Rivers. Located in a renovated old factory, the museum has vintage machinery and patterns for the production of wood type. Also displayed is one of the first home clothes dryers ever produced and other household mechanical aids. Hours vary, so call (920) 793-2490.

WHERE TO EAT

Kurtz's Family Restaurant. 1410 Washington Street, Two Rivers. The restaurant has been a Two Rivers dining spot since it opened in 1904. Some of the best hot fudge sundaes in Wisconsin are made here. Open from 11:00 A.M. to 11:00 P.M. Monday through Saturday. Closed Sunday. Call (920) 793-1222. $; ☐

WHERE TO STAY

Red Forest B&B. 1421 Twenty-fifth Street, Two Rivers. Built in 1907, the Red Forest sports magnificent oak paneling, a fireplace, queen-size beds, and plenty of antiques to admire. A full breakfast is included. Call (920) 793-1794 or (888) 250-2272; or visit www.redforestbb.com. $$-$$$; ☐

POINT BEACH STATE FOREST

The Point Beach State Forest, located 5 miles north of Two Rivers on Manitowoc County Highway O, blankets 2,900 acres of pine and hardwoods bordered by Lake Michigan on the east. It has 6 miles of excellent beach frontage open for running in the sand, studying shells, and bird-watching. Pine plantings were begun here in the early 1950s, with red pine being the hardiest. The forest has 127 campsites, 59 of which have electricity. There are 10 miles of hiking trails, plus a nature center, concession stand, and plenty of picnic areas.

Rawley Point, site of a maritime light tower just off County Highway O in the heart of the forest, was named after fur trader Peter Rawley, who opened a post here in the 1800s. His jut of rock is probably better remembered as a ship killer, with more than thirty brigs and schooners sunk here over the years. Often pieces of the old wrecks wash ashore. The Coast Guard has maintained a light here since 1853, with the cur-rent steel tower being constructed in 1894. The light, one of the brightest on the Great Lakes—visible more than 20 miles out on the water—operates from thirty minutes before sunset to thirty minutes after sunrise. For information on the forest, contact the site manager, who has an office at 9400 County Highway O, (920) 794-7480.

WHERE TO GO

Hiking. There are numerous excellent trails through the pine woods at Point Beach. The Blue, Yellow, and Red Loops are sandy up-and-down routes that require good pumping power in the legs, ranging from 5 to 7 miles each in length. The ½-mile Swales Natural Trail is perhaps best suited for the day-tripper in a hurry. Located at the north end of the playground and picnic area, the trail has signage describing the flora and fauna in the vicinity. The path is covered in wood chips for easy walking, weaving in and out of the stands of beech, maple, pine, and cedar trees.

The 3-mile-long Ridges Trail will take about two hours to traverse, with the trailhead at the nature center parking lot and running along a hummock through swamp areas. The Red Pine Trail is about the same length but might take longer because of its hilly nature. Both require liberal use of bug repellent during the wet season (which can be almost anytime because, after all, this is Wisconsin). On the latter route you'll pass through a group camp area, not far off County Highway O. Tune into the frog chorusing as you stroll along. Talk about nature's music!

WHERE TO GO NEARBY

Point Beach Energy Center. 6400 Nuclear Road, Two Rivers. The energy center is about 7 miles north of Two Rivers on State Highway 42 and 2 miles north of the Point Beach State Forest. From State Highway 42, turn east on the well-marked Nuclear Road. An alternate, more picturesque route, however, is via Manitowoc County Highway O from Two Rivers to Manitowoc County Highway V. Turn west on V and drive about a mile or so. Turn north on Sandy Bay Road, which runs into Lakeshore Road through the Point Beach State Forest. Lakeshore Road takes you to Nuclear Road.

The energy center has been closed to the general public since the terrorist attacks of 9/11. It's now only open to educational groups, who must call ahead (920-755-6400) to arrange a tour. The center features audiovisual and hands-on learning experiences for those interested in how energy works, and has a gallery entrance and an auditorium for programs. The building is handily accessible for those with physical challenges. A wood-chipped nature trail meanders through a nearby forest area. Adjacent to the center is Wisconsin Electric's Point Beach nuclear power plant. You will not—repeat not—see Homer Simpson working there.

Kaytee Avian Education Center. 585 Clay Street, Chilton (about 24 miles west of Manitowoc on State Highway 151 on the way to Lake Winnebago). Exotic birds from around the world strut their stuff in a wonderful display of rainbow-colored preening. The facility is open to the public from 9:00 A.M. to 5:00 P.M. Monday through Wednesday. Group tours only are scheduled Thursday through Saturday. Admission. Call (920) 849-2321 or (800) 669-9580 or use the center's Web site, www.kaytee.com.

The Old School Shops. 315 Elizabeth Street, Mishicot (9 miles north of Manitowoc on Manitowoc County Highway B or 6 miles northwest of Two Rivers on State Highway 47). The old schoolhouse houses one of the country's largest collections of Norman Rockwell memorabilia. The building was constructed in 1905. Hours are 10:00 A.M. to 5:00 P.M. Monday through Saturday and 11:00 A.M. to 4:00 P.M. Sunday. Admission. (920) 755-2291 or (920) 755-4560.

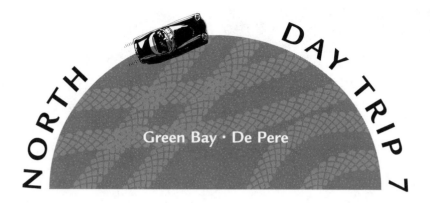

Green Bay · De Pere

Explorer Jean Nicolet visited Green Bay in 1634 in his search for a route to the Orient. He found an abundance of furs instead, prompting the French government to eagerly claim every inch of the new landscape in order to capture the market. Nicholas Perrot established a trading post here in 1665, which established the region as an economic powerhouse. But the first permanent settlement wasn't established in Green Bay until 1745. Because of its strategic location in those early days, Green Bay was always factored into the international scene. The British controlled the bay prior to the American Revolution and the War of 1812, ceding the area back to the United States after each conflict.

When the first Europeans arrived in the 1600s, the Green Bay region was a dense forest. The abundance of easily cut wood allowed some early families to earn a great side income by making shingles that were sold in Milwaukee and Chicago for $1.50 per bundle of a thousand. Because of the surrounding natural resources and location on the bay and rivers, the region quickly became an economic force, especially when the railroads arrived in the 1860s.

Green Bay has a strong industrial base, but everyone in Wisconsin knows the city best as the home of the championship Green Bay Packers football team. In the 1920s the Green Bay meatpacking industry provided a name for the city football team. The Packers became one of two charter NFL members, going on to win NFL league championship twelve times and the Super Bowl in 1966, 1967, and 1997. During the football season the state lives and breathes the green and gold, the club's colors.

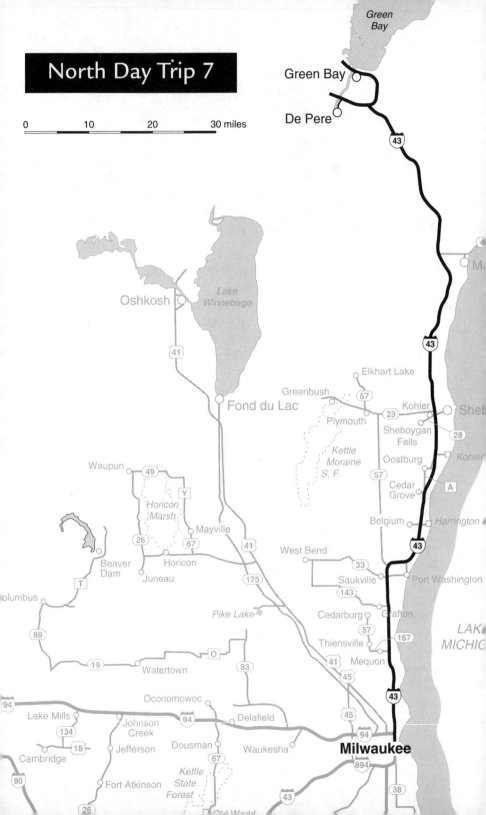

For more information about the city, contact the Green Bay Area Visitors & Convention Bureau, 1910 South Oneida Street, Box 10596, Green Bay, WI 54307-0596. Call (920) 405-1176 or (888) 867-3342. The Web site is www.greenbay.org.

GREEN BAY

Green Bay is located in northeastern Wisconsin, 113 miles north of Milwaukee at the union of the Fox and East Rivers. The water pours into the bay of Green Bay, which ultimately links with Lake Michigan and the world beyond. The city, incorporating about 50 square miles, is the county seat of Brown County. The urban area includes Howard, De Pere, Ashwaubanenon, and Allouez, names attesting to the region's French heritage.

GETTING THERE

The quickest and easiest route to the Green Bay area from Milwaukee is along I-43, a distance of about 180 miles. The trip takes a bit longer than two hours, but thousands of motorists from southern Wisconsin make the round-trip every time the Packers have a home game. Many fans arrive early for a tailgate party or a visit to some city attraction. They then attend the game, stay for supper, and return home relatively early.

If the day-tripper is poking along the western rim of Lake Winnebago after visiting Oshkosh, Neenah, Menasha, and Appleton, U.S. 41 is an easy alternate route to U.S. 43. Many other county and state roads also link the Green Bay area, providing numerous highway options.

WHERE TO GO

Green Pay Packer Hall of Fame. 855 Lombardi Avenue, Green Bay. Since this is Green Bay, most day-trippers want to see what the football fuss is all about. The team's hall of fame is across from Lambeau Field in the Brown County Expo Centre Complex. Look for the statue of the Packer player atop the giant football, which stands outside the hall of fame building. The museum displays just about everything that has to do with the Packers, from Super Bowl trophies to a helmet collection. Photos of all the Packer teams from 1919 to the present are exhibited, in addition to a showcase of player lockers inducted into the NFL Hall of Fame. Video presentations replay highlights of famous games. Packer archives are available to researchers by appointment. Of course, there is a gift shop to purchase all the requisite green-and-gold memorabilia required by a diehard fan. If you don't have your fill of Packer football after all this, there's always therapy. Admission is charged. Open 9:00 A.M. to 5:00 P.M. daily year-round, except Christmas Day. Call (888) 442-7225.

National Railroad Museum. 2285 South Broadway Street, Green Bay. After World War II a group of Green Bay business leaders investigated the establishment of a national railroad museum. They formed a committee to obtain a steam locomotive and display it in a city park. In 1956 they purchased their first engine: Milwaukee Road #261. In 1958 the committee acquired the twenty-two-acre Cooke Memorial Park from the city of Green Bay and opened the museum in 1961. The Hood Junction depot, which houses research material and memorabilia, was built that same year. Other structures were then added to house the museum's special pieces of equipment, including Dwight D. Eisenhower's wartime staff train and cars. The museum eventually acquired ten acres south of Dutchman's Creek from Brown County and completed the 1-mile loop of track now used for a train ride around the grounds. Now there are more than seventy-five pieces of rolling stock in the collection.

To get to the museum, turn north off U.S. Highway 172 onto Ashland Avenue. Drive to the first stoplight. Turn right onto Cormier Road; then drive east 4 blocks to South Broadway Street. The museum is at the intersection of Cormier Road and South Broadway. Admission is charged. Hours are 9:00 A.M. to 5:00 P.M. Monday through Saturday and 11:00 A.M. to 5:00 P.M. Sunday. Call (920) 437-7623.

Weidner Center for the Performing Arts. 2420 Nicolet Drive (located on the campus of the University of Wisconsin (Green Bay). The center has an excellent 2,021-seat performance hall, hosting a range of individual productions, Broadway musicals, and the Green Bay Symphony. For stage productions UWGB also has a theater department, which produces four full-length productions of classics and newer pieces each year at the center. Call the Weidner ticket office for shows and times; (920) 465-2217 or (800) 328-TKTS. The center's Web site is www.uwgb.edu/weidner.

The Neville Public Museum. 210 Museum Place (located on the Fox River downtown), Green Bay. The museum features interesting and educational exhibits of art, history, and science. Changing exhibits cover a range of topics, ranging from UFOs to bats. Hours are noon to 4:00 P.M. Sunday, 9:00 A.M. to 4:00 P.M. Tuesday, 9:00 A.M. to 9:00 P.M. Wednesday, and 9:00 A.M. to 4:00 P.M. Thursday through Saturday; closed Monday. Call (920) 448-4460.

Heritage Hill Living History Museum. 2640 South Webster Avenue (overlooking the Fox River), Green Bay. Visitors can experience what life was like for pioneers in the Green Bay area. Wisconsin's history is showcased at the site through twenty-five original or reconstructed buildings. Interpreters are on hand to show what daily life was like during Green Bay's settlement years. Four time periods are represented within the park, beginning in 1672 and ending in 1905. La Baye showcases the earliest, when French missionaries and fur traders were the only Europeans in the area. The next time period portrays Fort Howard, a United States Army post in 1836. Green Bay's business community of the 1870s is next, where visitors can watch a working blacksmith and visit the refurbished homes of prominent citizens such as Beaupré Place and Tank Cottage, the oldest building in Green Bay. Finally, you can explore a typical Belgian farm and study century-old agricultural practices. Another display shows a turn-of-the-last-century cheese factory and tells how important this business was in the rural development of Wisconsin.

The free Music on the Green concerts, with nationally known jazz and big band performers, are fun during summer. The shows are held on various dates from June to August. Concerts begin at 7:00 P.M. but the gates open at 6:30 for picnicking. The last festival of the season is *The Spirit of Christmas Past*, which will be held the first three weekends of December. This production shows how Christmas was celebrated throughout Green Bay history.

Hours during the summer season are 10:00 A.M. to 4:30 P.M. Tuesday through Saturday and noon to 4:30 P.M. Sunday, from May 23 to September 7. The museum is also open weekends in September and the first three weekends in December. Call (920) 448-5150 or (800) 721-5150.

Great Explorations Children's Museum. Port Plaza Mall, in downtown Green Bay. If the kids are along on a day trip, take them to the kids' museum for hands-on fun. Don't say it's a learning experience. Great Explorations likes to tie in history and science to local themes in its displays. Subsequently, you can learn about Green Bay's paper-making industry, the community's ethnic diversity, and how energy is made and consumed in the city. Admission is charged. Hours are 10:00 A.M. to 5:00 P.M. Monday through Saturday and 11:00 A.M. to 5:00 P.M. Sunday. Other times are by appointment. Call (920) 432-4397.

Bay Beach Wildlife Sanctuary. 1660 East Shore Drive, Green Bay. The sanctuary, the city's largest park, is a 700-acre urban wildlife refuge with an education center and observation and rehabilitation facility for injured animals. There are 6.5 miles of trails to hike. Free. Hours change, so please call (920) 391-3671.

Lambeau Field. Located between Lombardi Avenue on the north, Ridge Road on the west, State Highway 172 on the south, and Oneida Street on the east, Green Bay. For the Packermania set, touring the field is almost better than dying and going to heaven. What is better is actually attending a game. But unless you know someone who knows someone, good luck in getting tickets. The stadium is sold out well in advance of a playing year, with a waiting list for almost every game. Subsequently, although a tour seems second best, it will do in a pinch.

See the press box, executive skybox, kitchens, visitors' locker room, and many of the venerable structure's nooks and crannies. The stadium for the NFL's only community-owned ball club was renovated in the early 2000s. The spirits of past players seem to be everywhere, but there are real guides to show you around and bring up memories of fabled games. It's hard to stump these knowledgeable folks with trivia, even when asking how many hot dogs the stadium vendors peddle in a season and how many gallons of paint are used to stripe the field. The stadium is named after Curley Lambeau, club founder and early Packer coach. Ninety-minute walkabouts through the Packer's home are held daily from 10:30 A.M. to 4:30 P.M. from mid-June to Labor Day. Group tours are by appointment from May to December, but not on home-game weekends. Admission is charged. Call (920) 499-4281.

Oneida Bingo. Irene Moore Activity Center, 2020 Airport Drive, Green Bay. Try your luck at slots, video poker, blackjack, or bingo.

Three restaurants are on-site in case you need sustenance. Eating facilities include The Gathering (sit-down), Three Sisters (buffet style), and a snack bar. Open twenty-four hours a day every day. Call (920) 494-4500, (920) 497-8118, or (800) 238-4263.

Green Bay Botanical Garden. 640 Doty Road (adjacent to the Northeast Wisconsin Technical College), Green Bay. In 1995 construction of the sixty-acre botanical garden was started. Now those first plantings have blossomed beautifully amid the gentle hills and open spaces. A magnificent rose garden and the children's area are special highlights. The kids can scamper through a floral maze, study plant life under microscopes, and even plant their own vegetables in an urban youth garden program. If you'd like some assistance in looking over the grounds, free daily tours are offered from 9:00 A.M. to 6:00 P.M. The complex offers numerous workshops and lectures that attract thousands of dedicated gardeners from around northeastern Wisconsin. Call (920) 490-9457.

Fishing. Regardless of the season Green Bay is rich with fishing possibilities. Even in winter the Fox River yields a great crop of walleye and northern pike. Veterans say that using a jigging Rapala or Swedish Pimple tied with a minnow are best baits when going for lunkers. Then there's the western and eastern shores (from the lower bay to Chaudoir's Dock) of Green Bay itself for northerns and other species. Be sure to stick a pole and tackle box in the car trunk when visiting the city. You should be ready when the angling mood strikes.

New Zoo and Reforestation Camp. Situated on the north side of Green Bay. With more than 1,600 pine-shaded acres and 25 miles of hiking and biking trails, the complex offers plenty of outdoor adventure. There are picnic areas, trout ponds, and animal exhibits with an observation tower for a look over the grounds. Snowshoers and cross-country skiers have fun exploring the trails in winter, and horse-drawn wagon rides are available most weekends in summer and for special events in winter.

The thirty-five-acre New Zoo is the second largest in the state, after the Milwaukee County Zoo. The Green Bay zoo is located 11 miles northwest of Green Bay, within the Brown County Reforestation Camp. Drive 8 miles north of Green Bay on Highway 4 and exit Brown County Highway B (Sunset Beach Road). Follow Highway B 2 miles west to Brown County Highway IR. Follow Highway IR 1 mile north to the New Zoo. Brown County Reforestation Camp serves more than half a million visitors each year who enjoy watching the more than one hundred mammals of thirty-four species on display. The ninety birds represent thirty-three species, and there are reptiles, amphibians, fish, and insects exhibited, as well.

Feeding time for the animals is particularly fun. Approximate chow time in the Children's Zoo is from 9:00 to 11:00 A.M. Feeding at the Wisconsin Trail section is from 2:30 to 4:00 P.M.; bison and elk are fed from 10:00 A.M. to noon; and birds from 11:00 A.M. to 12:30 P.M. Grub is dished out in the international area between 1:00 and 2:30 P.M. Sorry, but there's no viewing of the bears, lions, lynx, or bobcats when they feed around forty-five minutes before closing.

For more information contact the New Zoo's Visitor Center (920-434-7841) or the Brown County Park Department (920-448-4466). Hours are 9:00 A.M. to 5:30 P.M. daily from March through September and 9:00 A.M. to 4:00 P.M. daily from October to January. The New Zoo is closed during January and February. A gift shop and concessions can be found in the visitor center, which closes its doors thirty minutes prior to closing hour.

ComedySportz. 211 North Washington Street, Green Bay. Goofy, zany comedy routines keep the laughs coming. Originating in Milwaukee, the ComedySportz gang is now in Green Bay and a dozen other cities. For show times call (920) 432-9374.

WHERE TO EAT

Titletown Brewing Company. 200 Dousman Street, Green Bay. The microbrewery, located in the former Chicago & Northwestern Railroad depot, offers six of its own beers on tap, plus root beer. But if brew isn't on your mind, try the Scotch and cigars. Plus pub grub. Look for the five-story clock tower as a landmark. Live music. The restaurant is open 11:00 A.M. to 11:00 P.M. Friday and Saturday and 11:00 A.M. to 10:00 P.M. Sunday through Thursday. The bar is open from 11:30 A.M. until bar time. Tours are at 2:00 P.M. Saturday. Call (920) 437-2337. $; ☐

Victoria's Restaurant. 2641 Bay Settlement Road, Green Bay. It's gotta be good, it's Italian. Pasta, pasta, pasta . . . the long, the round, the flat, the thin is served in grand style here, with a large selection of Italian wines. Hours are Sunday through Thursday 11:00 A.M. to 9:00 P.M. and Friday and Saturday 11:00 A.M. to 10:00 P.M. Call (920) 468–8070. $$.

River's Bend Supper Club. 792 River View Drive, Green Bay. Noted for its fresh fish and roast duck, the club has been a Green Bay fixture since the 1970s. Serves lunch and dinner. For hours call (920) 434–1383. $$; ☐

Rock Garden Supper Club. 1951 Bond Street (easy access off Highways 41, 141, 29, and 32), Green Bay. Lunch is served from 11:00 A.M. to 2:00 P.M. Monday through Friday, with a Sunday brunch from 10:00 A.M. to 2:00 P.M. Dinner is served from 5:00 to 10:00 P.M. Monday through Saturday and from 4:00 to 9:00 P.M. Sunday. Call (920) 497–4701. $$

Backgammon. 2920 Ramada Way, Green Bay. Good mix of steaks, seafood, and specials. Hours are 11:00 A.M. to 10:00 P.M. Monday through Thursday and 11:00 A.M. to 10:30 P.M. Friday and Saturday. Call (920) 336–0335. $$; ☐

Chanterelles. 2638 Bay Settlement Road, Green Bay. European dining, with daily specials. Open 5:00 to 9:00 P.M. Tuesday through Sunday. Call (920) 469–3200. $$; ☐

Kropp Supper Club. 4570 Shawano Avenue, Green Bay. Hours are 4:00 to 9:00 P.M. Wednesday, Friday, and Saturday, and after home Packer games on Sunday from 3:00 to 8:00 P.M. Call (920) 865–7331. $$; ☐

Ziggey's Inn. 741 Hoffman Road, Green Bay. Look for the sixteen-ounce rib-eye special served Tuesday through Thursday and on Sunday. Hours are 5:00 to 10:00 P.M. Tuesday through Saturday and 4:00 to 9:00 P.M. Sunday. Closed Monday. Call (920) 339–7820. $; ☐

Highpoint Supper Club. 2850 Humboldt Road, Green Bay. Specials served daily. Hours are 4:30 to 9:00 P.M. Tuesday through Thursday, 4:00 to 10:00 P.M. Friday and Saturday, and 4:00 to 9:00 P.M. Sunday; closed Monday. Friday features an all-you-can-eat fish fry. Call (920) 406–1017. $$; ☐

WHERE TO STAY

Regency Suites. 333 Main Street, Green Bay. Ask for the complimentary full breakfast and evening beverages with the midwinter specials, plus other deals throughout the year. Call (920) 432-4555. $$; ☐

Americinn of Green Bay. 2032 Velp Avenue, Green Bay. Jacuzzi rooms and suites are perfect if you are in Green Bay for a theater getaway or a Packer weekend. Call (920) 434-9790 or (800) 634-3444. $$; ☐

DE PERE

The Fox River built De Pere, as it connects the waters of Green Bay and Lake Winneago. The flowage brought trappers, traders, missionaries, and settlers to this region 100 miles north of Milwaukee, opening this section of the state to development and economic progress. Although that river was Wisconsin's first highway, the daytripper doesn't need to canoe north anymore. Where voyageurs' canoes once plied the Fox at De Pere, pleasure boaters now putt-putt. The river, however, is billed as Wisconsin's "first main street."

The river divides De Pere in an east-west manner, linked by a drawbridge above a 150-year-old boat lock that once helped ships up the rapids. At present, everything is politically quiet between both sides of the river, but it wasn't like that more than a century ago, when folks on either bank argued whether to join forces as one community or to stay independently separate. As realized now, the more level-headed won the day and De Pere forged ahead.

WHERE TO GO

Voyageur Park. De Pere. There's a history lesson taken with every step strolled through the park alongside the smoothly flowing Fox River. It is in the general vicinity where Father Claude Allouez built a mission church in 1671. And the redoubtable explorers Marquette and Jolliet departed from here in 1673 to explore the Fox and Wisconsin's hinterland, eventually becoming the first known whites to see the upper Mississippi River far to the southwest. The park is adjacent to the city's historic district.

De Pere Historic District. The community has set aside a 6-block area near Voyageur Park as a historical district, containing more than fifty businesses and homes that bring the good old days alive.

White Pillars. 403 North Broadway, De Pere. De Pere's historical museum is housed in the city's oldest building. It's a fitting repository for all the town's memorabilia. The structure was at various times an office, a bank, a barbershop, a newspaper office, and a church, in addition to being a home. Now you can browse through city records, look over old photos, and generally get in touch with De Pere's past. Hours are noon to 4:00 P.M. Monday through Friday. Call (920) 336-3877.

WHERE TO EAT

Black and Tan Grille. 101 Fort Howard Avenue, De Pere. That delightful Irish drink mix of dark Guinness stout and Harp beer gives its name to the Black and Tan. Even some of the other foods in the grille earn the appellation, such as the Black and Tan cheesecake and a steak drizzled with wine and balsamic vinegar. Hours are 5:00 to 9:00 P.M. Sunday through Thursday and 5:00 to 10:00 P.M. Friday and Saturday. Call (920) 336-4430. $$$; ☐

Ye Olde Chatter House. 614 George Street, De Pere. Hours are 7:00 A.M. to 9:00 P.M. Monday through Friday and 4:00 to 10:00 P.M. Saturday; closed Sunday. Call (920) 336-7337. $$; ☐

Union Hotel. 200 North Broadway (1 block north of the bridge), De Pere. Four rooms upstairs are rented out in the old hotel, built in 1832. The Swiss steak is worth the visit, and the Friday-night fish fry "ain't bad either," as they say here. Dining room is open 5:30 to 9:00 P.M. Monday through Thursday, 5:30 to 9:30 P.M. Friday and Saturday, and 5:00 to 8:30 P.M. Sunday. Call (920) 336-6131. $$; ☐

WHERE TO STAY

James Street Inn. 201 James Street, De Pere. Originally a flour mill dating from the nineteenth century, the all-suites inn is comfortably snug and tucked away. Many of the rooms have whirlpools, fireplaces, and decks overlooking the river. Call (920) 337-0111 or (800) 897-8483. $$-$$$; ☐

Northwest Day Trip 1

0   10   20   30 miles

Green Bay

De Pere

43

Point Bea
S. F.

42   Two Rivers

Manitowoc

Oshkosh

Lake
Winnebago

41

43

Elkhart Lake

Greenbush   67

23   Kohler   Sheboygan

Fond du Lac

Plymouth

Sheboygan
Falls   28

Kettle
Moraine
S. F.   Oostburg   Kohler-Andrae S. P.

49   57   Cedar
Grove   A

Horicon
Marsh   Belgium   Harrington Beach S. P.

26   Y

67   Mayville   43

Horicon   41   West Bend

175   33

Juneau   Saukville   Port Washington

143

Pike Lake   Cedarburg   Grafton   LAKE
MICHIGAN

57

Thiensville   167

Watertown   O   41   Mequon

83   45

Oconomowoc   45

Johnson   94   Delafield   43
Creek

efferson   Dousman   Waukesha   94   **Milwaukee**

67   894

Atkinson   Kettle
State

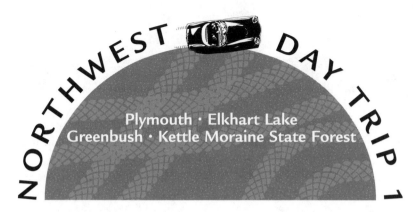

Plymouth · Elkhart Lake
Greenbush · Kettle Moraine State Forest

This region is easily accessed from a continuation of North Day Trip 5 (Sheboygan–Sheboygan Falls–Kohler). Plymouth is only 6 miles due west of Sheboygan on State Highway 23 or from Sheboygan Falls via Sheboygan County Highway C. Coming directly from Milwaukee, however, take I-43 north to State Highway 57, which leads directly into Plymouth. The rolling countryside is resplendent with maple, oak, and birch marking woodlots between the farmsteads. A drive here makes a lovely getaway, especially in autumn when the leaves change, the Canada geese honk their mournful way south, and the smell of harvest is in the air.

Historical attractions seem to be around almost every curve of the road. And they are. So be sure there is plenty of film in the camera, in order to take advantage of the scenic overlooks in the northern unit of the Kettle Moraine State Forest. Don't just sit in the car for this day trip. Get out and stretch your legs with all those hiking and cross-country ski opportunities, depending on the season. Scattered along the way are fruit and vegetable stands to explore and antiques shops to visit, plus a great range of bed-and-breakfasts and restaurants. Crossroads communities in the area, such as Glenbeulah, Cascade, Waldo, German Corners, and New Paris, might seem to be mere blips on the map, but they usually have a country pub or a small store in which to poke around.

PLYMOUTH

Plymouth was originally a stagecoach stop on the run from Sheboygan into the interior of pioneer Wisconsin. The first home-owners were Yankees from the East Coast, who named the town after Plymouth, Connecticut. The original settlers were soon followed by hardy German and Irish farmers. With the arrival of the railroads between 1859 and 1871, Plymouth quickly became a thriving rail-road hub. Several cheese factories were started, with the railroads hauling the dairy products throughout the Middle West. The quality of Plymouth cheese was so great that the town earned the nickname as the Cheese Capital of the World well before the turn of the nine-teenth century. The National Cheese Exchange, an organization responsible in the old days for setting cheese pricing, set up its head-quarters in the town in 1882 and stayed for years. Two local dairy managers, Elmer Eldridge and J. H. Wheeler, even perfected several processing methods that are still used today by major cheese compa-nies.

Plymouth was incorporated as a city in 1877 and is now a major tourist stop when taking drives through the Kettle Moraine State Forest.

WHERE TO GO

Arndt's Evergreen Golf Course. 1776 Eastern Avenue, Plymouth. This nine-hole, par-three course is adjacent to the Americinn Motel. An adjacent driving range gives everyone in the family who can tote a club an opportunity to practice swings before hitting the links. The pro shop offers clubs and carts for rent if the mood for a golf match suddenly strikes. Hours are 7:30 A.M. to dusk weekdays and 7:00 A.M. to dusk weekends from mid-April through late October. Call (920) 893–8822.

Tom & Jerry's Mini-Golf and Batting Cages. State Highway 67 and Suhrke Road, Plymouth. If members of your family are sports nuts—and if everyone is out for a drive—drop by Tom & Jerry's for a round on the thirty-six-hole mini-course. The tree-lined Shady Trails course makes for a comfortable workout, whereas the Stony Creek route offers tough water hazards. There are also six automatic batting cages, three of which are for baseball and three for slow-pitch softball. The facility is open from 10:30 A.M. to 9:00 P.M. weekends in May and daily in summer. Call (920) 893–0045.

Historic Plymouth Walking Tour. This self-guided tour can take as long as you wish, but a two-and-one-half-hour stroll takes the dedicated walker past more than fifty historic sites in town. Several of the buildings, such as the old Laack Hotel at 52 Stafford Street and the Henry H. Huson house, are listed on the National Register of Historic Places. For brochures outlining the tour sites, call the Plymouth Chamber of Commerce at (888) 693–8263 or pick up a map at the tourism booth in the Plymouth Center, 520 East Mill Street.

The Plymouth Center. 520 East Mill Street, Plymouth. The town's cultural center used to be an automotive dealership. It now houses a history museum with a marvelous collection of arrowheads and other Native American artifacts that were found in area fields over the years. The museum also displays antique fire equipment, desks and chairs from an old school, and an early print shop. In addition, the center is home to an art gallery and the local information service, staffed by volunteers.

The gallery features major Wisconsin artists, plus a permanent exhibit and regular art classes. Concerts, ranging from classical to folk music, are held in the building throughout the year, as well. The information center hours are 9:00 A.M. to 4:00 P.M. weekdays, noon to 4:00 P.M. Saturday, and 1:00 to 4:00 P.M. Sunday. The gallery and museum hours are noon to 4:00 P.M. Tuesday through Saturday and 1:00 to 4:00 P.M. Sunday. Both are closed Monday. Call (920) 893–5242.

WHERE TO SHOP

Plymouth Cheese Counter. W4882 State Highway 57 and Sheboygan County Highway PP, Plymouth. Capitalizing on the town's dairy heritage, the Cheese Counter presents more than one hundred varieties of cheese delights, including mild cheddar, Monterey Jack Veggie, and fat-free Koch Kaese. You can also pick up cheese spreads and summer sausage for in-car munching. Hours are 9:00 A.M. to 6:00 P.M. Monday through Friday, 9:00 A.M. to 5:00 P.M., Saturday, and 10:00 A.M. to 5:00 P.M. Sunday. Call (920) 892–8781 or (888) 60–SWISS. Check the Cheese Counter's Web site at cheesecapitol.com. The folks here even offer a gift shipment "cheese-a-month" club.

The Sewing Basket. 426 East Mill Street, Plymouth. The shelves here are lined with sewing products, fibers, fabric, felt products, and other needlework supplies. Product demonstrations are—as owners Patti Fohr, Betty McCartney, and Sheryl Schwochert say—a "stitch" in this cozy shop. For hours call (920) 892-4751.

WHERE TO EAT

Ella's Deli. 607 Eastern Avenue, Plymouth. Just like the delis of Milwaukee and Chicago, Ella's serves up a mighty line of sandwiches and soups. The subs are somethin' special, too. The latter always hit the spot when on a quick day tour in the Plymouth area (*hint*: you can also find other Ella's Deli outlets in Sheboygan and Sheboygan Falls). The shop is open 8:00 A.M. to 7:00 P.M. Monday through Friday, 9:00 A.M. to 5:00 P.M. Saturday, and 10:00 A.M. to 2:00 P.M. Sunday. Call (920) 893-3022. $; ☐

The Creamery Family Restaurant. 506 East Mill Street, Plymouth. This used to be an old Red Owl grocery store; now it's a laid-back eatery for fish fries, burgers, pie, and great malts. Hours are 6:00 A.M. to 8:00 P.M. Monday through Thursday, 6:00 A.M. to 8:00 P.M. Friday, 7:00 A.M. to 9:00 P.M. Saturday, and 8:00 A.M. to 2:00 P.M. Sunday. Call (920) 893-1770. $; ☐

WHERE TO STAY

B. L. Nutt Inn. 632 Main Street, Plymouth. This cream city brick home, which was built around 1875, offers two guest rooms and beautiful period furnishing. The full breakfast is worth the trip. Nutt was a local farmer who became a nationally-known wool broker. Call (920) 892-8566. $$; ☐

52 Stafford, An Irish Guest House. 52 Stafford Street, Plymouth. Listed on the National Register of Historic Places, the guest house was at one time the Laack Hotel. Over the years it served many other uses before renovator Rip O'Dwanny found it and renovated the property. Tapping deep into his Irish roots, O'Dwanny repaired the place and installed twenty rooms, which he named after Gaelic heroes and heroines. The rooms feature whirlpool baths and queen-size four-poster beds. The guest house also has a great lobby for lounging, a bar that serves up grand pints of Guinness, and a restaurant that offers lip-smacking delights. Irish music is a regular feature in the pub area. The Milwaukee-based Blarney folk group has been almost a house band because it has played here for so many years. So come to the 52 Stafford ready to party. And then relax. It's for good reason that "An Irish Guest House" is part of the name. Innkeeper O'Dwanny also runs the County Clare guest house in Milwaukee and a small hotel in Ireland. Call (920) 893-0552 or (800) 421-4667. $$-$$$; ☐

Harmony Hills in the Hollow. W7625 Sheboygan County Highway North, Plymouth. This remodeled farmhouse sits on forty acres of woods and fields that are great for exploring. The bed-and-breakfast is near the Kettle Moraine State Forest. Call (920) 528-8233. Cash or check only. $$

Spring Tulip Cottage. N4502 Sheboygan County Highway South, Plymouth. This private country cottage sits in the Kettle Moraine hills, making it a wonderfully romantic getaway. The snug little house has a fully equipped kitchen, parlor, bedroom loft, and picture windows. The cottage is 5 miles southwest of Plymouth—and worth the drive. Call (920) 892-2101. $$; ☐

Timberlake Inn Bed & Breakfast. 311 Madison Avenue (State Highway 28), Cascade. This rustic landmark building dates from 1895, with six rooms open for lodging. A powerful breakfast ensures that you will get off to a head start in the morning—only if you want to rise to the occasion. Cascade is about 5 miles south of Plymouth. Call (920) 528-8481. $$; ☐

ELKHART LAKE

Elkhart Lake was a resort community since the late-nineteenth century, with visitors attracted by resorts and cabins tucked along the lake and in the surrounding forest. It was the Midwest's gambling center from the 1920s to the 1950s. In fact, most businesses had at least one slot machine in the back room during those wild, wide-open days. The long-gone and much-lamented Fun Spot was a house converted into a gambling parlor in the 1940s by Otto Osthoff, a local entrepreneur who knew how to attract big-city high rollers from Milwaukee and Chicago. The state of Wisconsin eventually had to use its own mighty muscle to shut down his place, the Tern and Anchor, and other hot spots that had begun drawing Windy City mobsters and their lovely molls.

WHERE TO GO

Who cares if it snows in Elkhart Lake. Folks always have plenty to do regardless of the season. Schnee Days in early February features a cross-country ski clinic, snow golf, a chili cook-off, sleigh rides, and children's activities. All the goings-on are free, so call (920) 876-2922 for the details. No one needs to be a pro for the Down Hill Snow Bowling in mid-February, when Elkhart Lake hillsides become bowling "alleys" for a weekend of fun on the slopes. A fee is charged for competing, so check in at (920) 458-3310 for times and specifics. But by the time spring and summer roll around, hikers are hitting the trails.

Road America. N7390 State Highway 67 (2 miles south of Elkhart Lake). The 4-mile, 14-turn track hosts numerous events throughout the racing season, when the country's top drivers compete on the track's intricate course. Activities heat up with the June Sprints and the Texaco-Havoline-FedEx Championship Weekend in early July, among the many pro races. Motorcycle racing, vintage auto competitions, and other special events round out the race card. The track rests on 525 acres of rolling, tree-carpeted hills. Film star Paul Newman is a regular visitor, among the other entertainment stars who come to Road America to compete and to watch (and be watched). This is also a kid place, with youngsters age twelve and under admitted free. Call (800) 365-RACE.

Elkhart Lake Depot Museum. 104 East Street, Elkhart Lake. The museum, listed on the National Register of Historic Places, is housed in an old depot in the heart of the historic village. It contains most of the facility's original furnishings, bringing to mind those long-ago railroad days. Newspaper clippings, photos, and other memorabilia provide a good insight into the old Elkhart Lake, long a tourist destination for folks wishing to escape the rush of big-city life. The museum is open from 9:00 A.M. to 4:00 P.M. Monday through Saturday, from June 1 to Labor Day. Free admission. Call (920) 876-2922.

Henschel's Indian Museum. N8661 Holstein Road, Elkhart Lake. The Henschel homestead was settled in 1846. Since then, the family has made a concerted effort to find and catalog Native American artifacts on its property. By now thousands of stone and bone tools, copper implements, and pottery fragments have been recovered and are displayed. The museum is reached via Sheboygan County Highway J from Elkhart Lake; turn west on Sexton Road and then turn south on Holstein Road and go about ½ mile. Flint-knapping demonstrations show how the stone was turned into arrowheads and spear points. Henschel's also has a trout pond for fishing. Hours are 1:00 to 5:00 P.M. Tuesday through Saturday, Memorial Day through Labor Day. Call (920) 876-3193.

WHERE TO STAY

Siebken's Resort. 284 South Lake Street, Elkhart Lake. This bed-and-breakfast hotel dates from the turn of the nineteenth into the twentieth century. Packed with antiques, it makes an interesting place to visit. The resort has its own beach, ice-cream shop, bar, and sandwich shop. Call (920) 876-2600. $$; ☐

The Osthoff. 101 Osthoff Avenue, Elkhart Lake. The hotel and golf resort, on the shore of Elkhart Lake, offers one-, two-, and three-bedroom suites with kitchens, whirlpools, private balconies, and fireplaces. Located about five minutes away from Road America, the hotel caters to the race crowd during the season. Call (920) 876-3366. $$$; ☐

GREENBUSH

Greenbush is a crossroads community directly west of Plymouth on State Highway 23, or south from Elkhart Lake. Take Sheboygan County Highway J to A, then to P, and back to A. On the way from Elkhart Lake, detour around Crystal Lake, a delightful fifteen-minute drive on Sheboygan County Highway C, which rejoins P. Greenbush is only 53 miles north of Milwaukee.

Dedicated outdoors folks love the cross-country ski trails at the Greenbush Recreation Area in the North Kettle Moraine State

Forest, 15 miles northeast of Fond du Lac. Take Highway 23-E to N1765 County Highway G, which is just south of County Highway T. The park is open from 10:00 A.M. to 3:00 P.M. Remember that a state park sticker is required for the car.

WHERE TO GO

The main attraction here is the Wade House and Wesley Jung Carriage Museum, owned and operated by the State Historical Society of Wisconsin. The Wade House was a major stagecoach inn in the 1850s and an assembly point for Wisconsin troops on their way to fight in the Civil War. Visitors can ride in horse-drawn wagons around the extensive grounds, used as a battlefield for a Civil War reenactment early each October. Hours are 9:00 A.M. to 5:00 P.M. Tuesday through Sunday, May 1 through October 31. For a rundown on all the other activities at the Wade House, call (920) 526–3271.

KETTLE MORAINE STATE FOREST

The northern unit of the Kettle Moraine State Forest covers 29,000 acres in Sheboygan, Fond du Lac, and Washington Counties. The extensive oak- and maple-blanketed spread of rolling hills, interspersed with marsh and meadowland, lies approximately between Glenbeulah in the north to Kewaskum in the south. The northern edge of the forest is about a ninety-minute drive north from Milwaukee via State Highway 23 west out of Plymouth. Or you can head north on U.S. Highway 45 from Milwaukee to Kewaskum. Look at a map to determine the county roads that traverse the forestland.

The Kettle Moraine derives its name from the land formations created during the last Ice Age, between 25,000 and 10,000 years ago. Reminders of that frosty era are everywhere in this water-dappled countryside. Kettles are lakes formed by melting chunks of ice, buried under silt after the departure of the glaciers. When the ice melted, the ground caved in to create a pothole. The depression in the ground reminded early settlers of a kettle. On the other hand, a moraine is a long ridge of glacial debris left behind after the ice sheets retreated. From the air a keen-eyed viewer can trace the squiggly lines of rock that the untidy glaciers deposited throughout the region. Conical hills called kames and meandering glacial riverbeds termed eskers provide more dimension to the varied topography.

In the eighteenth and nineteenth centuries, trappers and traders for the Northwest Fur Company and the American Fur Company roamed the rugged hills and ridges of the Kettle Moraine in their quest for quality pelts. At present that same roller-coaster landscape makes great challenges for the hiker, cross-country skier, snowshoer, snowmobiler, and others enjoying outdoor fun. Yet even if the day-tripper prefers to remain carbound, the roads and byways in the forest take the traveler to many hidden retreats.

It doesn't cost anything to drive through the forest, but a park sticker is required for stopping at one of the trailheads or a campsite. For information about the Kettle Moraine State Forest, stop at the forest headquarters, N1765 Sheboygan County Highway G, or call (262) 626-2116. The forest headquarters are open from 7:45 A.M. to 4:30 P.M. weekdays. Offices at the area campgrounds are open from 9:15 A.M. to 10:30 P.M. Monday through Saturday and from 9:15 A.M. to 7:00 P.M. Sunday, between Memorial Day and Labor Day. The forest also has backpacking shelters and group camps. Visitors can hike, fish, hunt, ride horses, and bird-watch. Nature hikes and free evening naturalist programs are held regularly during the camping season. The recreation areas are open until 11:00 P.M.

Explore the forest by candlelight for a truly memorable night away from hearth and home. Hot drinks, snacks, and a bonfire to help warm the toes are usually found along the forest's Zilmer Trail on the first Saturday in February. That date, of course, depends on the weather. The trail is 18 miles southeast of Fond du Lac. Take State Highway 23 to County Highway SS between County Highway G and State Highway 67. The trail is lighted between 5:30 and 8:30 P.M. A state park sticker is required.

Mid-July is perfect for cyclists wishing to brave a twelve-hour endurance run through the North Kettle Moraine's New Fane Trail. The kick-off point is 18 miles east of Fond du Lac off Highway 23. The run begins at 8:00 A.M., with the last riders pulling into the finish line at 8:00 P.M. Call (262) 334-0171.

The Sargento Northern Kettle Moraine Challenge usually takes place on the last Sunday in January, depending on the weather and snow conditions. This cross-country ski challenge features a 2K kids' race and a 15K freestyle in eight classes on the forest's Greenbush trail system. Call Gerry Leiterman, (262) 626–2116.

WHERE TO GO

Henry South Reuss Ice Age Interpretive Center. The center is along State Highway 67 about 8 miles southwest of Plymouth, just south of the Long Lake Nature Trail and north of the Zillmer Hiking and Ski Trail. The information center overlooks the heart of the Kettle Moraine countryside. The facility is the center of activity for the state's 1,000-mile-long Ice Age hiking trail, following the debris rim left from the last retreating glacier covering Wisconsin. A mere 10,000 years ago this region was buried under a mile-high sheet of ice. The center has exhibits that describe that frosty era and orients visitors to the Ice Age Scientific Reserve, which stretches along the trail's paths. The center is named after a nature-loving congressman from Wisconsin, Henry S. Reuss, who helped establish the Ice Age Trail. Hours are year-round from 8:30 A.M. to 4:00 P.M. Monday through Friday and 9:30 A.M. to 5:00 P.M. Saturday and Sunday. A state park sticker is required for admission. Call (920) 533–8322.

Kettle Moraine Scenic Drive. A marked 25-mile drive takes motorists into some of the most scenic parts of the forest. Look for signs indicating KETTLE MORAINE SCENIC DRIVE. You can pick up the drive almost anywhere because all the area's major roads intersect with the system. Highlights along the drive include the Greenbush Recreation Area, Moraine Ridge Trail, Long Lake Nature Trail, and Mauthe Lake Recreation Area.

Climb the ninety-six steps to the top of Parnell Tower, an observation post astride one of the highest hills in the area. From this vista Sheboygan County rolls off to the horizon in all directions. The entrance to the tower site is 2 miles north of State Highway 67 on Sheboygan County Highway A. Turn left (west) on Sheboygan County Highway U and drive a quarter of a mile to the road leading to the tower. It is well marked. The tower itself is about a quarter mile into the forest, up a steep ridge. There are benches along the way for resting. A great hiking trail extends beyond the trail and runs for about 3 miles through the forest and meadows.

Once you've mastered the Scenic Drive, consider exploring the side roads on your own. One of the best alternate routes is along Sheboygan County Highways S and A, which cut along the east side of the forest. Another colorful route—especially vibrant in autumn— is along Sheboygan County Highway C, north of State Highway 23 out of Glenbeulah.

Ice Age Trail. Since the landscape was formed by the glaciers, it is fun to hike through the area and study the geology. The Ice Age Trail section that cuts through the Kettle Moraine State Forest presents one of the best walking experiences of any trail close to Milwaukee. One exceptional section of the trail is the 2.6-mile leg that loops over rough terrain, so be prepared for some muscle-stretching exercise. This is not a loop, so you will need to backtrack, travel with a partner in two cars (leaving one at the end of your walk), or have someone pick you up. There are two entrances to the trail. The first is on the south end, along Sheboygan County Highway U. This is not recommended because cars have to be parked alongside the road, a dangerous situation. The best parking is on State Highway 67, about 1.5 miles west of Sheboygan County Highway A. Pull up a small rise to the south of the highway, where there is a gravel patch well off the main road. Across the highway to the north is the Greenbush link to the Ice Age Trail. The southern part will take about two hours to traverse. On your trek you might see deer, wild turkey, and other denizens of the forest, lake, and prairieland.

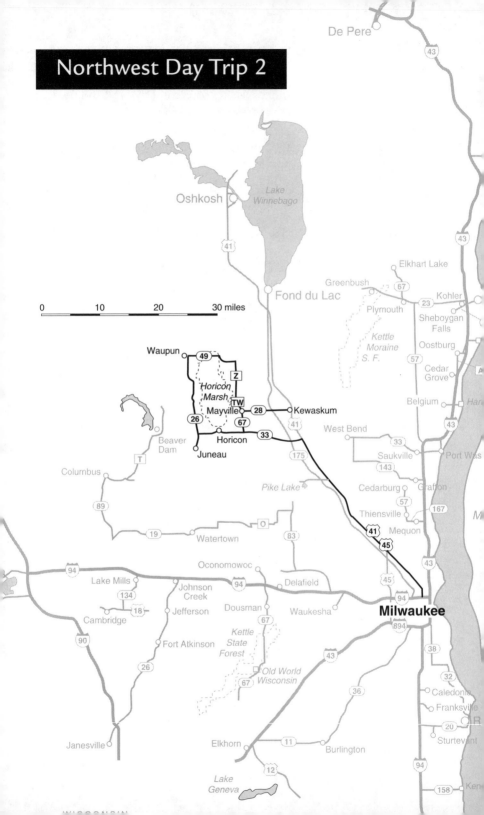

Northwest Day Trip 2

0 10 20 30 miles

Dodge County was settled in the early 1800s by East Coast Yankees looking for rich farmland. This part of Wisconsin was perfect, far from the rocky, worn soil of the East Coast. And there was so much of it! It wasn't long before the word spread that this region made for great homesteads. By 1836 there were enough local folks on hand for eager-beaver Henry Dodge to organize a grassroots political organization that sought official county status for their region. When this came about, the county was named after Dodge, who eventually went on to become a governor of Wisconsin.

Dodge County is now best known for its natural attractions, with its centerpiece of Horicon Marsh and its regional recreational trails. A day trip is easy from Milwaukee, which is only about 40 miles to the southeast.

If driving directly up from Milwaukee, take U.S. Highway 45/41, turn northwest on 41, and then exit on State Highway 33 at the Allenton/West Bend exit. Allenton is a friendly collection of pubs such as Proud Mary's and Silver Spurs (which brags of its pig roasts), the Carmel Lanes Bowling Alley, and a scattering of stores along the highway. Keep driving west 11 miles to State Highway 67 and turn north to Mayville, to start a tour around Horicon Marsh. Or, if you are extending a drive from Northwest Day Trip 1 (Plymouth–Elkhart Lake–Greenbush–Kettle Moraine State Forest), drive west on State Highway 28 from Kewaskum on the south end of the state forest. The highway leads directly to Mayville and the marsh.

Wildlife viewing is especially good in autumn along the marked Horicon Marsh Parkway, which rings around the marsh. It's a time when thousands of Canada geese migrate through the region. Their in-flight honking as they gracefully swoosh overhead fills the air like a New Orleans brass band on parade. Among the other common birds of the marsh are the pied-billed grebe, great blue heron, terns, doves, ducks, swallows, and dozens of other species.

The Dodge County Tourism Council can provide information on recreational opportunities throughout the vicinity. Call (800) 414-0101. For park information and reservations, contact the Dodge County Parks Department at (920) 386-3700 or access the county Web site at www.co.dodge.wi.us/plannng.

HORICON MARSH

Horicon Marsh covers 31,653 acres of bog and backwater created by melting glaciers about 10,000 years ago. Prehistoric burial and effigy mounds dating from hundreds of years ago show that the marsh was settled generations before the first white pioneers moved into Dodge County. The settlers, however, wanted to drain the marsh and plant crops on what they hoped would be resultant fertile farmland. A dam was built on the Rock River in 1846, creating a 51-mile-long lake. But the farming efforts failed, as well as efforts to build canals through the marsh to haul commercial goods. The dam was finally removed in 1869, and the marsh refilled naturally. After a twenty-year battle between other land developers and the state's conservation groups, the marsh was made into a protected preserve in 1941. Presently Wisconsin administers 10,587 acres on the south side of State Highway 49, and the federal government is responsible for 20,796 acres on the north side.

Horicon Marsh, located in east-central Wisconsin, is bordered on the south by State Highway 33, on the west by State Highway 26, on the north by State Highway 49, and the east by State Highway 28 and Dodge County Highways TW and Z. It is 13 miles west of U.S. Highway 41. The marsh is accessible year-round.

For more details on the marsh, contact the supervisors of the visitor center at the Horicon Marsh National Wildlife Refuge, W4279 Headquarters Road, Mayville; (920) 387-2658. The visitor center is open year-round from 7:30 A.M. to 4:00 P.M. Monday through Friday and open weekends in autumn. Check the center's

Web site at www.fws.gov/horicon.html. The Wisconsin Department of Natural Resources, Horicon Service Center, N7725 Highway 28, can also answer questions. Hours are 7:45 A.M. to 4:30 P.M. weekdays year-round. Closed weekends. Call (920) 387-7860.

WHERE TO GO

Hiking. The 2.5-mile Horicon Marsh Redhead Trail is about a two-hour walk from the parking area on the north side of the marsh, along State Highway 49. Wear the proper footgear for the weather because the trail can be wet and messy after a rain. Mosquitoes are also a challenge in early summer, so wear protective sprays or long-sleeved shirts. Yet don't let that deter you from a great day of bird- and animal-watching. If you prefer to drive, a road through the area is open from 8:00 A.M. to 3:00 P.M. weekdays from April 15 to September 15. Vehicles are prohibited there on weekends and holidays, so walking is a better bet to get close to the animal action. An information kiosk is at the trailhead, indicating several different loops in this section of marsh, such as the Red Fox Nature Trail and the Egret Nature Trail. Both are connected with the Redhead Trail for an expanded day of trekking. Rest rooms are also available at the parking lot.

Canoeing. Public and private boat-launching sites make it easy to get into the Rock River, the Horicon Marsh, and Lake Sinissippi. Not all sites are marked by signs, so it is best to use the public facilities. Among the most accessible public launch sites is the River Bend Park in downtown Horicon, which has plenty of space for trailers and cars. The park is below the Horicon Dam, offering about 15 miles of waterway on the route down to the Hustisford Dam to the south. The Rock River expands there into Lake Sinissippi at Hustisford. There are many back channels, bays, and islands to explore on the way.

The Ice House Slough is located off Horicon's Chestnut Street, around the corner from the Rock River, which flows under the Lake Street Bridge. From here canoeists can paddle south to the Horicon Dam and then reverse and go back to the Federal Dike in the marsh. The Arndt Ditch Landing is just off Dodge County Highway E, northwest of Horicon, opening directly into the marsh. The Burnett Ditch Landing is on the west side of the marsh, via Dodge County Highway E to State Highway 26. Turn right to Burnett and then make another right on Burnett Ditch Road.

Launchings are also possible at the Green Head Club, located on the marsh's east side. Take State Highway 28 out of Horicon; turn left on Bay View Road, go 1 mile and turn left onto Green Head Club Road.

WHERE TO GO

Marsh Haven Nature Center. The center is along State Highway 49 on the north side of Horicon Marsh. The long, low building, with its adjacent hiking paths and a pond, is fronted by a large parking lot, which makes it easy to find. To walk in the nearby woods, follow the east trail from the lot. To hike along a marsh and the pond, follow the trail to the west from behind the building. If you want more hiking or even biking opportunities, a section of the 34-mile-long Wild Goose Trail serves as the center's western border. Part of the building is partially underground, with windows opening on eye level with the land outside. This makes it perfect for watching animals and birds.

Marsh Haven is a forty-seven-acre private, nonprofit education facility run by volunteers. It was the brainchild of Lawrence Vine, a Wisconsin Department of Natural Resources researcher who lived in nearby Juneau. Wildlife exhibits and educational displays in the center tell the history of Horicon Marsh. Often artists work on paintings in the building and will happily explain how they plan and execute a piece. Admission is charged. Hours are 9:00 A.M. to 5:00 P.M. on Saturday and Sunday and 10:00 A.M. to 4:00 P.M. weekdays from May to December. Call (920) 324-5818.

MAYVILLE

Mayville's claim that it is the "Historic Gateway to the Horicon Marsh" is well deserved. The town dates from the middle of the nine-teenth century as a farming hub. Many of the buildings in the down-town area were built in the mid-1800s. Driving down the main street is like taking a step back to Wisconsin's early history. Local passersby still say, "Hello."

WHERE TO GO

Horicon Marsh Parkway. The parkway, formerly known as the Wild Goose Parkway, is a 36-mile auto-tour route around the Horicon National Wildlife Refuge and the Horicon Marsh State Wildlife Area. The route meanders along state and county highways through the communities of Burnett, Kekoskee, Horicon, Mayville, and Waupun. Visitor centers, recreational trails, and observation sites along the roadway are well marked and easily accessed. The parkway is most easily reached from U.S. 151 or U.S. 41 by following State Highway 33 to access the south end of the marsh or by State Highway 49 to reach the northern end of the marsh.

Audubon Days. Mayville. Held annually in early October, the three-day weekend festival celebrates the return of the geese to the marsh. Mayville offers live music, bed races, a flea market, art shows, kids' activities, a parade, sporting events, a bike tour, a run/walk, and scenic boat trips on the Rock River. For details contact the Mayville Area Chamber of Commerce at (800) 256–7670 or check the Dodge County Web site, www.dodgecountywi.com.

Downtown Holiday Heritage Fest. Mayville. Mayville's winter festival in mid-December kicked off in 1999, with fifteen professional ice sculptors competing for prizes throughout the downtown. There was also a holiday home tour, a secret Santa shop, caroling, a live Nativity, wine and cheese tasting, and other activities. Call (920) 387–1167.

WHERE TO SHOP

Old Fashioned Foods Cheese Factory Store. 331 Main Street (across from Mayville City Park), Mayville. Cheese lovers enjoy this store with its range of great flavors. Garden Jack, Butter Kase, and numerous other varieties are made on-site, along with several varieties of squeeze cheeses in bottles and cheese logs. The building was originally the old Ziegler Brewery, which was shuttered during Prohibition and subsequently reopened as a cheese factory. Current owner Gary Youso has managed the facility since the 1970s. Hours are 9:00 A.M. to 5:00 P.M. Monday through Friday and

10:00 A.M. to 3:00 P.M. Saturday and Sunday. Call (920) 387-7930 or (800) 346-0154.

WHERE TO EAT

Lee's Chinese Restaurant. 101 South Main Street, Mayville. Who says East doesn't meet West? In Mayville it certainly does at Lee's. Hours are 11:00 A.M. to 9:00 P.M. Tuesday through Thursday, 11:00 A.M. to 10:00 P.M. Friday, 11:30 A.M. to 10:00 P.M. Saturday, and 11:30 A.M. to 8:30 P.M. Sunday. Call (920) 387-0288. $$; ☐

WHERE TO STAY

Audubon Inn. 45 North Main Street, Mayville. This National Historic Landmark is located on State Highways 28 and 67, across from the Rock River in downtown Mayville. The building was built in 1896 and renovated in 1989 by Rip O'Dwanny, whose 52 Stafford, An Irish Guest House, in Plymouth, and the County Clare, in Milwaukee, are also popular getaways. The inn's reputation ranges far afield. Among its honors, the *National Geographic Traveler* magazine has called the Audubon Inn one of the top fifty-four great inns in the United States. There are seventeen individualized rooms with whirlpool tubs, quilt-covered, queen-size four-poster beds, and writing desks. The inn's restaurant is also considered one of the best one hundred in the state, according to Dennis Getto, food critic at the *Milwaukee Journal/ Sentinel*, the state's largest daily newspaper. The hearty foods and homemade desserts there would be worth walking to Mayville. Dinner is served from 5:00 to 9:00 P.M. Monday through Saturday. The inn's pub is open from 5:00 to 10:00 P.M. Monday through Thursday and from 5:00 P.M. to closing time on Friday and Saturday. The etched-glass skylight above the pub features a flock of Canada geese. Call (920) 387-5858. $$$; ☐

Addison House Bed & Breakfast. 6373 State Highway 175, Addison (9 miles east of Mayville). Addison, once a thriving farming crossroads, is now a blip on the map. The Addison House, a restored 1860s home with three decorated guest rooms, has always been a featured building here. Each room has a private bath and air-conditioning. Owner Suzanne Fish started the B&B in 1989 and has turned an adjacent bowling alley, dating from 1880, into the dining room. That room has a Federal-style cherry dining table seating twelve, with expansion to twenty-four. The house also has a large collection of antique dolls, teapots, and antique plat maps. The Home Sweet Home antiques shop is across the highway from the Addison House. Call (262) 629–9993. $$; □ 5 percent charge for use of credit cards

WAUPUN

As with other pioneer communities in Wisconsin, Waupun started as a farming village. In 1839 Seymour Wilcox was the first white man to stake a claim in the fertile Rock River Valley. A mix of Irish, Scottish, German, Norwegian, and Dutch emigrants followed him, clearing the woods for plantings of wheat and corn. In 1858 rail service linked Waupun to Chicago, providing a quick marketing route for these valuable cash crops.

In 1851 Wilcox gave twenty acres of land to the state for the construction of a prison, which opened the following year. The massive, high-walled complex still remains in use. Although the prison aids the community's strong economic base, Waupun would probably rather have visitors remember it as "The City of Sculpture." Seven original bronze pieces are featured in the town, including James Earl Fraser's noted *End of the Trail* in Shaler Park on Madison Street. The statue has become the symbol of the plight of Native Americans, with its lamenting horseman and downturned spear.

This National Historic Landmark was originally only an 18-inch-tall statue, made in 1894 and exhibited at the Panama Pacific International Exposition in San Francisco in 1914. Fraser was then commissioned to cast a larger statue in bronze by Clarence Shaler, a Waupun sculptor. Shaler created *Dawn of Day* (dedicated in 1931) on the City Hall terrace at the corner of Main and Forest Streets, as well as several other pieces around the city. Shaler wanted Fraser's Indian work to be a city centerpiece, and he encouraged the other artist to enlarge on his original idea. Maps of the sculpture sites are available from the Waupun Chamber of Commerce, 121 East Main Street; (920) 324–4357, extension 25. Or visit the city's Web site at www.waupunchamber.com.

WHERE TO GO

City Parks. If picnicking is on your mind, there are plenty of Waupun parks to enjoy. Dodge Park has two tennis courts in its four-and-one-half-acre spread, plus barbecue grills, rest rooms, a shelter, and a water fountain. Johnson's West End Park also has tennis courts, basketball courts, a softball field, and other recreational space. Other Waupun parks include McCune, Meadow View Heights, Shaler, Wilcox, Zoellner, and the Spring Street Recreation Area/Tanner Park.

WHERE TO SHOP

C&J Rock Shop and Craft Mall. 417 East Main Street, Waupun. C&J repairs and makes jewelry. There are also more than sixty other crafters throughout the 5,000-square-foot three-story mall area. For hours call (920) 324-4697.

WHERE TO EAT

Helen's Kitchen. Parkview Plaza, Waupun. Breakfast specials at Helen's are a good way to start any day. Plus, Saturday night boasts all the broasted chicken you can eat. Hours are 5:45 A.M. to 9:00 P.M. Monday through Thursday and 6:00 A.M. to 9:30 P.M. Friday and Saturday. Closed Sunday. $; ☐

Chit Chat Cafe. 435 Main Street, Waupun. Owners Jeff and Liza Schulz have added bluegills to their Friday night fish fry. This makes it one of the few places in east-central Wisconsin where you can nibble something fishy beyond haddock for this traditional pre-weekend dinner. Open twenty-four hours. Call (920) 324-5065. $; ☐

HORICON

The Horicon Chamber of Commerce is very helpful in describing what to see and do in the region. Its offices are located on Barstow Street in Horicon, with the tourism department hours there from 10:00 A.M. to 4:00 P.M. Monday through Friday and Sunday and from 9:00 A.M. to 5:00 P.M. on Saturday, May through October.

WHERE TO GO

Horicon Marsh Bird Festival. This annual event is held in early May for birding fans. Activities include banding and early-morning hikes. Kids of all ages are welcome. The Horicon Chamber of Commerce operates a food stand downtown for the birders from 10:00 A.M. to 4:00 P.M. during the festival. Check with the chamber for dates at (920) 485-3200 or visit the state's Department of Natural Resources Web site at www.dnr.state.wi.us/org/land/wildlife/reclands/horicon.

Blue Heron Landing. State Highway 33, downtown Horicon. One of the best ways to see the marsh if you don't have your own boat are the spring, summer, and autumn tours given by Blue Heron. Visitors ride on pontoon boats deep into the marsh, giving everyone the opportunity to see black-crowned night herons, wood ducks, geese, otters, and other creatures living in the marshland. Daily lecture tours run for about an hour, departing at 1:00 P.M. May through September. In October tours depart at 1:00 P.M. Monday through Friday, with varying times posted for Saturday and Sunday departures, depending on the weather. Two-hour bird-watching tours are also available on some weekends during May through September. Call for dates. The Saturday excursions depart at 6:00 P.M., and Sunday tours are held at 9:00 A.M. Each run leaves from the Blue Heron Landing on State Highway 33 by the bridge in downtown Horicon. Blue Heron also rents canoes. Call (920) 485-4663 or check its Web site at www.horiconmarsh.com. Bring your own binoculars.

John Deere Horicon Works. Downtown Horicon (by the bridge). John Deere, the area's largest employer, offers free tours of its factory complex that makes lawnmowers and garden tractors. The company started in 1861 as Van Brunt Inc., making planting equipment for farmers. The firm eventually became the world's largest manufacturer of grain drills. In 1911 Van Brunt joined with John Deere to make other farming equipment and started the lawn line in 1963. A complete walk around the manufacturing plant takes about three hours, beginning at 9:15 A.M. You'll see the press area and assembly lines. A tour of a downtown finishing facility takes about two hours, beginning at 10:00 A.M. Children must be at least age twelve. Tours are by appointment only. Call (920) 485-4411.

WHERE TO EAT

Mother's Day Restaurant. 417 East Lake Street (across from the post office), Horicon. Homemade cake, pie, and bread here makes this a place another mother can love. And it has cinnamon rolls to die for! Call (920) 485-4493. $; ☐

Shell's Place Bar & Grill. 315 East Lake Street, Horicon. This is Horicon's "Home of the Frosted Beer Mug," making it a perfect stop on a hot summer day. Bartenders Melissa and Gayle pour a grand tap. Hours are 3:00 P.M. to closing Monday and Tuesday and 10:00 A.M. to closing Wednesday through Saturday. Closed Sunday. Call (920) 485-0619. $; ☐

WHERE TO STAY

Royal Oaks Motel. W4419 Highway 33, ¼ mile east of Horicon; (920) 485-4489. The motel has sixteen units with queen-size beds, cable TV, and showers. $; ☐

JUNEAU

Juneau is the county seat of Dodge County. The friendly little city is named for Paul Juneau, who was the son of Solomon Juneau, an early Wisconsin settler and founding father of Milwaukee. The young man was accidentally shot and killed in a hunting accident and was buried between two oak trees in the Juneau cemetery. One of the oaks, however, was felled in a violent windstorm that slapped down on Juneau in 1998.

Juneau offers a wide range of things to do for the day-tripper. A farmers' market is held every Friday from June through September on the county courthouse lawn. Get there early to be sure of securing the best buys. The city also hosts a communitywide rummage sale in mid-August.

WHERE TO GO

Wild Goose State Trail. The Wild Goose State Trail is a 34-mile, multiuse recreational pathway in Dodge and Fond du Lac Counties along the abandoned Chicago & Northwestern Railway corridor. The packed limestone trail is flat and easy for hikers, cyclists, horse riders, and cross-country skiers. It runs from the southern trailhead at State Highway 60 (about 4 miles south of Juneau) in Dodge County to the northern trailhead at Rolling Meadows Drive in Fond du Lac. You can link with the trail at numerous points. Several of the best are at the Marsh Haven Nature Center parking lot, ¼ mile east of the trail on State Highway 49; the Horicon National Wildlife Refuge parking lot, ¼ mile east of the trail on State Highway 49; Burnett Fireman's Park in the village of Burnett; Whitty Park on the west edge of Horicon along Dodge County Highway E; Dodge County Airport on State Highway 26 north of Juneau; and Juneau City Park on Lincoln Street in Juneau. Rest rooms, picnic facilities, and restaurants are along the way.

The Wild Goose was the first such "co-operative" state trail in the state. It is owned by the Department of Natural Resources, with Dodge and Fond du Lac Counties providing the upkeep.

Camping near the trail is available at the Horicon Ledge County Park, 4 miles east of the trail near Horicon and overlooking the marsh (920-387-5450) and Waupun County Park, 5 miles west of the trail in Waupun (920-324-2769).

WHERE TO EAT

P.J.'s Family Restaurant. 255 West Oak Street, Juneau. Owners John and Pat Fabisch are rightfully proud of their nonsmoking place, which offers homemade pizza, plus full dinners, breakfasts, and all the extras. The restaurant is open 5:00 A.M. to 3:00 P.M. Monday through Thursday, 5:30 A.M. to 8:00 P.M. Friday, and 6:00 A.M. to 2:00 P.M. Saturday; closed Sunday. Call (920) 386-5691. $; □

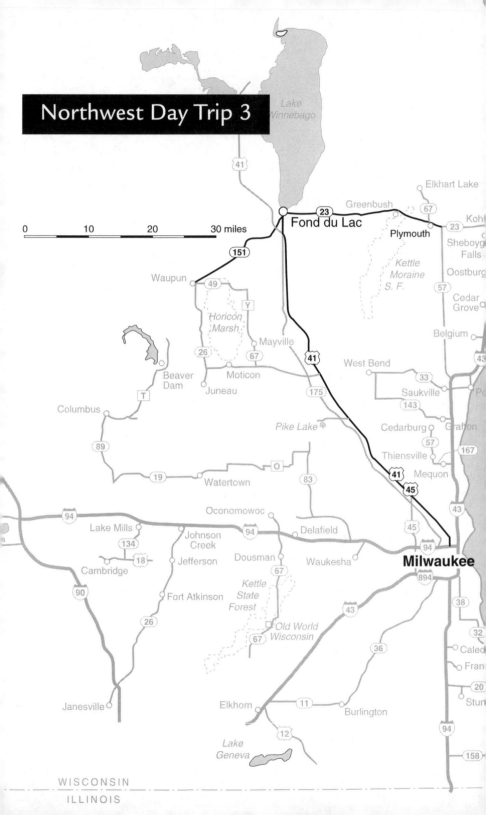

Northwest Day Trip 3

0   10   20   30 miles

Lake Winnebago

Elkhart Lake

67

23   Greenbush

Fond du Lac

Plymouth

Kohl

23

Sheboyg Falls

41

151

Waupun

49

Y

Horicon Marsh

Mayville

26

67

Moticon

Juneau

Beaver Dam

T

Columbus

89

19

Watertown

O

83

41

West Bend

33

175

Saukville

143

Pike Lake

Cedarburg

57

Thiensville

41

45

Mequon

Kettle Moraine S. F.

Oostburg

57

Cedar Grove

Belgium

43

Po

Grafton

167

43

Oconomowoc

Lake Mills

134

18

Cambridge

90

Johnson Creek

94

Delafield

Jefferson

Dousman

67

Waukesha

45

94

Milwaukee

894

Fort Atkinson

Kettle State Forest

26

67

Old World Wisconsin

43

38

32

Caled

Fran

36

20

Janesville

Elkhorn

11

Burlington

Stur

12

94

Lake Geneva

158

WISCONSIN

ILLINOIS

FOND DU LAC

French explorers first visited the Fond du Lac area in the early 1700s and established a trading outpost on the south shore of Lake Winnebago, Wisconsin's largest body of water at 215 square miles. Winnebago is 30 miles long and from 5 to 10 miles wide, extending from Winnebago County in the west to Fond du Lac County on the south and Calumet County on the east. The city name is derived from the French, meaning "the far end of the lake." The lake is a fantastic recreational outlet.

Fond du Lac's economic strength grew over the generations due to its geographic location on the lake and at the head of the fertile Fox River Valley. The Fox flows into the west side of Lake Winnebago at Oshkosh on its way east to Green Bay. The river flows out of the lake at its northern end in Menasha. All this water made it easy to transport goods and people. Loads of money was earned in the early century of Fond du Lac's life by smart entrepreneurs who secured control over the transportation outlets, whether stagecoaches, wagons, barges, or railroad concessions.

In 1837 only fifteen people lived where today's community sprawls. But by the time Wisconsin became a state in 1848, Fond du Lac was the second-largest city in the state. Lumber mills and agriculture attracted additional thousands of settlers, who arrived in large numbers with the advent of railroad service. Commercial fishermen once plied the lake, seeking monster sturgeon and other catches. They hauled in so much finny tonnage that the city earned the name "The Sturgeon Capital of the World." Many of the homes built by the community's early wealthy business families still stand.

Among the city's famous sons was King Camp Gillette, the inventor of the safety razor, who was born in Fond du Lac on January 5, 1855. Gillette went on to become president of the American Safety Razor Corp., which was renamed the Gillette Safety Razor Company in 1902. He remained as a company director until his death in 1931. A social reformer, Gillette dreamed up the idea of a giant world corporation to control industry, with the people as stockholders. He even wrote several books about his utopian philosophies.

The Fond du Lac Convention and Visitors Bureau is a wealth of information. Drop by 19 West Scott Street for armfuls of descriptive literature or call (920) 923–3010 or (800) 937–9123. The Web site is www.fld.com. Hours are 8:00 A.M. to 5:00 P.M. Monday through Friday and 9:00 A.M. to 1:00 P.M. Saturday, from Memorial Day Weekend through September.

To get to Fond du Lac, take U.S. 41 northwest out from Milwaukee. The ride on the four-lane highway is only 62 miles. If coming from Northwest Day Trip 1 out of the Plymouth area, a distance of about 30 miles, drive west on State Highway 23. From Northwest Day Trip 2 from Waupun, drive northeast on State Highway 151 about 20 miles.

WHERE TO GO

Fond du Lac's Talking Houses & Historic Places. This self-drive auto tour takes visitors around the city, with street directions on maps starting at the visitor information center at Fond du Lac Plaza, 19 West Scott Street. Sites indicated as "Talking Houses" are equipped with radio transmitters that fill you in on the history of the home or building. Stay in your car and tune in to whichever AM frequencies are indicated on signs near the sites (AM 1020, 1100, or 1620). Fourteen of the twenty-four homes on the tour are included in the program. Each message runs from two to four minutes.

Sabel's Misty Valley Gardens. Guests can hike through the gardens' acreage, which include a 2.5-acre section devoted to wood-land plants. Group tours are available weekdays by appointment, so get a gang together with strolling boots and appropriate-weather clothing. The gardens are 10 miles east of Fond du Lac. Take Fourth Street (County Highway T) to Oak Road to W2977 Walnut Road. Hours are 1:00 to 5:00 P.M. or call for an appointment, (920) 921-5849.

Wander Country Roads. A map suggesting backcountry meanderings in Fond du Lac County can be secured from the Fond du Lac County Planning Department at (920) 929-3135 or the Fond du Lac Convention and Visitors Bureau at (920) 923-3010 or (800) 937-9123. The driving will take the day-tripper through the county's wonderful rolling countryside to farm markets, hiking and biking trails, museums, and small villages such as Eden, Byron, Oakfield, Alto, Brandon, Fairwater, Mount Calvary, St. Cloud, and many other picturesque communities. One area just a few miles outside Fond du Lac has so many country churches it is called "The Holy Land."

Lakeside Park. Stroll through this 400-acre park, which had its beginnings in 1809. It has one of the best views in this part of the state, as it overlooks Lake Winnebago. On the grounds are a petting zoo and a Victorian bandstand that hosts regular summer concerts. A fun excursion is chugging along on the miniature train that rolls through the park. The marina at Park Avenue and Oregon Street has everything for the boater, from snacks to gifts, temporary moorings, slips, and pumps. There are eighteen free launch sites for fishing fans.

Among the neat things to see in the park is the 1920s-era carousel built by the famed Allen Herschel Co. All the animals are wooden pegged, held together without nails. A local businessman, Sam Costas, bought the unit from the Jack Vomberg Carnival in 1946 and placed it at his outdoor theater after three years of renovation work on the old machinery and woodwork. The carousel still gives thousands of rides to kids and oldsters every year.

The park's landmark, the Lookout Lighthouse, is open in summer to the public. Built in 1933, it became the city's symbol and can be see on flyers, letterheads, signage, and all sorts of other materials used in the community. Of a Cape Cod design, it is 40 feet high, with a 10-foot, 8-inch base of concrete and flagstone. The lighthouse has long been used to mark the entrance to the Fond du Lac harbor on Lake Winnebago. More about the lighthouse can be learned on the Talking Houses Tour by tuning in to AM 1620 on your car radio.

Jim Baldauf Collector Cars. 220 Morris Court, Fond du Lac. Baldauf's carpeted showroom is home to fifteen vintage vehicles, including a 1949 Oldsmobile, which is supposedly only one of five in the world. Lots of auto memorabilia can be found here, as well. Tours are by appointment. Usually open from 11:00 A.M. to 4:00 P.M. weekdays. But call (920) 923-2211 to double-check.

Buttermilk Performance Center. South Park Avenue at Old Park Road, Fond du Lac. The Fond du Lac Symphonic Band alternates with numerous guest artists during a free summer music series. Performances are held at 7:15 P.M. Wednesdays from June through August. In addition, local bands in the Music Under the Stars series are featured at 7:00 P.M. concerts on Mondays. Call the Convention and Visitors Bureau (920-921-5500) for playbills.

St. Paul's Cathedral. 51 Division Street, Fond du Lac. Magnificent wood carving by German craftworkers makes the cathedral an emotional and spiritual artwork. Stained-glass windows were designed and installed by skilled Canadian and American artists in the nineteenth and twentieth centuries, allowing explosions of colored light to illuminate the building's incense-perfumed interior. The cathedral also houses the tomb of Charles Chapman Grafton, the second bishop of Fond du Lac. A selection of traditional and historic vestments can also be viewed inside St. Paul's. The church is open weekdays from 8:00 A.M. to 4:00 P.M., but check in with the church office if you want to look around. Self-guided tours are available from 8:00 A.M. to noon on Sunday, with guided tours by reservation and a small fee. Be respectful if church services are being held. Masses are set at 7:30 and 10:00 A.M. Sunday. For a weekday schedule of Mass or to book a tour, call (920) 921-3363 or (920) 922-1833.

Galloway House and Village. 336 Old Pioneer Road (midway between State Highway 175 and U.S. 45), Fond du Lac. The original portion of the house was built in 1847 and enlarged on by a subsequent owner in 1868. It was again remodeled in 1880, which gave it today's appearance. The thirty-room home served four generations of Galloways, with its four fireplaces, stenciled ceilings, and one of the first indoor bathrooms in the state. Edwin P. Galloway, grandson of the original owner, donated the home, carriage house, and land to the Fond du Lac Historical Society in 1954. The grounds now include a "village" of twenty buildings, which include a railroad depot, a print shop, and a school brought to the site from around the county. Admission. Hours are 10:00 A.M. to 4:00 P.M. daily from

Memorial Day weekend through Labor Day and on weekends in September. Call (920) 922-6390.

The Adams House Resource Center and historical society office have been on the grounds since 1989. The house was built by Edwin H. Galloway for his wife's widowed aunt, Mrs. August Adams. Two of Mrs. Adams' sons were killed in the Civil War. The center is open year-round for society meetings and for historical research on Fond du Lac County. Hours are 10:00 A.M. to 5:00 P.M. daily. Appointments can be made by calling (920) 922-1166 or (920) 922-6390.

Tapping into the Civil War theme, the Galloway House usually holds a Civil War reenactment in mid-June. Military life of the era, along with drills, musket firing, posting of camp guards, and other duties are demonstrated from 10:00 A.M. to 5:00 P.M. Capitalizing on World War I, a Doughboys reenactment in mid-July brings back the days of an early Wisconsin state guard unit. Admission is charged at both events, with preschoolers admitted free.

WHERE TO SHOP

Kristmas Kringle Shoppe. 1330 South Main Street, Fond du Lac. Christmas-ornament collectors from around the state know they can get the latest decorations here from craftworkers in Germany, Poland, and Italy. Look for Byer's Patricia Breen, Radko, Boyd's Bearstones, Hummel, Swarovski silver crystal, and numerous one-of-a-kind pieces. Dozens of individually decorated theme trees are scattered around the two-story chalet-like structure to give a festive air. Kids are welcome if supervised closely. Take them to see the train sets and dioramas in the basement. The shop buyers regularly visit design studios and factories in Europe and elsewhere to arrange supplies of the holiday goodies. Hours are 9:00 A.M. to 6:00 P.M. Monday, Tuesday, Thursday, and Saturday, 9:00 A.M. to 8:00 P.M. Wednesday and Friday, and 10:00 A.M. to 5:00 P.M. Sunday. Call (920) 922-3900 or (800) 721-2525.

Farmers Market. Downtown Fond du Lac. Fresh fruit and vegetables are popular items when the farmers bring their produce to town early every Saturday June through October, with sales starting at 6:30 A.M. and running until noon.

Trinkets 'n Treasures Arts & Gifts. 47 South Main Street, Fond du Lac. This two-story art gallery and gift shop has Thomas Kinkade prints, Mill Creek sculptures, Europia glassware, and hundreds of other items. Hours are 9:30 A.M. to 3:00 P.M. Friday and 9:30 A.M. to 4:00 P.M. Saturday. Hours are extended for the Christmas holidays. Call (920) 922-5667.

Pat's Gallery of Antiques. 861 Grove Street, Fond du Lac. Toys, glassware, furniture, and loads of unusual items are displayed for sale. Hours are 11:00 A.M. to 5:00 P.M. Monday and Wednesday through Friday, 10:00 A.M. to 4:45 P.M. Saturday, and noon to 5:00 P.M. Sunday. Closed Tuesday. Call (920) 923-9237.

Living Light Studio. 314 Fourth Street, Fond du Lac. The studio has the city's largest collection of Native American art for sale, plus kaleidoscopes and blown-art glass. Hours are 10:00 A.M. to 5:30 P.M. Monday through Friday and 10:00 A.M. to 4:00 P.M. Saturday. Call (920) 921-1962.

Truly's Cake & Candy. 248 South Park Avenue, Fond du Lac. Nostalgia-plus here. All candy is mixed, measured, and dipped here for that extra touch of old-fashioned flavor. Hours are 10:00 A.M. to 6:00 P.M. Monday through Friday and 10:00 A.M. to 1:00 P.M. Saturday. Call (920) 923-3933.

The Lightsmith Shop. 262 Doty Street, Fond du Lac. Looking for stained glass? Tiffany-style lamp shades, angels, jewelry, and other handmade objects are presented. Crystal prisms can also be purchased. Open daily 9:00 A.M. to 5:30 P.M. and Saturday 9:00 A.M. to noon from October through April. Call (920) 922-3492.

Forest Mall. 835 West Johnson Street (junction of U.S. 23 and 41), Fond du Lac. This is Fond du Lac's largest mall, with fifty-five shops featuring such department stores as Younkers, Sears, Penney's, and Kohls, as well as specialty shops. The mall was entirely remodeled and reopened in spring 1999. *The Savings Times*, an in-mall shopper, is packed with coupons for bargains. Hours are 10:00 A.M. to 9:00 P.M. Monday through Friday, 10:00 A.M. to 8:00 P.M. Saturday, and 11:00 A.M. to 5:00 P.M. Sunday. Call (920) 922-5730.

WHERE TO EAT

Jukebox Charlie's. 248 North Hickory Street (just off State Highway 23), Fond du Lac. If you have blue suede shoes, this is the place to wear 'em because this dance hall/restaurant offers '50s and '60s tunes from the jukebox and platter-spinning (or CD buzzin')

DJs. Naturally a place like this has burgers, shakes, and fries. Hours are 4:00 to 9:00 P.M. Tuesday, Thursday, and Sunday, 4:00 P.M. to midnight Wednesday, and 4:00 to 10:00 P.M. Friday and Saturday. Closed Monday. Call (920) 926-1950. $; ☐

Old Country Buffet. 835 West Johnson Street, Fond du Lac. Melt-in-your-mouth roast beef or ham are the specialties during each dinner hour. Plus there's homemade soup, fresh fruit, casseroles, hot sweet rolls—and all the other comfort foods, from macaroni and cheese to potatoes and gravy. Daily breakfast hours are 8:00 to 11:00 A.M. Lunch hours are 11:00 A.M. to 3:30 P.M. Monday through Saturday. Dinner hours are 3:30 to 8:00 P.M. Monday through Thursday, 3:30 to 9:00 P.M. Friday and Saturday, and 11:00 A.M. to 8:00 P.M. Sunday. Call (920) 924-7619. $$; ☐

Rolling Meadows Family Restaurant. Corner of Rolling Meadows Drive and U.S. 151, Fond du Lac. The restaurant's motto is "You Can't Afford Not to Eat Here." Carryout is available. Open daily from 6:00 A.M. to 9:00 P.M. year-round. Call (920) 922-9140. $; ☐

Sunset Supper Club. N7364 Winnebago Drive, Fond du Lac. Steaks and prime rib are specialties at the Sunset, where the sun never sets on good food and service. Hours are 5:00 to 10:00 P.M. Tuesday through Thursday, 4:30 to 10:30 P.M. Friday and Saturday and 4:30 to 9:30 P.M. Sunday. Closed Monday. Call (920) 922-4540. $$; ☐

WHERE TO STAY

Ramada Plaza Hotel. 1 North Main Street (at North Main and Division Streets) downtown Fond du Lac. The hotel was constructed in 1923 by Walter Schroeder, a Milwaukee-based builder and innkeeper. Originally known as the Retlaw, which is Walter spelled backward, the building is now on the National Register of Historic Places. Take a look at the ornate crystal chandeliers and open balcony above the front lobby. The hotel is AAA approved and has rooms for the physically challenged, plus a health club, an indoor pool, a lounge, and a restaurant. The 132 rooms have in-room coffeemakers. Call (920) 923-3000 or (800) 2-RAMADA. $$; ☐

Costello's Irish Guest House. N5254 Martin Road (1 mile south of Fond du Lac). The four-bedroom, smoke-free home was built in 1879.

It has a game room, a full bath on each of the two floors, an outdoor grill, a kitchen, and a screened-in porch. Up to seven guests can take the entire old farmhouse for a visit. Call (920) 922-5725. $$; ☐

White Picket Fence Bed & Breakfast. 213 East First Street (corner of Park and First Streets), Fond du Lac. This Italianate-style home dates from the Victorian era, but its service and ambience is totally today. The two upstairs bedrooms have queen-size beds and air-conditioning, but there is a shared bath. Call (920) 922-0870. $$; ☐

Dixon House. W7190 Forest Avenue Road (2 miles west of Fond du Lac off State Highway 23). The century-plus old farmhouse sits on eighty acres. The upstairs bedroom has a private bath and air-conditioning. Extended-stay rates are negotiable. Call (920) 923-3340. $$

Holiday Inn Holidome. 625 Rolling Meadows, Fond du Lac. One of the city's larger convention hotels, it still provides a good getaway for the day-tripper. The indoor pool is especially handy if traveling with kids. Call (920) 923-1440 or (800) HOLIDAY. $$$; ☐

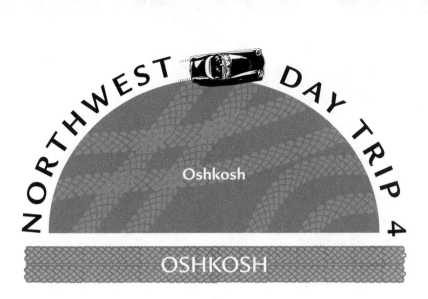

OSHKOSH

Oshkosh is the seat of Winnebago County, located on the west shore of Lake Winnebago and the mouth of the Fox River. The city is only 19 miles north of Fond du Lac (Day Trip Northwest 3) and 80 miles north of Milwaukee, making it an easy drive. French explorers poked around here as early as 1634, with fur traders and trappers following soon afterward. The first permanent settlement was a cluster of log cabins around a trading post in 1836. Oshkosh was incorporated as a village in 1846 and as a city in 1853, named after a local Menominee leader. By 1870 it was the state's third-largest city. Over the years it became a rail hub and remains a major Wisconsin manufacturing center. One of its most notable products was the legendary Oshkosh B'Gosh bib overalls, which originated here in 1895. The University of Wisconsin has a major branch here as well, which adds to the community's cultural tone. The city's chamber of commerce is located at 120 Jackson Street. Call (920) 303-2266. To get here, take U.S. 41/45 north out of Milwaukee and continue northwest when U.S. 41 splits from 45 at Richfield. The route is well marked.

WHERE TO GO

Historic Tours. The chamber has an excellent little guide to the city's more notable architecture, covering five districts listed on the National Register of Historic Places and a range of other properties. The Osborn House, 840 Osborn Street, is thought to be the oldest

surviving home in Oshkosh. The building was constructed in 1844 by Robert Osborn, one of the first land surveyors in the community. One of the most interesting districts is along Algoma Boulevard, once considered the Gold Coast of Oshkosh, where many of its most prominent citizens of the nineteenth century had their mansions. Many of these citizens were in the timber and lumber business, with rich woodwork subsequently being shown to good advantage in the houses. The majority of homes are in the Queen Anne and Period Revival styles, but the neighborhood also includes the one house in town designed by Frank Lloyd Wright.

Air Adventure Museum & Pioneer Airport. 3000 Poberezny Road, Oshkosh. The Experimental Aircraft Association (EAA) museum opens the eyes to the wonders of flight. Starting with displays on the Wright Brothers, the facility traces the evolution of aircraft up to the present. The museum has more than 200 historic aircraft, with about ninety on display at any one time (which encourages additional visits). The Eagle Hangar is dedicated to the memory of World War II aviators, with its display of planes and other military hardware of the era. You can also tour the restoration center and watch mechanics refurbishing old aircraft. During summer a tram ride of only a few minutes takes guests to the Pioneer Airport, a re-creation of an airport during the early days of air travel. If the weather is good, rides are available for a charge in a 1929 Ford Tri-Motor or an open cockpit biplane. The EAA Aviation Foundation's Boeing Aeronautical Foundation's Library has more than 10,000 books, thousands of journals and publications, and a collection of historical aircraft photos. Research facilities are available from 8:30 A.M. to 5:00 P.M. Monday through Friday.

At the end of each July, the EAA hosts the world's largest air show, attended by more than 800,000 people and attracting 12,000 planes. Military aircraft from around the world are part of the display. The EAA Housing Hotline (920-235-3007) can help with accommodations. Attendees fill almost every available room in Oshkosh and adjoining communities, so be prepared if you wish to stay over. Some visitors even hunker into a Milwaukee hotel and fly in and out of Oshkosh for the event. Even many day-trippers who are fanatic about flying simply drive to the EAA each day and return in the evening.

For general information on the EAA, call (920) 426-4800 or look at the Web site at www.eaa.org.

Frederic March Theater. 926 Woodland Avenue (University of Wisconsin/Oshkosh). The theater seats an audience of 500, with four main stage productions presented each year, as well as hosting traveling professional shows. Call the theater at (920) 424-4417 for the schedule.

Oshkosh Public Museum. 1331 Algoma Boulevard, Oshkosh. The museum was organized in 1905, when a group of town residents gathered to plan for a display on the history of Oshkosh and the Lake Winnebago region. Originally located in the public library, the museum became its own entity in 1924. The facility is now located in the historic Edgar Sawyer home, which holds more than 250,000 artifacts in geology, art, botany, and other fields. An extensive collection of letters, diaries, and manuscripts document the personal lives of Oshkosh residents over the years. Admission. Hours are 9:00 A.M. to 5:00 P.M. Tuesday through Friday and 1:00 to 5:00 P.M. Saturday. Call (920) 424-4731.

Paine Art Center & Arboretum. 1410 Algoma Boulevard, Oshkosh. This Tudor Revival mansion, built in the 1920s, has a series of rooms containing nineteenth-century French and American paintings, plus sculpture, rugs, and other art works. The art center also hosts demonstrations, lectures, tours, and family events throughout the year. The late Oshkosh lumber magnate Nathan Paine built the house for his wife, Jessie, and he'd be proud of what cultural events are now held in his former home. Admission is charged. Hours are 11:00 A.M. to 4:00 P.M. Tuesday through Sunday with hours extended to 7:00 P.M. on Friday. Outside, you'll enjoy strolling through the six gardens on the art center property. The Rose Garden is one of the more spectacular gardens when all the scented blooms are doing their flower thing. The arboretum is free. Call (920) 235-6903.

Morgan House. 234 Church Street, Oshkosh. Speaking of old homes, a tour of this 1884 Queen Anne is a pleasant way to spend a rainy afternoon or a pleasant day, as well. The house was built by John Rodgers Morgan, who helped found Morgan Lumber Products. It still has its original wallpaper, woodwork, and fireplaces. The Morgan House now houses the Winnebago County Historical and Archeological Society, which holds programs here. Admission. Hours are 2:00 to 4:00 P.M. Sunday, from Memorial Day to Labor

Day. You can also always get an appointment to walk through the building. Call (920) 232-0260.

Grand Opera House. 100 High Avenue, Oshkosh. The building, a restored 1883 Victorian theater, plays host to a diverse production lineup. The opera house features dance companies, theatrical performances, concerts, children's programming, and numerous other activities. For an entertainment rundown call the box office at (920) 424-2350. Tours of the building are available, and the casual daytripper almost expects to see a phantom or two in the opera's back row of seats. Call the administration office at (920) 424-2355 to set up an appointment. The facility's Web site is www.grandoperahouse.org.

Water Recreation. Lake Winnebago, the largest freshwater lake in Wisconsin, along with the Fox and Wolf Rivers and several smaller lakes cover more than 165,000 acres, with 168 miles of shoreline. The expanse of water is perfect for fishing, boating, waterskiing, canoeing, and other sports. Pioneer Princess excursion cruises puddle around Lake Winnebago, for a relaxed way to explore the lake. The line has the only excursion boat on the lake. The 63-footer has enclosed and outside decks. Call (920) 233-1980 or (800) 683-1980 for departure times and to make reservations. If you've forgotten your own boat or watercraft, rent what you need at Adventure Outfitters, 451 North Main Street (920-235-8893); Pioneer Inn Marina, 1000 Pioneer Drive (920-233-1981); or Performance Marine, 501 South Main Street (920-236-4220). Fishing licenses can be secured at local sporting-goods stores or from the Department of Natural Resources, 905 Bay Shore Drive (920-424-3050).

Boat launches in Oshkosh can be found at the following sites:

Bowen Street Launch, end of Bowen Street

Fugelberg Park, South Main Street and Fugelberg Terrace

Miller's Bay, Menominee Park, off Hazel Street

Mill Street Boat Ramp, Mill Street and Bay Shore Drive

Rainbow Park, Oshkosh Avenue and Rainbow Drive

William Steiger Park, Campbell Road, adjacent to the Oshkosh Senior Center

24th Avenue Boat Launch, South Main Street and Twenty-fourth Avenue.

Menominee Park and Zoo. Hazel Avenue and Merritt Street, Oshkosh. This is the city's premier park, with one hundred acres of picnic areas, a petting zoo, tennis courts, ball diamonds, boat launches, and a 2-mile paved recreation trail. A garden explodes in color during the growing season. For tykes there is a miniature train on which to ride, plus a merry-go-round, bumper cars, and other whirly-twirly-gigs. The Oshkosh Community Playground, built by 6,000 volunteers, is wheelchair accessible and features all sorts of play options from tunnels to slides. It's enough to make a day-tripper wanna be a kid again. Ah, go ahead. Explore the castle. The park is open daily from 8:00 A.M. to 11:00 P.M., with seasonal hours. Call (920) 236–5080.

Oshkosh Youth Symphony. If the opportunity arises and your visit coincides with a performance of the Oshkosh Youth Symphony Orchestra, be sure to take advantage of the concert. The symphony was founded in 1969 when Oshkosh area schools agreed that pupils with musical interests should have an outlet for their talents. Kids in grades 6 through 12 audition for places in the group, which has reached up to 105 young performers in size. Rehearsals and most performances are held at the University of Wisconsin/Oshkosh. The youngsters have also performed in the Twin Cities and communities throughout Wisconsin, demonstrating that they certainly know what they are doing. For schedules and other information, contact the symphony at (920) 233–7510 or www.athenet.net/~loofboro/badger/oyso/index.html.

Oshkosh Symphony Orchestra. Park Plaza Complex, Oshkosh. Since 1940 the symphony has brought together the Fox River Valley's top musicians. One of the most popular presentations is the annual holiday show, along with at least four other major concerts a year. The orchestra often collaborates with the youth symphony. All concerts are held in the Alberta Kimball Auditorium. Call (920) 233–7510 or try the Web site at www.vbe.com/~oso.

Rebel Alliance Theater. 445 North Main Street, Oshkosh. The community theater produces classics, children's programs, and original plays. Theater buffs often drive up from Milwaukee for a show, spend an overnight, and return. Diehards can even do the jaunt in an evening. Call (920) 426–8560 or use the Web site at www.rebel.oshkosh.net

Fratello's & Fox River Brewing Company. 1501 Arboretum Drive (State Highway 21 and the Fox River), Oshkosh. The Fox River Brewing Company was founded in 1995 by the Supple brothers, who grew up in their parents' restaurant business. Live music is presented every evening in the brewery bar from Memorial Day through Labor Day. Fox River has also an outside beer garden that is great for summer loafing. The attached restaurant has a full menu, offering steaks, seafood, and daily specials ($$; ☐). Hours are 11:00 A.M. to 10:00 P.M. Sunday through Thursday and 11:00 A.M. to 11:00 P.M. Friday through Saturday. To make it easy for boaters during the season, slips at the rear of the brewing building accommodate up to forty boats.

Brewery tours are available from 1:00 to 4:00 P.M. Saturday or by appointment. If they aren't too busy, one of the bartenders from the restaurant area can often take a break and show you around. The brewmasters are on duty only during the week. Call (920) 232–BEER. The brewery, which produces thirteen main beers and two seasonals, has a second location at the Fox River Mall, 4301 West Wisconsin Avenue, Appleton.

WHERE TO SHOP

Miles Kimball Warehouse Outlet. 2185 South Koeller, Oshkosh. Shoppers seeking discounts of up to 60 percent on items flock to this outlet to scoop up bargains. A drive from Milwaukee means nothing when it comes to trimming the bottom line on a cash register receipt. Miles Kimball was only twenty-nine when he went into business for himself in the 1930s. He devised a Christmas card with a verse that spelled out the name "Johnson." With a $500 loan and the Twin Cities phone book, he printed and mailed samples to every Johnson home in that area. The response was overwhelming, and he soon had enough cash to produce a batch of cards and expand his line through a catalog. From that beginning the company has grown to be one of the nation's leading direct-market mail-order houses for household items. The firm mails out more than 70 million catalogs each year. Hours are 10:00 A.M. to 9:00 P.M. weekdays, 10:00 A.M. to 6:00 P.M. Saturday, and 11:00 A.M. to 6:00 P.M. Sunday. Call (920) 231–1070.

Prime Outlets-Oshkosh. U.S. Highway 41/44, Oshkosh. More than sixty outlets for clothing, books, cutlery, toys, and other retail items attract shoppers from around Wisconsin. Brand names include Black & Decker, Dansk, Casual Corner, OshKosh B'Gosh, Nautica, and loads more. Since Prime Outlets is only 82 miles north of Milwaukee and 50 miles west of Green Bay, it is a day-tripper shopping mecca. The drive takes only about ninety minutes from Milwaukee. Hours are 10:00 A.M. to 6:00 P.M. Monday through Thursday, 10:00 A.M. to 9:00 P.M. Friday and Saturday, and 11:00 A.M. to 6:00 P.M. Sunday. Closed Easter, Thanksgiving, and Christmas. Call (800) 980–SHOP or check the Web site at www.primeoutlets.com.

WHERE TO EAT

Lara's Tortilla Flats. 715 Main Street, Oshkosh. Salsa, fajitas, nopalitos, corn bread, burritos, and the whole range of Tex-Mex foods can be found here in downtown Oshkosh. Hours are 11:00 A.M. to 10:00 P.M. Monday through Saturday. Call (920) 233–4440. $

Ardy & Ed's Drive-In Restaurant. 2413 South Main Street (across from Lake Winnebago), Oshkosh. The business has been at the same location since 1948 and still has carhops on roller skates and '50s and '60s music playing. The draft root beer goes well with a burger and fries. This place is so special it's worth some specific directions. From U.S. Highway 41, exit on Ninth Avenue and take Ninth east through Oshkosh to South Main Street. Turn right (south) and travel about 1 mile. From the south on U.S. Highway 45, follow the highway into Oshkosh to Twenty-fourth Avenue, and there it is. Open 11:00 A.M. to 10:00 P.M. weekdays March through September. Call (920) 231–5455. $

Granary Restaurant. 50 West Sixth Avenue (between Oregon and Main Streets downtown), Oshkosh. The restaurant calls home a century-old flour mill that was the first electric mill in Wisconsin. The menu ranges from piles of pasta to platters plied with pounds of barbecued ribs. House specials include chicken teriyaki, veal Siciliano, and veal Oscar. Lunch hours are 11:00 A.M. to 2:00 P.M. Monday through Friday. Dinners are from 5:00 to 10:00 P.M. Monday through Saturday, 5:00 to 10:30 P.M. Friday, and from 5:00 to 9:00 P.M. Sunday. Call (920) 233–3929. $$$; ☐

Jeff's on Rugby. Corner of Tenth and Rugby, Oshkosh. Smoke-free! That's the way to enjoy the prime rib special on Wednesday and Saturday evenings, with Alaskan whitefish on tap for Friday night. Lunch is served from 11:30 A.M. to 2:00 P.M. Monday through Friday. Happy hour is 3:00 to 6:30 P.M. Monday through Thursday. Dinner is offered from 5:00 to 10:00 P.M. Friday through Sunday. Open seven days a week. Call (920) 231-7450. $$; ☐

Brooklyn Food & Spirits. 607 South Main Street, Oshkosh. Steak, chicken, and gourmet burgers. Hours are 11:00 A.M. to 10:00 P.M. Sunday through Thursday and 11:00 A.M. to midnight Friday and Saturday. Call (920) 233-0303. $$

WHERE TO STAY

Baymont Inn, 1950 Omro Road; (920) 233-4190. $$; ☐

Pioneer Inn and Marina, 1000 Pioneer Road; (920) 233-1980. $$$; ☐

Americinn Motel, 1495 West South Park Avenue; (920) 232-0300. $$; ☐

Park Plaza Hotel, 1 North Main Street; (920) 231-5000. $$$; ☐

Holiday Inn, 2251 Westowne Avenue; (920) 303-1300. $$; ☐

Howard Johnson, 1919 Omro Road; (920) 303-1300. $$; ☐

Josef's Motel, 4645 South U.S. Highway 45; (920) 231-9350. $; ☐

Ramada Inn, 500 South Koeller Street; (920) 235-3700. $$; ☐

Super 8 Motel, 1581 West South Park Avenue; (920) 426-2885. $$; ☐

Town Motel, 215 Division Street; (920) 233-0610. $$; ☐

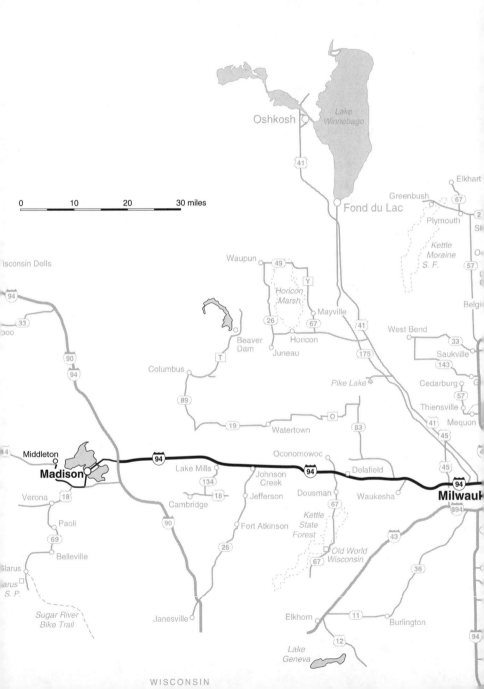

West Day Trip 1

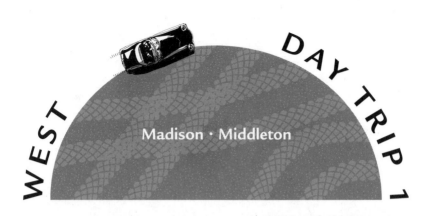

Madison · Middleton

MADISON

Wisconsin's capital, Madison, is affectionately called "Mad City" by the locals. This is probably for good reason. Not only is the city the state's political power center, with all the attendant intrigues, but it is also home of the University of Wisconsin, with a supporting cast of professorial types, eager young minds, and a liberal outlook on life. *Forward*, the statue atop the state capitol, looks down at the entire scene from her perch. One wonders what she thinks about all the hustle and bustle.

Madison is a city of lakes; the largest is Mendota, followed by Monona, Waubesa, and Wingra. Parks and observation points are scattered around the waters, with one of the best vistas from the deck atop the downtown Monona Terrace Convention Center. The center design was a brainchild of famous architect Frank Lloyd Wright, and his signature look is stamped everywhere in the building, from the carpet design to the roof line. The center is open daily from 9:00 A.M. to 5:00 P.M., with the Willliam T. Evjue Rooftop Garden open daily from 8:00 A.M. to midnight, depending on the weather. Public guided tours are given daily at 11:00 A.M. and 1:00 P.M. Tours are free on Monday and Tuesday; on other days a small fee is charged.

The city is built on an isthmus between Lakes Mendota and Monona, hence its nickname as "The Isthmus City" and the name of its weekly alternative newspaper, the *Isthmus*. Madison touts itself as "being on everyone's short list." *Money* magazine consistently ranked the city as among the best places to live in America. *Ladies Home Journal, The Utne Reader, Expansion Management,* and *Outside* magazines are among the others who have tooted Madison's horn. The combination of geography, cultural and social amenities, business opportunities, and the mix of politics and academia contribute to the city's high ranking. One publication even called Madison's Picnic Point one of the ten most romantic places in the country in which to kiss. The narrow, wooded jut of land pokes its finger about a mile into Lake Mendota.

For tour and travel details on the Madison buzz, stop at the Greater Madison Convention and Visitors Bureau, 615 East Washington Avenue. A visitor information hotline can be called at (608) 255-2537 or (800) 373-6376. For walk-ins the office is open from 8:00 A.M. to 4:30 P.M. weekdays. An additional info center is located at the Dane County Regional Airport from noon to 10:00 P.M. weekdays and from 11:00 A.M. to 8:00 P.M. Saturday and Sunday. Or visit the CVB Web site at www.visitmadison.com.

GETTING THERE

Madison is a mere ninety-minute drive—give or take a couple of nanoseconds, depending on traffic—from Milwaukee via I-94. The heavily traveled corridor is a commuter route for politicos, bureaucrats, and even book-laden scholars who make the trip each day. Many travelers prefer to leave their cars at home and utilize the regularly scheduled Badger Bus Lines. The motor coaches depart the Milwaukee depot at 635 North Seventh Street, Milwaukee (414-276-7490), destined for the Madison terminal, 2 South Bedford Street (608-255-6771). From there it is easy walking distance, or cab and local Madison bus service, to sites around the capital city. Rates are $22 round-trip for anyone one and older, or $12 one way. Beverages and snacks are allowed. With that in mind it is a comfort to know that on-board rest-room facilities are provided.

The company has almost a century of service accommodating travelers. Madisonian John Meier is Badger's current president, heading a family-run operation that was started in the 1920s by his grandfather. There's no better way to travel than to settle back, read a book, and occasionally look out at the countryside whether it's rain or snow or gloom of night. The coaches depart from both the Madison and Milwaukee terminals at 7:00 and 10:00 A.M. and at 12:30, 3:00, 5:30, and 8:00 P.M. daily, including Sundays and holidays.

Whether driving or using a motor coach, a day trip to Madison allows visitors to choose from a plethora of activities and then return home in reasonable shape. Weekend getaways are also popular, especially when tying in a morning shopping excursion with an afternoon athletic event at the university and a late-night theater engagement followed by dinner.

If driving, consider hauling along bicycles because Madison is one of the most user-friendly cities of its size in the country. In fact, *Bicycling* magazine has placed Madison in the top-five North American cities for biking. Special bike lanes are on most major roadways, with abundant racks outside stores and offices, in parks, and along the lakes. More than one nattily dressed business type is seen pedaling along with the pack of body-pierced, tattooed students.

WHERE TO GO

State Capitol. Capitol Square, Madison. The current white granite structure in the heart of the city is the third capitol. This building was designed by George B. Post and constructed between 1906 and 1917. Free daily tours track the building's history, art, and architecture. Each tour departs from the ground level of the rotunda at 9:00, 10:00, and 11:00 A.M., as well as at 1:00, 2:00, and 3:00 P.M. Sunday tours are held at 1:00, 2:00, and 3:00 P.M. An additional 4:00 P.M. tour is added in summer.

The walkabout allows a peek into the senate and assembly chambers to watch legislators in action. The supreme court hearing rooms are also open to the public. Tours usually run from thirty to forty-five minutes, allowing plenty of time to buttonhole a hometown representative for a question-and-answer session. Reservations are necessary for groups of ten or more; call (608) 266-0382. Of course, a visitor can roam on one's own to count the statuary. Check with the tour desk for general information on the building. The desk is open from 8:30 A.M. to 5:00 P.M. Monday through Saturday and from noon to 5:00 P.M. on Sunday.

Walking Tours. A ground-eye view of Madison is the best way to experience this city. Several walking tours have been developed by the Madison Landmarks Commission and the Madison Trust for Historical Preservation, with maps and booklets available from tourism outlets throughout town. The Third Lake Historic District is always a favorite. The district is one of Madison's earliest residential neighborhoods, located on the north side of Lake Monona. The tour usually begins at the west end of Jenifer Street and proceeds east through the district. Another excellent neighborhood tour meanders through the Greenbush-Vilas neighborhood bounded by Henry Vilas Park, Monona Bay, Regent Street, and Randall Avenue. A stroll through either area takes visitors past homes, old businesses, churches, and other historic sites that have figured prominently in the city's history. The Forest Hill Cemetery tour is also fun. Now the resting place of such Wisconsin luminaries as Alice Whiting Waterman (1820–1897), a redoubtable activist who cared for Confederate prisoners imprisoned in the Madison area during the Civil War; newspaper publisher George Merrick (1841–1931); and General Lucius Fairchild (1831–1896).

Madison City Parks. As early as 1894, the Madison Park and Pleasure Drive Association had acquired a system of trails for carriages and walking around the city's lakes. The group's original system eventually grew into the Madison Parks Division, now including 200 scenic properties, golf courses, play areas, hiking paths, and wetlands. Even Fido is accommodated in exercise areas at Quann and Sycamore Parks. Most areas are wheelchair accessible. For details call the Parks Administration Office at (608) 266-4711. Maps and flyers can be secured from the department in the Madison Municipal Building, Room 120, 215 Martin Luther King Jr. Boulevard.

Wisconsin Veterans Museum. 30 West Mifflin Street (Capitol Square), Madison. Part of the state's Department of Veterans Affairs, the museum presents fascinating displays of Wisconsin soldiery over the generations. Lifelike dioramas depict troops in action and behind the scenes. Hours are 9:00 A.M. to 4:30 P.M. Monday through Saturday and noon to 4:00 P.M. Sunday, April to September. Closed Monday and holidays during the rest of the year. Free admission. For details on programs and exhibits, call the museum at (608) 267-1799 or visit the Web site, www.badger.state.wis.us/agencies/dva.

Madison Children's Museum. 100 State Street, Madison. The Children's Museum is the city's only real hands-on museum. Of course, it helps if a guest is a youngster who loves to crawl, climb, and make music. Participatory programs are geared to kids from age one through twelve. Exhibits and events are regularly scheduled. Hours are 9:00 A.M. to 4:00 P.M. Tuesday through Sunday. Call (608) 256-6445.

The Elvehjem. 800 University Avenue (on the university campus), Madison. This art museum hosts a $50-million collection of paintings, sculpture, prints, and other artifacts, augmented by traveling collections for its 24,000 square feet of display space. The facility sponsors a Sunday Afternoon Live from the Elvehjem series of concerts throughout the school year, featuring top chamber music programs. The shows are then aired on Wisconsin Public Radio. Museum hours are 9:00 A.M. to 5:00 P.M. Tuesday through Friday and 11:00 A.M. to 5:00 P.M. Saturday and Sunday. Call (608) 263-2495.

The Entomology Museum. 1630 Linden Drive, Madison. Politics in Madison have been known to drive folks buggy. But the study of insects is in the interest of science at the Entomology Museum. The collection there includes 1.5 million insects, representing more than 15,000 species. One can only hope that the giant beetles and killer cicadas displayed at the facility won't ever wind up in a cupboard at home—either would be an exterminator's nightmare. But kids dig the live tarantulas and huge, hissing Madagascar cockroaches that happily call the museum their home. For hours call (608) 262-0056.

Madison Repertory Theater. 122 State Street, Madison. Roger Bean's *The Marvelous Wonderettes,* David Auburn's *Proof,* Noel Coward's *Blithe Spirit,* Fred Alley's *Guys in Ice,* Kenneth Lonergan's *Lobby Hero, The Laramie Project* by Moises Kaufman and the Tectonic Theater Project, and Craig Wright's *The Pavilion* are among the recent offerings at the Mad City Rep. Talkbacks are often held after performances, providing a chance to discuss a production with the cast and learn details about the play. Performance times are 7:30 P.M. Wednesday and Thursday, 8:00 P.M. Friday, 5:00 and 8:30 P.M. Saturday, and 1:30 and/or 5:00 P.M. Sunday. Call (608) 256-0029. Parking is available nearby in the Civic Center or State Street Capitol ramps, as well as other nearby lots or at on-street meters.

Comedy Clubs. It's not only the politicians who get the laughs in Madison. The city's two major comedy outlets bring in the best national, regional, and local chuckle-meisters and -mistresses. For late hour merriment, if extending a day trip to an overnight, choose from a laughter lineup at Laugh Lines Comedy Club, 6722 Odana Road (608-833-1055; remx0l@aol.com), and the Funny Business Comedy Nite Club, 118 State Street (608-256-0099).

Olbrich Botanical Gardens. 3330 Atwood Avenue, Madison. Garden lovers have long enjoyed the floral delights at the Botanical Gardens, on the northeast shore of Lake Monona. Trails traverse the site, weaving in and out of the rich plantings of seasonal and annual flowers and shrubbery. A horticultural library is open to the public. The site is open year-round, with the gardens available for touring from 9:00 A.M. to 5:00 P.M., with summer hours from 8:00 A.M. to 8:00 P.M. The conservatory hours are 10:00 A.M. to 4:00 P.M. Monday through Saturday and 10:00 A.M. to 5:00 P.M. Sunday. The gardens are closed Thanksgiving and Christmas. Admission is free to the outdoor gardens, with a fee for the conservatory. Call (608) 246-4550.

Madison Black Wolf Baseball. The team plays home games in Warner Park on the city's northeast side from the end of May through the beginning of September. Special promotion nights are regularly held. Bat Day for kids is a popular mid-June event, along with July's Helmet Night and an August Cap Night. Fireworks are also regularly scheduled. For tickets call (608) 244-5666.

Henry Vilas Park Zoological Society. 702 South Randall Avenue, Madison. This free zoo houses more than 700 animals of all shapes, sizes and facial makeup. They growl, howl, bark, woof, gurgle, meow, yowl, hoot, and holler their hellos to visitors. The zoo has a long, distinguished history in Mad City. In 1904 William F. and Anna M. Vilas donated land to the Madison Park and Pleasure Drive Association "for the uses and purposes of a public park and pleasure ground." The park was named after the Vilas' son, Henry, who died as a youngster because of complications from diabetes. In 1911 the first animal exhibits were set up, marking the "official" start of the zoo, reorganized in 1926 as the Henry Vilas Park Zoological Society.

The park is open year-round, with concessions and a gift shop as amenities. Hours are 9:30 A.M. to 5:00 P.M., Monday through Friday; and 9:30 A.M. to 8:00 P.M. Saturday and Sunday. Building hours are 10:00 A.M. to 4:00 P.M. The zoo is closed afternoons on Thanksgiving Day and the day after Thanksgiving, Christmas Eve and Christmas Day, and New Year's Eve and New Year's Day. Be aware that occasionally the zoo closes early, sometimes around 3:00 P.M. for special events, so call ahead to confirm hours. The Children's Zoo is open Memorial Day weekend through Labor Day. While at Henry Vilas, think desert! Take a free camel ride between 10:30 A.M. and noon most Sundays from June through August.

University of Wisconsin–Madison. Located in the heart of Madison, the sprawling campus is not easily missed. Most of the main buildings are clustered in the streets near the west end of State Street, less than a mile from the Wisconsin State Capitol. The Memorial Union, 800 Langdon Street, is a good place to start a tour.

Get caught up in the educational whirl on campus. Here's a few thrills for the junior set. After making an appointment, journey into the living sciences at the Outreach Program in the Biotechnology Center, 425 Henry Mall. Call (608) BIO–TREK. Visitors can tour a research lab and take part in a hands-on class on plant DNA and even use enzymes to make cheese. Death's Head cockroaches, four-inch-long Chilean rosehair tarantulas, and about two million other preserved insects can be ogled at the Insect Research Collection, 346 Russell Labs, 1630 Linden Drive. Call for an appointment, (608) 265-9500.

University of Wisconsin–Madison sports facilities. Camp Randall Stadium/Field House/McClain Center, 1440 Monroe Street. The university's major sports facilities can be discovered in one all-inclusive jaunt around the site, which is a couple of blocks from the main campus. Call for appointments, however. The forty-five-minute tours are scheduled at 10:00 A.M. Tuesday and Thursday. Built on what was originally a Civil War campground for Union troops, the stadium is now home to Badgers football. The field house hosts volleyball and wrestling, with the McClain Center used as an indoor practice facility for several sports. All tours begin at the Athletic Department's Welcome Center at Gate 21 at the stadium. Call (608) 262-1866.

The Kohl Center, 601 West Dayton Street, is named after university benefactor Senator Herb Kohl, a UW grad and owner of the Milwaukee Bucks professional basketball team. The $76 million facility opened in 1998, seating 17,142 for basketball and 15,237 for Badger hockey. Visiting the center's public areas is allowed from 8:00 A.M. to 4:30 P.M. Monday through Friday. Guided forty-five-minute tours are available by appointment. Call (608) 263-5645.

The Red Gym isn't quite so state of the art, having been dedicated in 1894. But, as university president Charles Adams said at the ceremony, it was "built to endure for all time." In 1993 the structure at 716 Langdon Street was named a National Historic Landmark. The restored facility is now a student and visitor center. The building is open 8:00 A.M. to 6:00 P.M., weekdays, 10:00 A.M. to 3:00 P.M. Saturday, and 11:00 A.M. to 2:00 P.M. Sunday. Drop-bys can wander around the public areas at will or a thirty-minute guided tour is available by appointment. Call (608) 265-9500.

Madison in the winter. There's no need to think that a Wisconsin winter would ever close up the state capital. Far from it. The more snow, the better these rugged residents love it (generally speaking, of course). Here are some fabulous cross-country ski trails that are easily accessible: Elver Park, 1301 Gammon Road; Odana Hills Golf Course, 4635 Odana Road; Own Conservation Area, 6021 Old Sauk Road; Warner Park, 1511 Northport Drive; and the University of Wisconsin–Madison Arboretum (enter on Fish Hatchery Road or Seminole Highway). Naturally, there are plenty of other urban trails to ski. Just follow the tracks. For skating, try the east side's Olbrich Park, 3330 Atwood Avenue; Elvejhem Park, 1202 Painted Post Road; and Reindahl Park, 1818 Portage Avenue. On the west side, there are Garner Park, 333 Rosa Road; Westmorland Park, 4114 Tokay Boulevard; and Arbor Hills Park, 3109 Pelham Road.

Special Events. There is always something to do in Madison. The proximity of the state capital from Milwaukee makes it an easy run to take in April's Midwest Horse Fair, the Hero's Madison Marathon in May, Cows on the Concourse during June Dairy Month outside the state capitol, Art Fair on the Square in July, and the Madison Blues Festival in August, among many others. One of the most fun is the Michael Feldman show "Whad' Ya Know?" on Wisconsin Public Radio. The talk/quiz program is aired on selected Saturday mornings from the Lecture Hall at Monona Terrace. For the broadcast schedule and ticket availability, call (800) WHA-KNOW.

WHERE TO SHOP

Dane County Farmer's Market. Ringing the State Capitol, area farmers set up stalls for their beets, honey, ginseng, bedding plants, and spuds. The veggies and flowers are augmented by goodies made by local bakeries, cheese makers, and sausage purveyors. Smart townies get there early for the best pickin's. Bring a reusable shopping bag or a cart with which to haul away your choice produce. Hours are from 6:00 A.M. to 2:00 P.M. from the last Saturday in April through the first Saturday in November. *A walking hint*: Pedestrians usually stroll counterclockwise around the square. The market also sets up on Martin Luther King Boulevard (just off Capitol Square) from 9:00 A.M. to 2:00 P.M. on Wednesdays between May and October. Call (608) 424–6714 or (866) 424–6714 for details on the market seasons or check the market Web site at www.madfarmmkt.org.

Bookstores. Madisonians and visitors seeking the best and latest in literary lore find plenty of opportunities for browsing and buying. The city overflows with independent bookstores. Many are specialty outlets. Mystery lovers flock to Booked for Murder, Ltd., Lakepoint Commons, 2701 University Avenue; (608) 238–2701. Rainbow Store Cooperative, 426 West Gilman Street (608–257–6050; rbc@supranet.com), focuses on cutting-edge titles in cultural and media studies, as well as social theory. The Canterbury Booksellers Coffeehouse, 315 West Gorham Street (608–258–9911 or 800–838–3855; canbookin@aol.com), offers a great range of titles, plus java, soup and sandwiches, author appearances, music, and children's storytelling. A bed-and-breakfast is on the upper floor, with plenty of books lining each room's shelving. Craving the latest news from overseas? Pic-A-Book, 506 State Street (608–256–1125; www.picabook.com; avalon@execpc.com), has one of the city's largest selections of international newspapers and magazines.

A map of the stores in Madison and nearby communities can be secured from the Madison Area Independent Booksellers Association, c/o 20th Century Books at (608) 251–6226 or via the MAIBA Web site at www.maiba/maiba.html. Hours and specialties of each outlet are listed.

Wisconsin Craftsmen. 14 North Carroll Street (Capitol Square area), Madison. This craft shop, which is located in the first skyscraper built in Madison, presents items made by artisans with physical challenges from around the state. The store is a project of the Easter Seal Society of Wisconsin. Open from 9:30 A.M. to 5:00 P.M. weekdays and from 10:00 A.M. to 4:00 P.M. Saturday. Call (608) 255–6301.

Monroe Street. An interesting mix of stores, businesses, and eateries can be found on Monroe Street between Odana Road and

Regent Street. For a wide selection of UW Badger and Green Bay Packer gear, try Stadium Sports, 1501 Monroe, (608) 255-4432. Move along to Maurie's Fine Chocolates, 1637 Monroe (608-255-9092), to satisfy a sweet-tooth craving. Need a bed to haul home? There's Affordable Futons, 1709 Monroe (608) 258-9888. Floor coverings? Don't miss Borokhim Oriental Rugs, 1801 Monroe, (608) 257-2222. Native American handicrafts are found at Katy's American Indian Arts, 1817 Monroe, (608) 251-5451. Pick up the latest Marvel and DC comics at Capital City Comics, 1910 Monroe, (608) 251-7688. All this walking builds up an appetite, which can be serviced at the Dardanelles Mediterranean Restaurant, 1851 Monroe (608-256-8804), and Deb & Lola's Relish Deli and Market, 1923 Monroe (608-255-8500).

WHERE TO EAT

Being a university town, Madison has a marvelous range of restaurants that cater to every pocketbook size and menu fancy. State Street, leading from the capitol to the campus, is one of the best places for inexpensive and moderately priced eats. The thoroughfare, closed to traffic except buses and emergency vehicles, is lined with Thai, Greek, Indian, vegetarian, and more exotic eateries. Doors open and close with regularity, so a walk along the street is the best way to see what's new in the culinary realm. When the weather is nice, many restaurants offer outdoor seating. When perched at an outside table, however, be aware of the bus fumes. This problem has long been a complaint of diners. Therefore, you may want to aim for a place that has a backyard garden or a second-floor view overlooking the passing crowd.

Babcock Hall Dairy Plant. 1605 Linden Drive on the University of Wisconsin campus adjacent to the Stock Pavilion. Since Wisconsin is the country's acknowledged Dairy State, a stop at the university's Department of Food Science and Center for Dairy Research is a must. The building is named after Dr. Stephen Babcock, who developed a butterfat test for milk in 1891. A store in Babcock sells twenty flavors of lip-smacking ice cream, plus yogurt and cheeses that are made on-site. Soup and sandwiches are also available. The store is open from 9:30 A.M. to 5:30 P.M. Monday through Friday. A second-floor balcony is open from 10:00 A.M. to 1:30 P.M. Saturday, for watching the dairy plant in operation. The ice cream is also sold at the Memorial Union, Union South, University Hospital, and during events in Camp Randall Stadium and the UW Field House. Call (608) 262-3046. $; □

Esquire Club. 1025 North Sherman Avenue, Madison. This is one of the city's longest-running restaurants under one-family ownership. The Kavanaughs purchased the property in 1947 and still serve up fine Angus beef and a variety of seafood. They offer lunch and nightly specials, including a Friday fish fry worth driving in from the North Sea to sample. Hours are 11:00 A.M. to 10:00 P.M. Monday through Thursday, 11:00 A.M. to 11:00 P.M. Friday and Saturday, and 3:00 to 9:00 P.M. Sunday. Call (608) 249-0193. $$$; □

Blue Marlin. 101 North Hamilton Street (on Capitol Square), Madison. This is one of the best places in town for fresh seafood and fine wines. It's a cozy little restaurant within shouting distance of the governor's office . . . in case you want to issue a dinner invitation. Lunch hours are 11:30 A.M. to 2:30 P.M. Tuesday through Friday, with dinner served from 5:30 to 10:00 P.M. Sunday hours are 5:30 to 9:00 P.M. Closed Monday. Call (608) 255-2255. $$$; □

Dotty Dumpling's Dowry. 116 North Fairchild Street, Madison. Dotty's bills itself as the world's hamburger headquarters, and international burger lovers agree. They have voted the restaurant as having the best patties in the state. Even the kids will be impressed. Hours are 11:00 A.M. to 10:00 P.M. Monday through Wednesday, 11:00 A.M. to 11:00 P.M. Thursday through Saturday, and noon to 9:00 P.M. Sunday. Call (608) 255-3175. $; □

Famous Dave's Bar-B-Que. 900 South Park Street, Madison. There are few other eateries where can you get St. Louis–style ribs (luscious sauce served with smoking-hot bones), Texas beef brisket, and Georgia chopped pork. Ask for the chicken, one of the most popular items. A children's menu is available for the smaller tummies. Call (608) 286-9400. $; □

Dog Eat Dog. 106 King Street, Madison. Get Chicago-style hot dogs, Italian beef and sausage, and some of the best cheese fries in the Cheese State. And, since this is Mad City, there are also vegetarian items on the menu. Hours are 11:00 A.M. to 9:00 P.M. daily. Call (608) 441-9364. $

Fyfe's Corner Bistro. 1344 East Washington Avenue, Madison. Holler for Angus steak here and ye shall be served . . . in great portions. Live music keeps the joint jumping Thursday through Saturday.

Lunch runs from 11:00 A.M. to 2:00 P.M. and dinner from 5:30 to 10:00 P.M. Monday through Friday. Call (608) 251-8700. $$; ☐

Great Dane Pub & Brewing Company. 123 East Doty Street, Madison. The Dane is Madison's original brewpub. Add a downtown location with billiards, garden dining, a kids' menu, and fourteen types of beer and it all comes up in a winning combo. Hours are 11:00 A.M. to 2:00 A.M. Sunday through Thursday and 11:00 A.M. to 2:30 A.M. Friday and Saturday. Call (608) 284-0000. $$; ☐

Cafe Rigoletto. 1109 Fourie Drive, Madison. Keep thinking Italian. This is a classic restaurant of the old style, serving breakfast, lunch, and dinner. Hours are 6:00 A.M. to 10:00 P.M. daily. Call (608) 826-0555. $$; ☐

Mountain Jack's West. 7315 West Towne Way, Madison. The word on the street here is that MJW serves the best prime rib in town. That may well be, or at the least, the folks here lay out one of the biggest slabs o' tender meat in the burg. You'll find the place tucked into a locale behind the Sears store in the West Towne Mall. Hours are 11:30 A.M. to 2:00 P.M. for lunch and 5:00 to 10:00 P.M. for dinner on weekdays. Dinner is also served 4:00 to 10:00 P.M. on Saturday and 6:30 to 9:00 P.M. on Sunday. Call (608) 833-7383.

Smoky's Club. 3005 University Avenue, Madison. This family-run business has been a staple on the city's west side for more than forty years. Homemade soup draws hungry diners from around the community. Also steaks that are "hmmmmm, good." Hours are 5:00 to 10:00 P.M. Monday, Wednesday, and Saturday. Closed holidays. Call (608) 233-2120. $$

Ella's Deli & Ice Cream Parlor. 2902 East Washington Avenue, Madison. While many longtime Madisonians still miss Ella's downtown location, this east-side site is available whenever cravings hit for kosher goodies like grandma used to make. An outside carousel, which runs from spring through autumn, is the signature landmark. Inside is a delightful melange of toys suspended from the ceiling. Hours are 10:00 A.M. to 10:00 P.M. Sunday through Thursday and 10:00 A.M. to 11:00 P.M. Friday and Saturday. Call (608) 241-5291. $; ☐

Smoky John's #1 BBQ. 2310 Packers Avenue, Madison. The phone number here is the giveaway as to the menu offerings. This north-side establishment has won the city's "best ribs" three years running, plus many other national and regional barbecue awards.

Smoky's is open from 11:00 A.M. to 9:00 P.M. Tuesday through Sunday. Closed Monday. Call (608) 249-RIBS. $; ☐

Nau-Ti-Gal. 5360 Wesport Road, Madison. Hungry Madison residents love the waterfront dining here, especially during warm weather. They're also drawn by the brunch that rates high on the tummy-filling charts. Hours are 11:30 A.M. to 10:00 P.M. Monday through Thursday; 10:30 A.M. to 10:30 P.M. Friday and Saturday; and 10:00 A.M. to 2:00 P.M. and 5:00 to 10:00 P.M. Sunday. Call (608) 246-3130. $$; ☐

Captain Bill's Seafood Company. 2701 Century Harbor Road. Fresh seafood earns kudos for this old salty dog. For a Key West atmosphere on Lake Mendota, this is the place to see. Lounge hours start at 4:30 P.M. until bar time, with dinners served from 5:00 P.M. until, well, when Captain Bill's ship comes in. Call (608) 831-7327. $$; ☐

J.T. Whitney's Brewpub & Eatery. 674 South Whitney Way. Brewmeister Dick Becker serves up great bubbly here, along with hearty lunches and dinners. Hours are 11:00 A.M. to midnight daily. Call (608) 274-1776. $$; ☐

WHERE TO STAY

As with any major city, Madison has a range of accommodations from inexpensive chain and mom-and-pop motels to convention hotels and delightful bed-and-breakfast facilities. Among the latter are The Livingston, a Victorian Inn, 752 East Gorham Street (608-257-1200), which is on the National Register of Historic Places, and the Mansion Hill Inn, 424 North Pickney Street (800-798-9070). The Edgewater, 606 Wisconsin Avenue (800-922-5512), and Madison Concourse Hotel and Governor's Club, 1 West Dayton Street (800-356-8293), are among the most popular larger hotels.

MIDDLETON

The western suburb of Middleton proclaims that it is a "Good Neighbor City." For info about what to see and do locally, drop by the chamber of commerce, which is open from 8:30 A.M. to 5:00 P.M. Monday through Friday; (608) 831-5696.

WHERE TO SHOP

Clasen's European Bakery. 7610 Donna Drive, Middleton. More than 500 pastries and bread styles are baked daily from scratch at Clasen's. Free coffee and cake are offered to hungry visitors every day. The butter-cream and whipped-cream tortes are to die for. Gourmet chocolates are also available if the Danish pastries are still not enough to satisfy a discerning sweet tooth. Tours are available of the kitchens, with their ranks and ranks of ovens and stainless-steel mixing bowls. *A warning:* Don't go there hungry. Call (608) 831-2032.

The Wine Boutique. 6220 University Avenue, Middleton. This shop has a Wine of the Month Club and weekly tastings. Call (608) 232-7040 to discover the details.

WHERE TO EAT

Capital Brewery Bier Garden. 7734 Terrace Avenue, Middleton. For lip-smacking brews, Capital is hard to beat. Popular beverages include award-winning special pilsner, Bavarian lager, Wisconsin amber, and specialty beers such as Blonde Doppenbock, Raspberry Wheat, Wild Rice, Maibock, and Kloster Weizen. In addition to beer Capital Brewery has its own root beer and cream soda for the kids or those who prefer an alternative to the bubbly. The Reptile Palace Orchestra, Balkan Lounge Funk, Moon Gypsies, and other popular local and regional bands perform on Saturday nights (cover charge). The brewery doesn't serve food, but area restaurants provide grub on Friday, Saturday, and Sunday, with menus ranging from brats and burgers to Caribbean style. Call (608) 836-7100. The Bier Garden can be $ or $$, depending on the amount of hops ingested. ☐

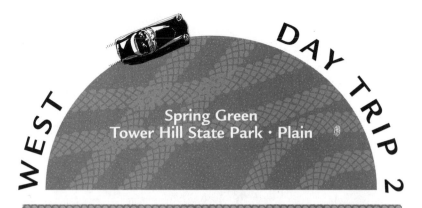

SPRING GREEN

The Spring Green area offers a ton of activities that capture the fancy of the day-tripper. A jaunt here—just to the west of Madison—can be an extension of West Day Trip 1 (a thirty-minute drive) or can be a direct run in from Milwaukee, which is about 110 miles to the east. Experienced travelers get up early and are on the footsteps of Frank Lloyd Wright's farm home by midmorning, even after pausing in Madison for a cuppa java.

So what's to see and do? The recreational menu is long: theater, golf, museums, nature preserves, hiking, canoeing, gallery crawls, shopping, bicycling, historic sites, and simply loafing.

GETTING THERE

Take I-94 from Milwaukee, turn south on I-90, and then pick up the Beltline (U.S. Highways 18 and 12) around the south side of the state's capital city. Turn north on U.S. Highway 12 and exit U.S. Highway 14 in Middleton. From there you'll drive through Cross Plains, Black Earth, Mazomanie, and Arena, all at the western edge of "Wright Country." Return the same way or go south on State Highway 23 to Dodgeville and pick up U.S. 18/151 for the run back to Madison. A loop such as that should be a weekend getaway, in order to take in as many attractions as possible. Or turn north on State Highway 130 out of Lone Rock and meander along Sauk County Highway B back to Plain and on to U.S. Highway 12.

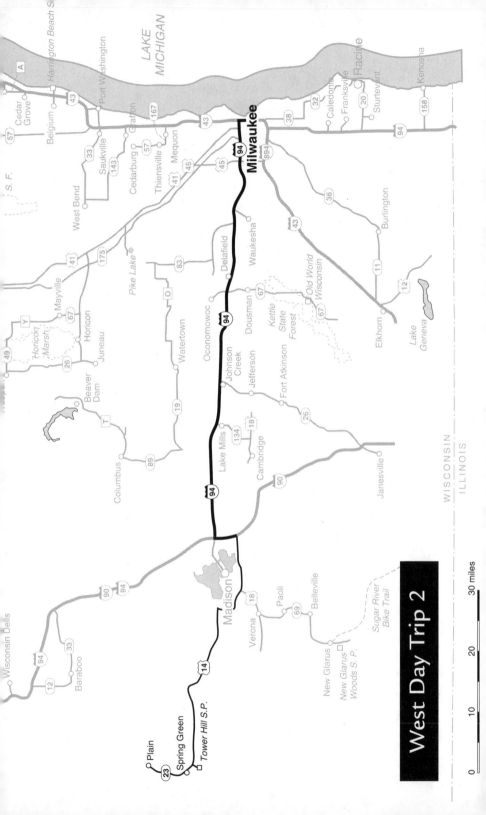

West Day Trip 2

Although it isn't far from Milwaukee, whether in distance or time, you don't want to rush your rural hiatus.

WHERE TO GO

Taliesin. Three miles south of Spring Green on State Highway 23 and Iowa County Highway C. Noted architect Frank Lloyd Wright loved the rolling countryside along the Wisconsin River where he grew up. From his workshops and studios in Spring Green, in a complex called Taliesin, he went on to confirm his fame as an internationally noted figure. Tours of varying lengths are offered around the 600-acre estate. The most extensive walking tours are held daily at 10:45 A.M. and 1:45 P.M. May through October. Other tours include that of the Hillside Home School, built in 1902, and Wright's 5,000-square-foot drafting studio. Another tour takes guests through Wright's home, showcasing his huge collection of Asian art. Admission charged for the tours. A nearby visitor center has a bookstore and a restaurant. Call (608) 588-7900. The Web site is www.TaliesinPreservation.org.

Other Wright-designed sites to see in the area include the M&I Bank on Jefferson Street in Spring Green and the windows in the town's St. John's Catholic Church, 129 West Daley Street. Unity Chapel, built in 1886, was Wright's family chapel, with several graves of relatives in the nearby cemetery. The plain little building is located on Iowa County Highway T, just off State Highway 23. Aldebaran Farm, the ancestral home of Wright's uncle James, is across Highway T (for touring call 608-588-2568). Bicyclists enjoy pedaling around the area to visit these attractions.

American Players Theatre. E 2930 Golf Course Road (4 miles south of Spring Green off Iowa County C). The open-air theater, across the road from the House on the Rock Resort, is located on 110 acres of woods and hills. Shakespeare's plays form the production backbone, augmented by those of Oscar Wilde, Molière, Goldsmith, and other great playwrights. On bright summer nights the stars rival the spotlights. Be prepared for whatever the weather presents by bringing a sweater or jacket if necessary. An extra smear of bug spray is a wise investment, as well. The seats are cushioned, and there isn't a bad view in the natural amphitheater, reached by a ten-minute walk up a hill. A shuttle bus is available for those wishing to ride. Bring a picnic or purchase a box supper on the grounds. Performances run from June until early October. Call the box office at (608) 588-2361. The Web site is www.americanplayers.org.

Gard Theater. Jefferson Street (downtown Spring Green). Look for a good movie in a historic setting. The old Gard, built in the early twentieth century, features films at 7:00 and 9:00 P.M. Friday and Saturday and 7:30 P.M. Sunday. The theater also hosts the River Valley Players, a community theater group. For performance times call the Spring Green Chamber of Commerce at (608) 588-2042.

Rural Musicians Forum. Jazz, folk, and chamber music are offered year-round at several sites in the Spring Green area. A summer concert series is held Monday evenings at Unity Chapel. A holiday concert is an annual tradition at the downtown Gard Theater. Winter and spring concerts are held in other locales. Call (608) 588-2042 for times and dates.

Wyoming Valley Methodist Church. Seven miles south of Spring Green on State Highway 23. The church regularly hosts concerts, choral events, and other musical productions. Call the chamber of commerce at (608) 588-2042 for the calendar.

House on the Rock. 5754 State Highway 23, Spring Green. In the early 1940s artist Alex Jordan built a house on a 60-foot chimney of rock overlooking the Wyoming Valley. While he never expected the place to be a tourist attraction, visitors kept showing up at his door, so he eventually began leading tours through his amazing home. Jordan then began collecting all sorts of memorabilia to display, from organs to ship models. To accommodate the growing crowds and additional exhibits, a foyer for the main house was built in 1961, followed by the Mill House in 1968. The Streets of Yesterday, with its old-time village feel, opened in 1971. Many other display areas opened later, including a Heritage of the Sea hall that features a 200-foot-high sea serpent battling a giant octopus. A holiday tour around Christmas features several thousand Santa Clauses. The entrance to the grounds is marked by giant flower-filled urns, with lizards and gremlins entwined around their rims, making the house easy to find. The complex is open from mid-March through the end of October, with holiday tours from early November through January 2. Admission. Call (608) 935-3639.

Spring Green Arts and Crafts Fair. Downtown Spring Green. Held since the early 1960s on the last weekend in June, the fair attracts more than 220 nationally known artists who exhibit and sell their works on Spring Green's downtown streets. Food, entertainment, and a children's area round out the event. Call (608) 588-2042.

Wisconsin River. Canoe along the wide Wisconsin, stopping at area parks and sandbars to picnic along the way. In 1989 the Wisconsin legislature created the Lower Wisconsin State Riverway to protect the river valley's natural beauty. The plan regulates recreation and management use along the riverbanks. It is estimated that there are at least sixty-two endangered, threatened, or special-concern-status wildlife species within the riverway boundaries, in addition to thirty-four plant species (including cactus) that are native to the region. The river runs through the "driftless area," a section of Wisconsin that escaped being leveled during the most recent Ice Age of 10,000 years ago.

River access in Spring Green is available at Peck's Landing on the north side of the State Highway 23 bridge and a public boat landing on the northeast side of the U.S. Highway 14 bridge. Other nearby put-in sites are the Arena boat landing (reached by driving north from U.S. Highway 14 at Arena School to Willow Street to River Road and north on to the river) and the Lone Rock boat landing on the south side of the river off State Highway 130. Most river users ply the 25-mile section between Prairie du Sac and Spring Green. Traffic can be heavy in summer.

Canoe rentals are available at Bob's Riverside Camp, 1 mile west of Spring Green on Shifflet Road. Call (608) 588-2826 for shuttle reservations. The Waz Inn in Lone Rock also offers shuttle service, as well as food provisioning. Call (608) 583-2086.

When on the water, remember to respect the other boaters, the wildlife, and the landscape. Don't pitch rubbish into the water. *A serious warning:* Don't drink and canoe at the same time. While basically presenting a pleasant adventure, the river is wide and can be fast and dangerous during high-water times.

WHERE TO SHOP

Art on 23. 355 Winsted Street (State Highway 23), Spring Green. Glassblower Colleen Ott showcases her work, along with dozens of other artists. Hours are 11:00 A.M. to 5:00 P.M. Friday through Sunday, and by appointment during the week. Call (608) 588-7718.

Jura Silverman Gallery, Wisconsin Artists Showcase. 143 South Washington Street, Spring Green. Fine arts and crafts from numerous state artists are offered for sale, along with Silverman's exquisite handmade papers and prints. Custom orders can also be taken. The showcase is located in a restored old cheese warehouse. Hours are daily, except Monday and Thursday, from 11:00 A.M. to 5:00 P.M. or by appointment. Call (608) 588-7049.

Wilson Creek Pottery. 2 miles north of Spring Green on State Highway 23, then right on Iowa County Highway WC for 3 miles. Peggy Ahlgren specializes in nifty tableware and kitchenware. For store hours call (608) 588-2195.

Stage Stop. 3334 South Winsted (State Highway 23, Winsted at Daley Streets), Spring Green. Pushcarts, buckboards, and oak furniture, plus smaller gifts, can be purchased here. Open year-round, but call (608) 588-7221 or (608) 588-7826 for hours.

Spring Green Cafe & General Store. 137 South Albany Street, Spring Green. Gourmet groceries, women's apparel, jewelry, rare books, and artwork from around the world fill this refurbished cheese warehouse. Hours are 9:00 A.M. to 6:00 P.M. weekdays, 8:00 A.M. to 6:00 P.M. Saturday, and 8:00 A.M. to 4:00 P.M. Sunday. Call (608) 588-7070.

Sew 'n Sew. 122 North Lexington Street, Spring Green. Two floors of quilting and sewing materials should be enough to delight any stitchery fan. Sewing machines for sale and a repair service make this an all-around stop. Hours are 9:00 A.M. to 5:00 P.M. Monday through Friday and 9:00 A.M. to 4:00 P.M. Saturday. Call (608) 588-2273.

Farm Markets. Since the Spring Green area is in a fertile farming region, roadside stands offer a fine selection of fresh produce in season. Heck's Marketplace on U.S. Highway 14 in Arena is one of the largest. Not only does it offer tomatoes, beans, and pumpkins, it also has an enormous selection of concrete lawn ornaments, to say nothing of bait, groceries, and beer. Daily hours are 7:00 A.M. to 8:00 P.M. May through October. A flea market is held on the grounds on Saturday and Sunday in those months, as well. Call (608) 753-2474. Peck's has two sites: Farm Market East, 2 miles east of Spring Green on U.S. Highway 14 (608-588-7177); and Farm Market West, 4 miles west of Spring Green on U.S. Highway 14 (608-583-4977). Daily hours for both facilities are 7:00 A.M. to 7:00 P.M. from June through the first week in November. The Oakwood Fruit Farm, north of Lone Rock on State Highway 130, is open from August through Christmas, offering apples, cherries, grapes, and other fruit. Open daily from 10:00 A.M. to 5:00 P.M. Call (608) 585-2701.

WHERE TO EAT

The Post House and Dutch Kitchen Restaurant. 127 East Jefferson Street, Spring Green. For the past 135 years, the Post House has been serving great meals in downtown Spring Green. The outdoor garden in summer is delightful, while the Flying Dutchman Bar was designed by West Wesley Peters, an architect from Taliesin. Owners Jack and Mary Ann Baryenbuch are excellent hosts. Hours are 11:00 A.M. to 2:00 P.M. Monday through Friday for lunch. Dinner is served Tuesday through Thursday 5:00 to 9:00 P.M.; and Friday 4:00 to 10:00 P.M. On weekends the restaurant is open Saturday 11:00 A.M. to 9:00 P.M. and Sunday 11:00 A.M. to 8:00 P.M. Call (608) 588-2595. $$; □

The Old Feed Mill. 114 Cramer Street, Spring Green. Enjoy the rustic decor of this restored 1857 stone flour mill. The two-story building includes a bakery and gift shop, as well as dining rooms. Hours are 10:00 A.M. to 9:00 P.M. Tuesday and Wednesday, 10:00 A.M. to 10:00 P.M. Friday and Saturday, and 10:00 A.M. to 8:00 P.M. Sunday. Closed Monday and Thursday. Call (608) 795-4909. $$; □

Riverview Terrace. Frank Lloyd Wright Visitor Center, State Highway 23 and Iowa County Highway C, Spring Green. The building was designed by Wright to provide a great, sweeping view of the Wisconsin River. The cafe in the center serves lunch from May through October. For hours call (608) 588-7900. $; □

WHERE TO STAY

Round Barn Lodge and Restaurant. State Highway 14, Spring Green. The lodge has a heated indoor pool and an outdoor pool with sundeck, augmenting the forty-four comfortable rooms. An excellent restaurant presents delicious steak, seafood, and large salad bar. $$; □ The complex was designed by associates of noted architect Frank Lloyd Wright. Nonsmoking and wheelchair-accessible rooms are available. Call (608) 588-2568. The Web site is www.roundbarn.com.

House on the Rock Golf Club Resort. 400 Springs Drive, Spring Green. The resort has eighty two-room suites alongside a twenty-seven-hole golf course. Tennis, a fitness center, and a spa make the resort a great day-tripper weekend. Hiking, biking, and cross-country skiing in the area are additional sports to enjoy. And don't pass up the casual and fine-dining restaurants there. Prior to 1999 the resort was known as The Springs. It is across the road from the American Players Theatre. Call (800) 822-7774. $$$; ☐

Spring Valley Inn. State Highway 14 and Iowa County Highway C, Spring Green. The inn is located on twelve acres of woods and prairie. The attached health club has the largest indoor pool in Spring Green. Call (608) 588-7828. The Web site is www.spring valleyinn.com. $$; ☐

The Silver Star. 3852 Limmex Hill Road, Spring Green. Innkeepers Jean and Michael Langer graciously supervise operations at this rustic, log cabin inn and its ten guest rooms. Fine-art and photography galleries and a cafe round out the accommodations. Call (608) 935-7297. Try the Silver Star Web site at www.silverstarinn.com. $$–$$$; ☐

TOWER HILL STATE PARK

Comprising only seventy-seven acres, Tower Hill is one of the state's smallest state parks, yet it is one of the richest in history. In the nineteenth century, it was the site of the village of Helena, one of the first incorporated communities in Wisconsin. Its major business was producing shot, made in a tower atop a high hill. Adding to the tower's height, miners using crowbars, picks, and shovels dug a vertical shaft through 120 feet of limestone and made a 90-foot horizontal tunnel near Mill Creek to connect with the shaft. Hot lead was poured out of a cauldron through screens at the top of the tower, cooling and forming musketballs as it fell to the bottom of the structure and hit a pool of cold water. Several trails make their snakelike way throughout the woods surrounding the hill and old tower, which contains photos of the shot-making process.

The park is open daily from May through October and is a popular stop for canoeists along the nearby Wisconsin River. Tower Hill is 2 miles south of Spring Green, via State Highway 23, then 1 mile east on Iowa County Highway C. If worried about directions, look for the easy-to-spot signage on Highways 23 and C. For camping info contact the Park Superintendent, Tower Hill State Park, Route 3, Spring Green, WI 53588, (608) 588-2116.

PLAIN

The Germanic heritage of Plain is, well, in plain view. Most of the townsfolk's ancestors came from the Waldmünchen area of Bavaria in the mid- to late-nineteenth century. They cultivated neat farms around their trim little town, which now sports a public nine-hole municipal golf course just off Main Street (Sauk County Highway B) a block south of downtown, paralleling the southeast side of State Highway 23. One wonders what the early settlers would have thought of that.

WHERE TO GO

The heart and soul of Plain is the Romanesque St. Luke's Catholic church, which overlooks the town from a bluff. Look around the interior to admire the stained-glass windows and Italian marble altars. St. Anne's Shrine, a chapel built in the 1930s, is reached higher up the hill by strolling along a path lined by the Stations of the Cross. Near the shrine is a replica of the famous Lourdes Grotto in France, where it is believed the Blessed Virgin appeared to a young girl in 1858. For details on the church history, talk with pastor Fr. Mike Resap; (608) 546-2482.

Summer events in Plain include St. Luke's annual parish picnic in mid-June, with a home-cooked dinner that rivals munchables anywhere. The local firemen also celebrate with a festival over the last full weekend in July with a parade of fire-fighting gear, music, and a chicken barbecue (never overdone, of course).

WHERE TO SHOP

Cedar Grove Cheese. Mill Road, Plain. This family-owned cheese factory has some of the best Colby in the state. Drop by for a tour. Hours are 8:00 A.M. to 4:30 P.M. Monday through Saturday, and 8:00 A.M. to 2:30 P.M. Sunday. Call (608) 546-5284.

WHERE TO EAT

I-Diehl Tap. 400 Main Street, Plain. Since 1978, Tap owner Emil Diehl has been running his popular getaway pub. Wide selection of sandwiches, soups, and daily specials. Hours are seven days a week from 5:00 A.M. to 1:00 A.M. Call (608) 546-2323. $

Ring's Bar. 950 Elma Avenue, Plain. Allen Ring, bar owner, presents a good place for sandwiches. Hours are Monday through Saturday from 9:00 A.M. until the last customer leaves. Call (608) 546-9231. $

WHERE TO STAY

Bettinger House. State Highway 23 (6 miles north of Spring Green), Plain. The Bettinger House is known for its full-course, table-groaning breakfasts. Call (608) 546-2951. $$; □

Classic Charms Bed & Breakfast. S10284 Dead End Road, Plain. The Victorian-era home is a neat, tucked-away place waiting to be discovered by the Milwaukee day-tripper. Call (608) 546-2439. $$

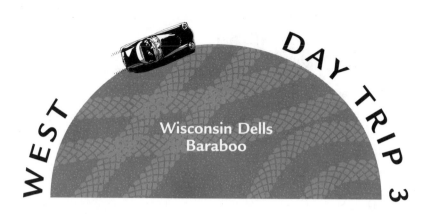

WISCONSIN DELLS

Around the turn of the nineteenth century, a boy supposedly climbed a tree overlooking a Ho-Chunk encampment in central Wisconsin and watched the Native Americans performing their ritual dancing. Whether or not that story is true, the kid—Glen Parsons—went on to develop a series of sunset cruises along the Wisconsin River that included a stop at Standing Rock. There, hidden in a natural amphitheater among the boulders fronting the river, he had arranged for the local Indians to put on a regular show. The program became a staple of Dell tourism until the mid-1990s. By that time, the Ho-Chunk were spending their time developing a casino in the Dells. Today, Te'e Esanahere Native American Dancing (for specifics call the visitor center at 608-254-4636) has picked up the tradition. The production company's canyon amphitheater site is now across from the Tommy Barlett Robot World & Exploratory, 1 block off Wisconsin Dells Parkway on Canyon Road.

The Wisconsin Dells symbolize tourism in the Midwestern consciousness. Flatlanders from Illinois, Cheese Heads from Milwaukee, and others from around the area have been flocking here since shortly before the Civil War. Lured by stereoscopic photographs taken by noted camera artist H. H. Bennett, visitors flocked to enjoy the boat rides, fresh air, and the chocolate fudge. Fifteen miles of waterway along the river make up the Upper and

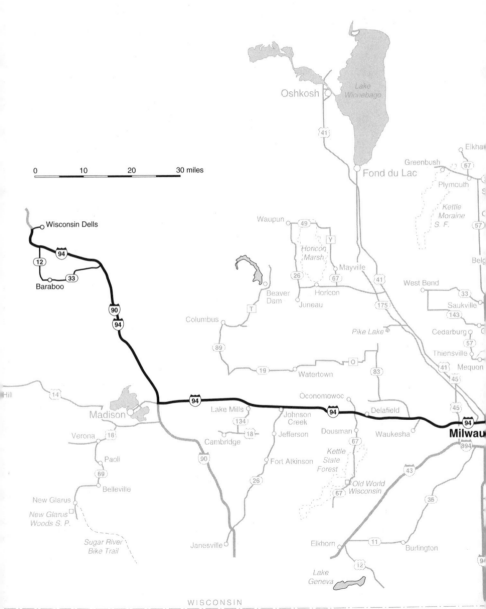

West Day Trip 3

Lower Dells, an evolution of the French word *dalles,* which means "river gorges." Conservation-minded environmentalists fought hard and won protection for the shoreline, which remains pristine, wooded, and quiet. The honky-tonk aspect of the Dells, with its animal parks, souvenir shops, haunted houses, and museums, is inland and well away from the river.

But step back for a minute to the tail-end of the Cambrian Period of the earth's formation. Five hundred million years ago, the stone found in Wisconsin Dells was originally the sandy shore of an ancient lake. Nineteen million years ago, a glacier edged within 4 miles of the Dells. This Driftless Area, untouched by those long-ago ice sheets, forms the rugged geography of the region. Fifteen thousand years ago, the glaciers began melting and created Glacial Lake Wisconsin, once the size of Utah and more than 150 feet deep. The Dells, of course, were submerged. Then the last ice that blocked the outflow from the glacial lake finally broke loose, and the flood that resulted dropped the water to 50 feet. The sandstone melted away beneath the deluge, and the rugged Dells we see today were formed.

In the late 1600s French explorers roamed through here, and settlers eventually made their way to the river by the 1830s. In 1849 Yellow Thunder purchased land for his Ho-Chunk nation, thus ensuring that his people would not be among the displaced Native Americans forced to leave their ancestral homes. By 1856 the first tourists were poking around the Dells, in the forefront of business that grew steadily over the next century. Between the late 1800s and the 1930s, local businessman George Crandall planted more than 100,000 pine trees along the river to conserve its natural look. At present those trees tower over the excursion boats, hikers, fishing fans, and other nature lovers.

GETTING THERE

The Dells are easy to reach from Milwaukee. It's about a ninety-minute drive west on I-94 to Madison and then north on I-90/94 to the Dells exits. Most of the attractions are ranged along U.S. 12/State Highway 13 (Wisconsin Dells Parkway in Lake Delton) and on Broadway in Wisconsin Dells. The twin towns have no problem of being lumped together under the "Dells" category. For all the latest on attractions, contact the Convention and Visitors Bureau, 701

Superior Street, Wisconsin Dells, WI 53965-0660. Call (608) 254-4636 to confirm seasonal hours. The area Web site is www.dells-delton.com.

WHERE TO GO

Tommy Bartlett's Ski, Sky & Stage Show and Robot World & Exploratory. 560 Wisconsin Dells Parkway. More than forty million spectators have seen the Bartlett show since it was launched in the early 1950s. Water-ski thrills, dancing waters, Polynesian drum dancers, aerial acrobats, daredevils dangling down from helicopters, throaty singers, sound-effects specialists, frantic plate spinners, and who knows what else have been a staple of Dells entertainment for years. Show times are 1:00, 4:30, and 8:30 P.M. daily rain or shine during the season, which usually runs from late May through early October. Three thousand seats are under cover, so ask for one of those when buying tickets when the outside is damp—or bring an umbrella.

You can also enjoy the adjacent Robot World & Exploratory, which combines hands-on science experiments with talking-robot kitsch. But it's all fun, anyway, and a great way to spend a couple of hours if the weather is nasty. Admission is charged. Hours are 8:00 A.M. to 11:00 P.M. daily April through October. Call (608) 254-2525. Check the Web site at www.tommybartlett.com.

Original Wisconsin Ducks. 1890 Wisconsin Dells Parkway (the main dock is 1 mile south of the Wisconsin Dells on State Highway 12). Yahoo! Ride the green and white Ducks, those famous World War II amphibious vehicles, which operate from April through mid-October. The ungainly looking all-terrain vehicles rumble across land and plunge through waterways to provide an exciting back-country look at the world. The 8½-mile-long trip hits the river at Echo Point and chugs downstream, crossing a sandbar en route to a portage around Newman's Dam and on to Dawn Manor, where it again pulls back into the forest. Call for a schedule of departures during the summer season; (608) 254-8751.

Water Parks. Summer fun means getting wet. And that's the secret of excitement at the Dells' plethora of water parks. They offer bumper cars, flume rides, tidal waves, and a host of other entertainment, including arcades, go-carts, amusement rides, mini-golf, and kid play areas. Most open at 9:00 A.M. daily, with extended evening hours depending on the weather, from Memorial Day weekend through Labor Day. Call each site to confirm, however. All-day passes can be purchased, and spectators can usually watch for free. Several offer free picnic groves. And be careful of the sunburn—it doesn't take long to scorch.

Noah's Ark. 1410 Wisconsin Dells Parkway; (608) 254-6351

Riverview Park & Waterworld. U.S. Highway 12, near the boat docks; (608) 254-2608

Family Land. U.S. Highway 12; (608) 254-7766

Timber Falls & Adventure Golf. At the Wisconsin River Bridge and Stand Rock Road (near downtown Dells); (608) 254-8414

Mini-Golf. Arnold Palmer or Tiger Woods probably won't be seen on these links, but almost every visitor to the Dells whacks at a golf ball sometime during a stay. Here's a few from which to choose:

Shipwreck Lagoon. U.S. Highway 12. Try your hand in the batting cages, or, if the day is slow, there's even bungee jumping. But the focus is mini-golf, with a choice of eighteen, thirty-six, or fifty-four holes. Players move across bridges and streams, climb aboard a pirate ship, and scale lookout towers, besides confronting other challenges. Admission charged. Call (608) 253-7772.

Pirate's Cove. At the Country Kitchen Corner (intersection of Highways 12, 16, and 23 and I-90/94. Take exit 57 from the freeway. Seventeen waterfalls make for plenty of hazards. Admission. Open daily at 8:00 A.M. from April through October. Call (608) 254-7500.

Golf. For big person's golf two courses stand out:

The Wilderness Golf Resort. Take exit 92 off I-90/94 and drive west 1 mile on U.S. Highway 12. Call ahead for tee times; (608) 253-GOLF.

Trappers Turn. Trappers Turn Drive. Call (608) 253-7000 or (800) 221-8876. The Web site is www.trappersturn.com.

Lost Canyon Horse & Carriage and **Canyon Creek Riding Stables.** Lost Canyon is on Canyon Road off I-90/94 and is open from 8:30 A.M. to 8:00 P.M. The stables are ½ mile north of I-90 on Hillman Road and are open from 9:00 A.M. to dusk. Both facilities operate daily from May through late September. At Lost Canyon carriages leave every ten to fifteen minutes from opening, with the last wagon departing at 7:30 P.M. The trips take about ninety minutes, beginning on the south shore of Lake Delton. The riding trails are easy, with horses that know the route, so don't expect wild stallions needing to be tamed. Just climb aboard and enjoy the guided jaunt. Little kids will enjoy the pony ring. Credit cards are accepted. Call (608) 254-8757 for Lost Canyon and (608) 253-6942 for Canyon Creek or use the Web site at www.dells.com/horses.html.

Fishing. You can do your own angling on the river but for a more sure catch, try the fish farms:

B&H Trout Fishing & Bait Shop. Seven miles north of Wisconsin Dells on State Highway 13 (look on the right side). B&H has trout pools that almost guarantee a catch. The attraction will clean, freeze, and store your fish until it's time to head home. Hours are 6:00 A.M. to 9:00 P.M. Call (608) 254-7280.

Wisconsin Dells Trout Farm & Canoe Trips. Five miles north of Wisconsin Dells on State Highway 13 at the intersection with Sauk County Highway K. Admission to the trout farm is free, but if you fish and land a big one, you are charged 10 cents per inch. Hours are 9:00 A.M. to 6:00 P.M. Call (608) 589-5353.

Dells Boat Tour. Early vacationers came to the Dells in order to tour the river. You still can. Both the Upper and Lower Dells provide enough images for any photographer, just as they did for H. H. Bennett more than a century ago. The 15-mile Upper Dells tour includes shore-landing strolls at Stand Rock and Witches Gulch, with excursions daily from early April to early November. The Lower Dells tour takes in the ghost town of Newport, as seen on the bank, with plenty of Native American and logging legends tossed in by the boat driver. These tours run from mid-April to early October. Both trips leave from the boat docks at the Wisconsin River in downtown Wisconsin Dells. Call (608) 254-8555.

WHERE TO EAT

With almost one hundred restaurants in the Wisconsin Dells–Lake Delton area, there are plenty of culinary opportunities with a wide range of pricing. There are the usual chain fast-food joints if familiarity is the day-tripper's requirement, but there are plenty of other eating establishments from which to choose. If you decide to lay in, contact Dine Inn (608–253–3463), which can deliver a full meal from one of nine restaurants it has as clients. Dine Inn delivers to homes, motels, campgrounds, and even poolside.

American Club & Polish American Buffet. 400 Sauk County Highway A and U.S. Highway 12, Wisconsin Dells. Home-cooking at its best. Try the pierogi and kielbasa for some Eastern European treats. And then there's the standard, but delicious, baked chicken. Hours are noon to 9:30 P.M. daily. Call (608) 253–6704. $$; ☐

Country Kitchen. 800 U.S. Highway 12 (junction with State Highways 16, 13, and 23), Wisconsin Dells. The restaurant claims it has the best pancakes in the Dells region. And who is to argue, especially whenever you get a griddle craving at some odd hour. The restaurant is open twenty-four hours a day, year-round. Call (608) 254–2593. $$; ☐

Ishnala Supper Club. Ishnala Road, Lake Delton. For calm, quiet, sit-down dining after a full day of activities, the Ishnala is the place if the day-tripper hungers after a steak or prime rib. Hours are 4:00 to 10:00 P.M. Monday through Friday, 4:00 to 10:30 P.M. Saturday, and noon to 9:00 P.M. Sunday. Pontoon boat cruises are also available. Call (608) 253–1771. $$$; ☐

BJ's Restaurant. 1201 Wisconsin Dells Parkway, Wisconsin Dells. A full breakfast menu provides selections on which to start the day right. Steaks, chops, and baked fish are dinner favorites. A kids' menu is offered, as well. Open 6:30 A.M. to late night, daily, year-round. Call (608) 254–6278. $$; ☐

Monk's Bar & Grill. 116 Fourth Avenue, Wisconsin Dells. There are burgers and then there are Monk's burgers. Since 1947 Monk's has been dishing up grand sandwiches. Open daily at 11:00 A.M. until late night. Call (608) 355–0977. $; ☐

WHERE TO STAY

Use the Dells hotel hot line to help find a room via the InnLine Information System. There are several dozen campgrounds, motels, hotels, and resorts from which to chose in a wide price range. Many of the larger facilities have indoor pools with water slides, game rooms, and other amenities, which is a great draw in the winter. The Dells is becoming an all-season destination whether for a day trip, a weekend, or a longer getaway. To check on the room situation, call (800) 223-3557. Operators are on call from 8:00 A.M. to 5:00 P.M. Monday through Friday. If no one can pick up your call, you can always leave a message and receive loads of flyers and other details about lodging and attractions.

BARABOO

Baraboo is a pleasant little community 12 miles south of the Dells and about 35 miles northwest of Madison on U.S. Highway 12 or readily accessed from I-90/94 on State Highway 33. The town square is typical of a nineteenth-century community, ringed by stores with the courthouse in the middle. The Al Ringling Theater and several other historic buildings are also on the square. From 1884 to 1918, Baraboo was the winter base for the Ringling brothers and their circus, just before it earned the title as "The Greatest Show on Earth" when it linked with Barnum and Bailey. A number of houses in the community were owned by circus folk.

WHERE TO GO

Circus World Museum. 426 Water Street, Baraboo. The museum, a National Historic Landmark, is operated by the State Historical Society of Wisconsin on the grounds of the old Ringling Brothers Circus winter quarters. Many of the show's animal barns and wagon shops have been refurbished and reopened with exhibits on all aspects of the circus and its personnel. See the three-legged chair used by animal trainer Clyde Beatty, a suit worn by Tom Thumb, and thousands of other show business artifacts. Dozens of old circus wagons were secured by the museum and they were repaired for display. They are hauled each summer to Milwaukee for the Great Circus Parade, usually held at the end of July or in early August.

The facility also has a large research library that is open year-round, plus daily circus performances during the summer season. Admission is charged. Hours are 9:00 A.M. to 6:00 P.M. Off-season hours are 9:30 A.M. to 4:00 P.M. Monday through Saturday and 11:00 A.M. to 4:00 P.M. Sunday from early November to early May. The ticket wagon closes one hour before the museum closes. For all the latest circus scoop, call the twenty-four-hour information line at (608) 356-0800. The museum Web site is www.circusworldmuseum.com.

International Crane Foundation. This is a chance to see all the world's fifteen crane species as well as a whooping-crane exhibit. Although you can walk around the pens by yourself, guided tours are given at 10:00 A.M. and 1:00 and 3:00 P.M. from Memorial Day to Labor Day and on weekends in May, September, and October. General hours are 9:00 A.M. to 5:00 P.M. daily May 1 through October 31. The foundation grounds are ten minutes from either the Dells or Baraboo. From Baraboo take U.S. Highway 12 West to Shady Lane Road; follow the signs 1½ miles to the foundation entrance. From the Dells and I–90/94, take U.S. Highway 12 east and follow the signs. Call (608) 356-9462.

Devil's Lake State Park. S5975 Park Road, Baraboo. The park sprawls over 10,000 acres, including the 368-acre, 50-foot-deep lake. Native Americans called this Spirit Lake, but early settlers didn't quite get the reasoning and wound up tagging it Devil's Lake. Other than the name and the occasional patch of poison ivy, there's nothing to worry about here. Oh, sure, there are some rattlesnakes in the bluffs, but leave them alone and they'll leave you alone.

The main ridge towers 500 feet above the glacially formed lake, allowing great rock-climbing challenges and wonderful vistas from the observation lookouts. Swimming, fishing, canoeing, and scuba diving are popular recreational activities. The park also has almost 20 miles of trails for hiking or cross-country skiing back to nature. There are also 415 campsites available during the season. Yet since this is one of the state's most used parks, be sure to call ahead for reservations. Only about a fifteen-minute drive south of Baraboo, the park is bounded by South Shore Drive (State Highway 123) on the west and State Highway 113 on the east, with the rock cliffs and South Lake Road on the south and Sauk County Highway DL on the north. Day-use hours are 6:00 A.M. to 11:00 P.M. A Nature Center on the lake's north shore is a good place to start a Devil's Lake visit. Interpretive displays on the region's history, geology, and flora and fauna are helpful to put everything into perspective. The center is open from 9:00 A.M. to 4:45 P.M. daily from June 1 to September 1 and from 9:00 A.M. to 3:00 P.M. Saturday and Sunday in September and October. For other information call the park office at (608) 356-8301.

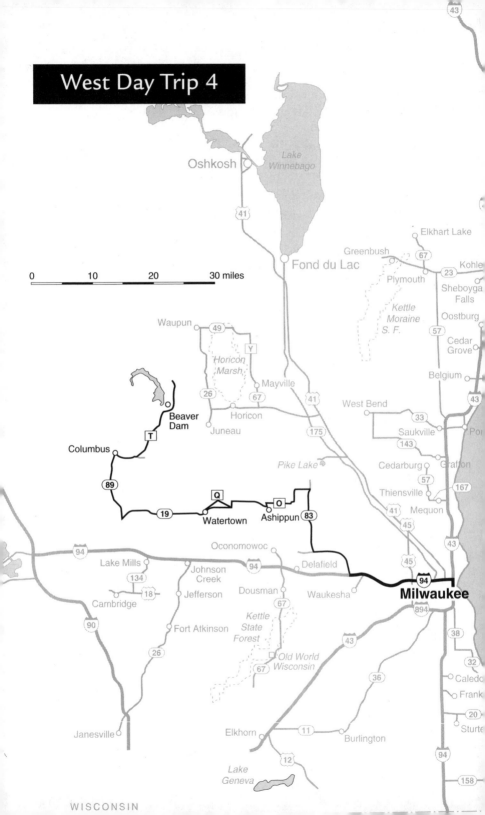

West Day Trip 4

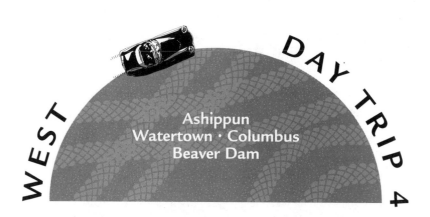

ASHIPPUN

Start your tour of Dodge County via Dodge County Highway O west from State Highway 83. County Highway O will take you to Ashippun, home of the Honey Acres, a real honey of a museum. Ashippun is also located on State Highway 67, about forty minutes northwest of Milwaukee. The museum is on State Highway 67, indicated by numerous signs. It is open from 9:00 A.M. to 3:30 P.M. weekdays, year-round, and also from noon to 4:00 P.M. on Saturday and Sunday, from mid-May through mid-October. Honey Acres includes many exhibits on bees and honey producing. One of the most interesting displays features spigots that drip clover and other honey flavors, allowing some comparison shopping.

WATERTOWN

After having fun in Ashippun tasting the various honeys, take your sweet old time south along Dodge County Highway O to Watertown, which was one of Wisconsin's most prosperous communities even before the territory became a state. The first white settler, Timothy Johnson, claimed 1,000 acres of land in 1836, realizing the value of the river and local natural resources. By 1849 Watertown, then known as Johnson's Rapids, had become a village of several hundred hardy souls, most of whom were from New York State or

149

were German and Irish immigrants. In 1953 Watertown became a city and adopted a charter. Two years later it was the second-largest community in Wisconsin, with more than 8,000 residents.

One of the most famous locals of the era was Carl Schurz, a German-born U.S. antislavery congressman noted for his support of Abraham Lincoln. Schurz went on to become a general in the Civil War. After the war he became a journalist and moved to Missouri and became a U.S. senator from that state. Later, he returned to newspapering and also wrote many political treatises while living in New York City.

In the 1860s Watertown's farmers were known for their "goosenoodling," the practice of force-feeding noodles to geese for rapid weight gain. This enlarged the birds' livers, which were made into *pâté de foie gras* and sold around the country. The German farmers brought their geese to the *viehrmarkt* for sale. Although Watertown now has a strong industrial base, its farmers' market in summer and autumn is a reminder of that early agricultural tradition.

WHERE TO GO

Berres Brothers Coffee. 101 Western Avenue, Watertown. Although primarily a wholesale coffee producer, Berres delivers gourmet coffees to many area grocery stores and offices and has a factory outlet on-site where the thirsty day-tripper can purchase a refreshing pickup cuppa java. No greasy aftertaste with Berres, which has developed a special roasting method that uses a machine similar to a popcorn popper instead of more traditional units that are more like a clothes dryer, exposing the bean surface to potential burning. The company also has a mail-order catalog. Hours are 8:00 A.M. to 5:30 P.M. weekdays and 9:00 A.M. to 4:00 P.M. Saturday. Call (920) 261-6158 or (800) 233-5443.

Octagon House and America's First Kindergarten. 919 Charles Street, Watertown. Operated by the State Historical Society, the museum was once a kindergarten, founded in 1856 by Margarthe Meyer Schurz, whose husband, Carl, was a noted U.S. general and politician. From Watertown the concept of early education for kids spread around the nation. The school was moved to the grounds of the eight-sided house in 1956. Hours are from 10:00 A.M. to 4:00 P.M. daily from May 1 to Memorial Day and after Labor Day through October; and from 10:00 A.M. to 4:00 P.M. daily from Memorial Day through Labor Day. Call (920) 261-2796.

The Market. From I-94, drive 7 miles north on State Highway 26, turn right (east) on Milwaukee Street, go 2 blocks, and turn left (north) on Water Street. The market is adjacent to the Rock River, 1 block south of Watertown's old-fashioned downtown. The complex is in a renovated 1870s lumberyard, with cobblestone walkways and plank boardwalks to give a feel for the past. Gourmet bath items, fifty antiques dealers, golf clubs, paintings, cigars, and a pie shop round out the market's offerings. Mall hours are 10:00 A.M. to 8:00 P.M. Monday through Friday, 10:00 A.M. to 5:00 P.M. Saturday, and 10:00 to 4:00 P.M. Sunday. Call (920) 262-2348 or try the Web site at www.themarketmall.com.

Parks. Watertown's hometown feel is augmented by its wide-ranging park system. Riverside Park, at twenty-nine acres the community's largest, features picnic areas, rest rooms, play areas, fishing, hiking trails, tennis and volleyball courts, ball diamonds, and swimming. The town's smallest park (one and one-tenth acres) is the cozily comfortable Fannie P. Lewis Park, a jewel of a picnic hideaway. Then there's Clark, Lincoln, and Tivoli Island Parks for more urban greenery. For more information call the Watertown Parks and Recreation Department at (920) 262-8080.

WHERE TO SHOP

James J. Chocolate Shop. 712 West Main Street, Watertown. Old-fashioned, handmade candy makes this shop a dieter's demise. Hours are 10:00 A.M. to 6:00 P.M. Monday through Friday and 10:00 A.M. to 5:00 P.M. Saturday. Call (920) 206-9787.

Watertown Homestyle Bakery. 411 East Main Street, Watertown. The luscious perfume of fresh pastries, cookies, pies, and cakes lures the innocent passerby. Forget the calories. Doors open at dawn with sweet, chewy offerings. Closed Saturday afternoons. Call (920) 261-4101 for hours.

The Craft Castle. 407 East Main Street, Watertown. The hobbyist can get everything needed for painting, printing, woodworking, plaster art, and wreath making. Hours are 9:00 A.M to 5:00 P.M. Monday through Thursday, 9:00 A.M. to 6:00 P.M. Friday, and 9:00 A.M. to 4:00 P.M. Saturday. Call (920) 261-9666.

River City Antiques. 204 West Main Street, Watertown. Furniture, toys, clothing, and other memorabilia are for sale. Hours are

10:00 A.M. to 5:00 P.M. Tuesday through Friday, 10:00 A.M. to 4:00 P.M. Saturday, and noon to 4:00 P.M. Sunday. Call (920) 261–8517.

Calico Cottage. 209 East Main Street, Watertown. Country furniture, barn-board reproductions, and Victorian-style furnishings set the Calico Cottage apart. Hours are 10:00 A.M. to 5:00 P.M. Monday through Friday, 10:00 A.M. to 4:00 P.M. Saturday, and noon to 4:00 P.M. Sunday. Call (920) 261–9460.

Fischers Department Store. 210 East Main Street, Watertown. In the same family for more than one hundred years, started by the current owner's grandfather, Fischers offers high-quality styles for men and women, plus home furnishings. This is one of the last old-time-style department stores in Wisconsin, located adjacent to the bridge in downtown Watertown. When they say, "discover the difference" here, they mean it. Friendly, informed clerks help guide the mall-shocked customer to the right racks. It is amazing how personal service means so much. Hours are 9:00 A.M. to 5:00 P.M. Monday through Thursday, 9:00 A.M. to 8:00 P.M. Friday, 9:00 A.M. to 5:00 P.M. Saturday, and noon to 4:00 p.m. Sunday. Call (920) 261–6965 or try the Web page at www.fischers.com.

WHERE TO EAT

Mullen's Dairy & Eatery. 212 West Main Street, Watertown. Since 1932 Mullen's has been serving delicious ice-cream sundaes, cones, and shakes. All the ice cream is made at Mullen's, ensuring only the best. You can also settle into one of the back booths for homemade chili or a burger and fries. Displayed around the rooms are antique milk bottles, advertising signs, and other artifacts. Hours are 9:00 A.M. to 10:00 P.M. daily. Call (920) 261–4278. $

Phil's Pizza Palace. 112 South Second Street, Watertown. Okay, here's another supremely delicious pizza joint. But Phil's has the plus of offering gyros, Greek salad, shish kabob, and other Mediterranean delights on its expansive menu. Hours are 4:00 P.M. to 1:00 A.M. Tuesday through Thursday, 4:00 P.M. to 2:00 A.M. Friday and Saturday, and 4:00 to 11:00 P.M. Sunday. Call (920) 261–0102. $; □

The Upper Krust. 210 South Water Street, Watertown. The Krust's home-baked pie and cheesecake are superb. Full range of soup, salad, and sandwiches. Hours are 11:00 A.M. to 7:00 P.M. Saturday, 11:00 A.M. to 4:00 P.M. Sunday, 10:00 A.M. to 8:00 P.M. Monday through Thursday, and 10:00 A.M. to 9:00 P.M. Friday. Call (920) 206–9202. $; □

Donny's Supper Club. N8240 Jefferson County Highway, Pipersville (4 miles south of Watertown). Hours are 5:00 to 9:30 P.M. Monday, Tuesday, and Thursday; 4:00 to 10:30 P.M. Friday; 5:00 to 10:00 P.M. Saturday; and 4:00 to 9:30 P.M. Sunday. Closed Wednesday. Call (920) 261-2651. $$; ☐

Steakfire Grille & Bar. 1726 State Highway 26, Watertown. If steaks are your nosh of choice, the Steakfire serves up savory delights. Daily lunch is offered from 11:00 A.M. to 5:00 P.M., with dinner served from 5:00 to 10:00 P.M. Call (920) 262-2222. $; ☐

Settler's Bay Restaurant. 1601 East Gate Drive (adjacent to State Highway 16), Watertown. The restaurant offers casual, family dining. Hearty portions help, with daily specials. The prime rib is ace, along with an excellent Sunday breakfast buffet. Settler's serves up five kinds of hot wings during its daily Wing-Dings extravaganza from 3:00 to 6:00 P.M. Kitchen hours are 11:30 A.M. to 9:00 P.M. Tuesday through Thursday, 11:30 A.M. to 10:00 P.M. Friday and Saturday, and 10:00 A.M. to 8:00 P.M. Sunday. Live music is offered from 8:00 P.M. to midnight on Friday. Call (920) 206-7774. $$; ☐

WHERE TO STAY

EconoLodge. 700 East Main Street, Watertown. Located near downtown, the EconoLodge is convenient to the shopping district along the river. Thirty-eight rooms are available for smoking and nonsmoking guests. Call (920) 261-9010. $$; ☐

Brandt-Quirk Manor. 410 South Fourth Street, Watertown. Innkeepers Wayne and Elda Zuleger keep a tidy house, an 1875 Victorian, by the way. The Brandt has four rooms, with antique furnishings, high ceilings, stained-glass windows, and marble fireplaces. A full breakfast is served every morning. Call (920) 261-7917. $$; ☐

COLUMBUS

Leaving Watertown, proceed west on State Highway 19 to State Highway 89. Turn north to Columbus, on the eastern rim of Dodge County. In mid-May each year, Columbus celebrates its nickname as the "Red Bud City" with a Red Bud Festival that includes music, the crowning of a prince and princess, bargains in the shops, and a library book sale. The color of the town's redbud trees during spring brings an explosion of crimson to the scene.

Just outside Columbus, on State Highway 16, is Astico Park, with sixty-nine acres of prairie and woods on a peninsula along the Crawfish River. There are 60 campsites in the park, with hiking trails, picnic areas, and shoreline access for canoeing and fishing. For more information on Columbus, contact the chamber of commerce at (920) 623-3699.

WHERE TO GO

Columbus Antiques Mall. 239 Whitney Street, Columbus. With 180 dealers utilizing 80,000 square feet, the mall is the largest antiques and collectible outlet in Wisconsin. It is open 364 days a year from 8:15 A.M. to 4:00 P.M. In one room look over the displays on Christopher Columbus and items from the 1893 Columbian Exposition. Call (920) 623-1992.

BEAVER DAM

After exploring the Columbus Antiques Mall, drive east on State Highway 60 to Dodge County Highway T at the crossroads community of Astico. Turn north onto T and drive 8 miles to Beaver Dam, a city of 15,169. It is the largest city in the county, located on the south shore of Beaver Dam Lake. The waterway, spreading over 6,600 acres, extends 14 miles north from Beaver Dam to Fox Lake (on State Highway 33) and is a great recreational resource. There are boat landings, play areas, and picnic grounds at Tahoe and Waterworks Parks. Fishing is allowed from shore and from the public piers at each park. Water-ski shows are held on Sunday evenings at Tahoe Park throughout summer. In addition, swimming is available at the beach at Crystal Lake Beach, a small lake within the boundaries of Beaver Dam. Swan City Park, adjacent to the town hospital, has a wading pond for youngsters under the age of eight.

Swan City Park hosts Wednesday night concerts in summer and has a restored 1880 springhouse to explore, along with picnic shelters and a play area. Golfers can take advantage of the links at Old Hickory and Beaver Dam Golf Club. A golf driving range is on Dodge County Highway B at the outskirts of town. For details on other activities in town, contact the Beaver Dam Chamber of Commerce, 127 South Spring Street, Beaver Dam, WI 53919-2320. Call (920) 887-8879 or use the Web site at www.beaverdam chamber.com.

WHERE TO GO

D&D Marine. W9276 Dodge County Highway G, Beaver Dam. You can rent pontoons, fishing boats, ski boats, and canoes for fun on the water at D&D Marine. Call (920) 885-4038 for rates and hours during the boating season.

Beaverland Must-skis. Tahoe Park, Beaver Dam. The club shows are held at 6:00 P.M. (weather permitting) on Sunday from the end of May through early September in Tahoe Park, as well as on Memorial Day and Labor Day. Call the chamber of commerce for more information; (920) 887-8879.

WHERE TO SHOP

Front Street Gifts. 127 Front Street, Beaver Dam. Toys, puzzles, bears, games, art glass, and other collectibles here can add to a day-tripper's collection. Hours are 10:00 A.M. to 5:30 P.M. Monday through Thursday, 10:00 A.M. to 6:00 P.M. Friday, 9:00 A.M. to 4:00 P.M. Saturday, and noon to 4:00 P.M. Sunday. Call (920) 885-5225.

Kornely's Craft & Hobby Center. 130 Front Street, Beaver Dam. Train supplies, doll-making material, paint, puzzles, cake-decorating equipment, rubber stamps, and almost everything else you can think of in the hobby line can be secured at Kornely's. Hours are Monday through Wednesday and Saturday 9:00 A.M. to 5:00 P.M., Thursday and Friday until 8:00 P.M. From November 1 through December 24 the store is open 9:00 A.M. to 4:00 P.M. Call (920) 887-3380 or (888) 875-2768. The Web site is www.kornelys.com.

Herter's Waterfowl Headquarters. 111 East Burnett Street, Beaver Dam. Need a new rod and reel? How about fillet knives, hooks, duck and goose decoys, camouflage clothing, tackle boxes? Herter's has it all. Please call ahead for hours; (920) 887-1765.

WHERE TO EAT

Park Plaza Pizza. 233 Front Street, Beaver Dam. Burgers and sandwiches, chicken, and shrimp are touted menu items. Hours are 11:00 A.M. to midnight Monday through Thursday, 11:00 A.M. to 1:30 A.M. Friday and Saturday, and 5:00 P.M. to midnight Sunday. Call (920) 887-8411. $$; ☐

Walker's Family Restaurant. Intersection of State Highway 33 and U.S. Highway 151, Beaver Dam. Baked chicken and homemade bread are signature items at Walker's. Open seven days a week, 6:00 A.M. to 11:00 P.M. Call (920) 885-9041. $$; ☐

WHERE TO STAY

The Victorian Bed & Breakfast. 518 North Center Street, Beaver Dam. The house, built in 1900, exudes warmth and charm—elegance, too. Two bedrooms. Call (920) 885-9601. $$; ☐

Grand View Motel. 1510 Center Street (1 mile west of downtown Beaver Dam on State Highway 33). The motel accepts pets, so Fido is welcome to come along on your day trip. Call (920) 885-9208. $; ☐

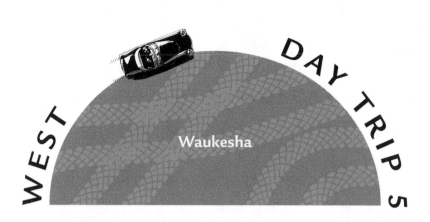

WAUKESHA

Originally called "Prairie Village" due to its proximity to a Potawatomi Indian village, Waukesha is one of the fastest-growing cities in Wisconsin. Located along the Fox River, the town name translates to mean "By the Little Fox." This active community first received its reputation as a destination in the late 1800s. The area's mineral springs were thought to hold curative properties. By the early 1900s as many as twenty-five passenger trains a day were dropping off some of the most wealthy and famous people of the era. Visitors to the area included Mrs. Abraham Lincoln and President Ulysses S. Grant.

People still flock to Waukesha, although now its business, cultural exhibits, and local parks are the main attractions. Even driving through the neighborhoods can yield great sights. Many of the homes that sprang up during the tourist boom of the last century are still standing, and the downtown buildings retain much of their original architectural look.

Only 20 miles west of Milwaukee on I-94, Waukesha offers quite a lot. You may have to go back a few times to get in everything. Contact the Waukesha Area Convention and Visitors Bureau, 223 Wisconsin Avenue, Waukesha, WI 53186-4926. Or call (262) 542-0330 or (800) 366-8474. Check out the Web site at www.wauknet.com/visit. If you are already in the neighborhood, stop in to say hello. Hours are 8:00 A.M. to 5:00 P.M. weekdays.

157

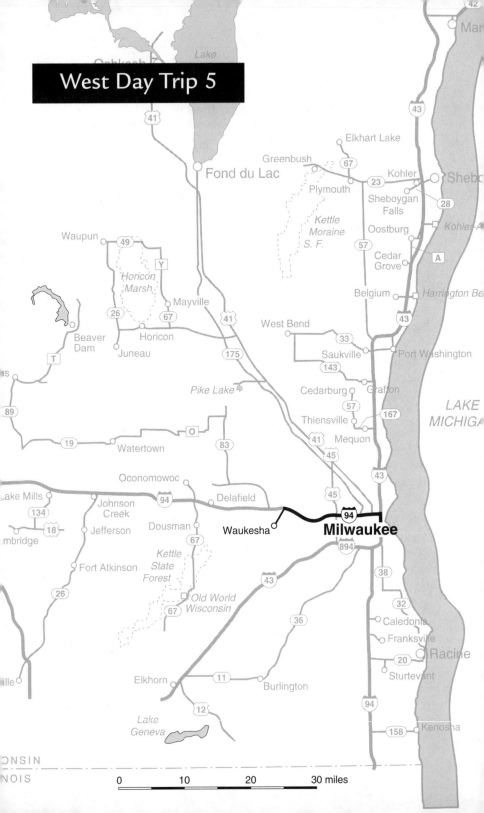

West Day Trip 5

WHERE TO GO

Skateland Roller Skating. 1931 East Main Street, Waukesha. This is a great place to roll with the family. If you are a bit shaky, then come along for lessons before attending one of the public sessions. Skateland's hours of operation vary according to season and the number of different-themed skating sessions. Call (262) 542-7971 or (262) 542-1549 for more information.

Sunset Bowl. 333 West Sunset Drive, Waukesha. One of the best alleys to enjoy Wisconsin's favorite pastime (outside of watching the Green Bay Packers). Nothing feels better than to slip on those crazy, multi-toned shoes and slide your fingers into the holes on a bowling ball, knowing that a strike is right around the corner. Open bowling hours vary often, so call (262) 542-9191 to get updated information.

Cutler Park. 321 Wisconsin Avenue, Waukesha. This park, located in downtown Waukesha, contains prehistoric Indian mounds and a Civil War monument. The real gem in the park, however, is the Carnegie Library. Established in 1912, this beautiful building now has an annual circulation of more than 1,248,768. It also has some great kids' programs throughout the year. Hours are 9:00 A.M. to 9:00 P.M. Monday through Friday, 9:00 A.M. to 6:00 P.M. Saturday, and 1:00 to 4:00 P.M. Sunday. Call (262) 524-3689 for more information about library activities.

Prairieville Park. 2507 Plaza Court, Waukesha. If you like the feel of the wind in your hair as you eye up the perfect putt, then Prairieville Park, a challenging mini-golf course, is your place. They also have batting cages, which include baseball, softball, and fast-pitch softball. Specializing in birthday parties and other group functions, they have packages that can cater to your needs. Summer hours are 10:00 A.M. to 10:30 P.M. Monday through Saturday and 11:00 A.M. to 10:30 P.M. Sunday. Call (262) 784-4653 for spring and fall hours.

Waukesha Civic Theater. 264 West Main Street, Waukesha. Starting in the 1950s, the Waukesha Civic Theater still packs in a tremendous amount of talent during its seasons. Performing Tony Award–winning musicals and plays, they also have great children's productions. Located in downtown Waukesha, it is an easy jump to all the great restaurants in the area. The theater is wheelchair-accessible. Business office hours are 12:30 to 5:00 P.M. Tuesday through Friday. Call (262) 547-4911. The box office hours are 5:00 to 7:00 P.M. Monday through Friday, noon to curtain on show Fridays, and two hours before curtain on show Fridays and Saturdays. The administrative office number is (262) 547-0708.

Retzer Nature Center. Native Wisconsin plants, birds, and animals are highlighted throughout this 330-acre park. Five miles of hiking trails range in length and difficulty. During winter the center offers challenging opportunities for cross-country skiing aficionados. Stop by for one of the center's guided tours, or you can pick up some audiocassettes at the nature center desk for your own information as you wander. They also offer an Adventure Trail, which is wheelchair-accessible, with a paved road and signs in braille. Nature Center hours are 8:00 A.M. to 4:30 P.M. daily; the park is open from sunrise to 10:00 P.M. Monday through Friday. The park is open year-round. Call (262) 896-8007 for more information about special events at the nature center.

Waukesha Symphony Orchestra. 100 North East Avenue, Waukesha. The *Milwaukee Journal-Sentinel* called this group "one of the most remarkable community orchestras in the nation." Celebrating more than fifty years in Waukesha, they offer jazz, chamber, and choral music throughout the year, as well as their fantastic full-orchestra concerts. Performances are held in the Shattuck Auditorium in Carroll College. Call (262) 547-1858 for more information about seasonal updates and special artists' series.

Minooka County Park. 1927 East Sunset Drive, Waukesha. Swimming, hiking, biking, and bridle and nature trails are a part of summer in this 580-acre park. During winter you can wander through the snowbound trails, cross-country skiing or snowshoeing while watching the silence of the season. Hours vary according to season, so call (262) 548-7801 for updated information.

WHERE TO SHOP

A Dicken's of a Place. 521 Wisconsin Avenue, Waukesha. A perfect place to browse through the aisles, this downtown Waukesha antiques store has some fantastic finds, including clothes, furniture, and more. Go pick up a table that reminds you of grandma's house as sunlight filtered through the lace curtains or of a lamp you saw in an old family picture. Hours are 10:00 A.M.

to 5:00 P.M. Monday through Saturday and noon to 5:00 P.M. Sunday. Call (262) 542-0702

Babbling Brook & Heirloom Doll Shoppe. 416 East Broadway, Waukesha. Famous for its collection of antique dolls and intricate glassware, this is a collector's dream come true. Hours are 10:00 A.M. to 6:00 P.M. Thursday and Friday, and 10:00 A.M. to 4:00 P.M. Saturday. Call (262) 544-4739 for more information.

Susan Kruger Antiques. 401 Madison Street, Waukesha. Just browsing through the aisles can take you back to a bygone era. Specializing in antique hardware and sterling silverware, the store also holds a cornucopia of other great items. Hours are noon to 5:00 P.M. Tuesday through Friday, and 10:00 A.M. to 5:00 P.M. Saturday. Call (262) 542-7722 for more information.

WHERE TO EAT

Christina's Family Restaurant. 350 Delefield Road, Waukesha. If you are looking for some great local grub, head on over to Christina's. Breakfast, lunch, and dinner are served with a smile, and there is always a pot of coffee on. Hours are 5:30 A.M. to 10:00 P.M. Monday through Saturday and 6:00 A.M. to 9:00 P.M. Sunday. Call (262) 542-6739. $; ☐

Kalypso Restaurant. 500 East Broadway, Waukesha. Another good home-style-cooking joint, the Kalypso serves up a mean breakfast. A great place to stop on the way to downtown Waukesha. Hours are 5:00 A.M. to 10:00 P.M. daily. Call (262) 549-9002. $-$$; ☐

Sunset Family Restaurant. 535 West Sunset, Waukesha. Come on in and fill up with some great comfort food. Sunset offers the basics to keep any family happy. Hours are 6:00 A.M. to 10:00 P.M. daily. Call (262) 524-9555. $-$$; ☐

Wildflowers. 2810 Golf Road (located in the Country Inn Hotel), Waukesha. For breakfast, lunch, or dinner, join the gang over at Wildflowers for some excellent grub. Dinner has barbecued ribs and New York strip steaks; lunch overflows with salads and sandwiches. Hours are 6:30 A.M. to 2:00 P.M. and 5:00 to 10:00 P.M. daily. You can also look them up on the Web at www.foodspot.com. Call (262) 547-0201. $$$; ☐

Hillcrest Deli. 2000 Davidson Road, Waukesha. If you are looking for the perfect place to grab the fixins' for a fine sandwich, a fantastic Friday Night Fish Fry, or a Saturday prime rib dinner, then drop by the Hillcrest Deli. The restaurant also has homemade soups, as well as an extensive beer and wine list. Hours are 11:00 A.M. to 2:00 P.M. Monday through Thursday and 10:00 A.M. to 5:00 P.M. Friday. Call (262) 650-8303. $-$$; ☐

Weissgerbers Gasthaus. 2720 Grandview Boulevard, Waukesha. No Wisconsin town is complete without its German restaurant, and Waukesha is no exception. From wienerschnitzel to steak, lobster, and duck, this place has it all. The Gasthaus also offers a full wine and beer list. Hours are 11:30 A.M. to 2:00 P.M. for lunch and 5:00 to 9:00 P.M. for dinner daily. Call (262) 544-4460 for more information. $$-$$$; ☐

Gyros Corner West. 1538 East Moreland Road West, Waukesha. This popular restaurant presents a wide variety of foods, many with a Greek twist. Gyros Corner serves breakfast, lunch, and dinner, each having distinct specials. Hours are 5:00 A.M. to 10:00 P.M. Monday through Saturday and 6:00 A.M. to 9:00 P.M. Sunday. Call (262) 544-0211. $-$$; ☐

Albanese's Roadhouse. 2301 Bluemound Road, Waukesha. If a down-home Italian place is what you're craving, head on over to the Roadhouse. Offering a variety of Italian and American cuisine, it has something for everyone. Call (262) 785-1930 for more information. $$; ☐

Matteo's Italian Ristorante & Bar. 1608 East Sunset, Waukesha. Another great place for a little bit of Italiana. Pastas and pizzas fill out the menu, along with appetizers and salads. *Mangia!* Hours are 11:30 A.M. to 2:00 P.M. Friday, lunch only; 5:00 to 10:00 P.M. Tuesday through Saturday, and 5:00 to 9:00 P.M. Sunday and Monday. Call (262) 544-6022 for more information. $$-$$$; ☐

Casa del Rio. 408 East Main Street, Waukesha. While you are out visiting Waukesha, go check out this south-of-the-border favorite. The Casa has all the regular south-of-the-border menu items, from taco to burritos, as well as a few other dishes for diners with a more adventurous palate. Voted by Dennis Ghetto, food critic for the *Milwaukee Journal-Sentinel*, as having the best chili rellenos. Hours are 11:00 A.M. to 10:00 P.M. Tuesday through Thursday, 11:00 A.M. to 11:00 P.M. Friday, 10:00 A.M. to 11:00 P.M. Saturday, and 9:00 A.M. to 10:00 P.M. Sunday. Closed Monday. Call (262) 542-4080. $; ☐

WHERE TO STAY

County Inn Hotel. 2810 Golf Road, Waukesha. This is a great place to stay after enjoying your travels around Waukesha. The hotel has more than 200 rooms, including suite accommodations. The hotel also has a workout center, an indoor pool, and a nature trail that wraps around the hotel. Wildflowers Restaurant and Coppers Pub and Grill provide the chance to sit and unwind after a long day. Call (800) 247-6640. Check out the County Inn Web page at www.countyinnhotel.com. $$-$$$; □

Ramada Limited. 2111 East Moreland Boulevard, Waukesha. This newly remodeled hotel offers standard, business, and whirlpool suites, as well as a fitness center and an indoor pool. Complimentary continental breakfast accompanies every room. Rooms are wheelchair-accessible. Call (262) 547-7770 or (800) 21-GUEST for more information. $$; □

Best Western. 2840 North Grandview Boulevard, Waukesha. For visitors looking for a first-class night to accompany a day of luxury, step into the Best Western. The facility offers deluxe king- and queen-size rooms, as well as whirlpool suites. Call (262) 524-9300 or (800) 547-3935 for more information. $$; □

Select Inn. 2510 Plaza Court, Waukesha. An inexpensive way to spend the night in Waukesha while getting excellent service. The Select Inn offers standard, suite, and extended-stay apartments. It is wheelchair-accessible, and pets are welcome with an advanced deposit. Contact the property at (262) 786-6015 or (800) 641-1000 for more information. $$; □

Super 8. 2501 Plaza Court, Waukesha. The motel offers double and king-size beds as well as rooms featuring kitchenettes. Continental breakfast is available, as well as nonsmoking rooms and cable TV. Call (262) 785-1590 or (800) 800-8000. $-$$

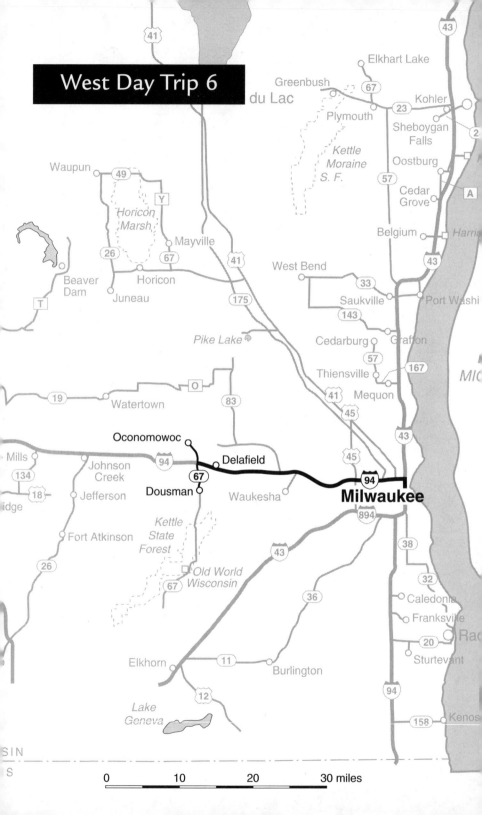

OCONOMOWOC, DELAFIELD, AND DOUSMAN

No matter the season, this westernmost section of Waukesha County offers plenty of things to do. Parks, lakes, campgrounds, and quaint little stores dot the area, connected by a series of state highways that pass through rolling hills and verdant valleys.

Originally settled by German and Norwegian farmers, the area had a huge population boom in the late 1800s, when the springwater in nearby Waukesha was thought to contain magical, curative properties. Oconomowoc, as well as the other cities, had its share of famous folk setting up palatial abodes. At one time Lake Road was referred to as Presidents' Avenue because Taft, Grant, Cleveland, Coolidge, McKinley, and Teddy Roosevelt had visited Draper Hall, one of the more prominent homes in the neighborhood. Many of the huge mansions went up around the area's many lakes, and historic walking tours in these communities can be a great way to experience the grandeur of yesteryear.

Delafield covers 9 square miles of gentle Kettle Moraine terrain surrounding Lake Nagawicka, which is more than 1,000 acres in size. Although settlers arrived here as early as 1839, the city was not incorporated until 1959 and now serves as a bedroom community for Milwaukee.

Water is still an important asset to this area. The many lakes in the region offer a variety of opportunities for boating and fishing. Even during winter folks gather on the ice to see if they can catch the "big one" that got away when shorts and T-shirts were in season.

This region isn't just about outdoor recreation. There are a number of theater companies, musical venues, and restaurants that can be a great destination after wandering through the forested parklands near Dousman and the other communities.

You can catch these cities off I-94 west, or you can meander off the beaten path by cruising west on State Highway 18 and picking up State Highway 67 north.

More information is available by contacting the Oconomowoc Visitors and Convention Bureau, 174 East Wisconsin Avenue; (800) 524-3744. Hours are 9:00 A.M. to 5:00 P.M. weekdays. The Delafield Chamber of Commerce is located at 421 Main Street. Hours are 9:00 A.M. to 5:00 P.M. weekdays; the phone number is (262) 646-8100, or check the Web site at www.delafield-wi.org.

WHAT TO DO

Oconomowoc Historical Society Museum. 103 West Jefferson Street, Oconomowoc. Walk through time and trace the rich history of this bustling community. Learn about the Native Americans who first populated the area and called it *Coo-No-Mo-Wauk*, or "where the waters meet." Journey with the white settlers as they set up farms in the area. See photographs and items from the different eras. Hours are 1:00 to 5:00 P.M. daily. For more information call the museum at (262) 569-0740.

Lapham Peak State Park. State Highway C, Delafield. If wandering through majestic trees on a warm summer day sounds like time well spent, then head over to Lapham Peak State Park. This park offers 671 acres of land with 14.6 miles of walking, biking, and horse trails. It also offers 2.3 miles of cross-country skiing trails, a picnic area, and a lookout tower on top of Lapham Peak. This is Waukesha County's highest point, towering 1,233 feet. The park is named for Increase Lapham, an early pioneer scientist whose weather studies led to the formation of the National Weather Service. For more information call (262) 646-3025.

Kettle Moraine Golf Club. 4299 Highway 67, Dousman. If golf is your game, then head on out to this eighteen-hole course built on the scenic edge of the Kettle Moraine Forest. The club also offers a complete pro shop and driving range with lessons from a PGA instructor. After a rousing game of golf, wander over to the new clubhouse, which features the Score Card Lounge and the elegant Kettle Room restaurant. Hours vary according to weather, so call (262) 965-6200.

Olympia Highlands. 965 Cannon Gate Road, Oconomowoc. As the snow settles over the ground across Wisconsin, minds wander toward ski slopes. Waiting the whole year to feel the wind in your hair as you whisk on down a mountain can be such a terrible thing. Well, patience is rewarded. Saunter over to the Olympia Highlands to get your skiing fix. For those of you who have never put a pair of skis on before, they do offer lessons on the slope adjacent to the Oconomowoc Spa and Resort. There are even things to do during summer, with an award-winning golf course, plus tennis and racquetball courts. With the resort directly across the street, skiing here makes a perfect day trip, with a night of luxury added on for good measure. Hours are 3:30 to 10:00 P.M. Monday through Friday and 10:00 A.M. to 10:00 P.M. Saturday, depending on weather. Call (262) 567-2577 for more information.

Lake Country Players. Waukesha County Highways K and E, Hartland. Started in 1959, this community theater still presents a fantastic collection of local talent. The troupe usually produces a musical in spring and a drama or comedy in fall, using the theater at Arrowhead High School. Also offering scholarships to budding actors, the Lake Country Players have helped a number of prominent artists get their start. Call (262) 367-3072 for updated information on performances.

Lake Country Dance Theater. Waukesha County Highways K and E, Hartland. Since the 1980s, local choreographers Nina Gaydos-Fedak, Sally Pfeiffer, and Shawn Dunn have been gathering dancers from around the community to put on shows throughout the year. Their biggest production, however, is during the Christmas season. With performances based at Arrowhead High School, they also do outreach into other area schools to teach dance and movement. Call (262) 369-5355 for performance dates or for information regarding dance workshops.

Lake Country Children's Theater. This company partners with other performing groups at University of Wisconsin/Whitewater and the Wauwatosa Children's Theater, as well as with national acts.

This gives kids in the area an opportunity to see live theater from great pros. During summer they also audition local children for various performances. Most of these productions take place in Nixon Park in Hartland, about an hour's drive from Milwaukee, which makes it easy for the day-tripper with a car full of theatrically inclined youngsters. Call Katie Weber at (262) 966-7012 for an updated performance schedule or for tickets to the show.

St. John's Northwestern Military Academy. 1101 North Genesee Street, Delafield. Founded in 1884, the school's Corps of Cadets come from around the world. Most of the academy's lannon-stone buildings date from the turn of the twentieth century. Tours are available. Call (800) 752-2338.

Nashotah House. 2777 Mission Road, Delafield. Founded in 1842 as a frontier mission and incorporated as a college in 1847, Nashotah House is now a theological seminary for Episcopal priests. You can take a self-guided tour of the campus by picking up a brochure at the college Development Office. Call (262) 646-6500 or visit the Web site at www.nashotah.edu.

Hawk's Inn. 426 Wells Street, Delafield. Built in 1846, the Hawk's Inn is now a renovated historic site. The old inn formerly served as a stagecoach stop and dance hall. The wainscoting, oak floors, and cherry banister in the main hallway are impressive. Demonstrations and special events are regularly held throughout the year, such as a May Quilt Show, a Haunted Inn in October, and other fun. The inn is open, with guides in period costumes, from 1:00 to 4:00 P.M. Saturday, May through October. Call (262) 646-4794.

WHERE TO SHOP

Marsh Hill Ltd. 456 North Waterville Road, Delafield. Very-high-quality European pine furniture graces this store. The graceful lines and edging complement the different woods of the Austrian, Swedish, Irish, French, and British fixtures. Hours are noon to 5:00 P.M. Thursday through Sunday. Call (262) 646-2560 for more information.

Delafield Antique Center. 803 Genesee Street, Delafield. With more than seventy-five dealers in one place, a shopper hits pay dirt. The vendors offer eighteenth-, nineteenth-, and twentieth-century furniture, jewelry, toys, and more. Hours are 10:00 A.M. to 5:00 P.M.

Monday through Saturday and noon to 5:00 P.M. Sunday. Call (262) 646-2746 for more information.

Curious Antiquities. 173 East Wisconsin Avenue, Oconomowoc. This gallery and store is a perfect place to come and see the odd, bizarre, and unusual. The owners have original Audubon prints and Paxton botanical prints, nineteenth-century Japanese woodblock prints, ancient Egyptian jewelry, antique Roman coins, armor, swords, archaic maps, pre-Columbian artifacts, and much, much more. Hours are 11:00 A.M. to 5:00 P.M. Monday, 10:00 A.M. to 5:30 P.M. Tuesday and Wednesday, 10:00 A.M. to 6:00 P.M. Thursday and Friday, and 10:00 A.M. to 5:00 P.M. Saturday. Call (262) 567-8280 for more information.

Oconomowoc Gallery, Ltd. 157 East Wisconsin Avenue, Oconomowoc. The shop boasts one of the largest displays of art in Wisconsin. Contemporary to traditional work, vintage European posters, etchings, serigraphs, natural and state wildlife artists, sculpture, jewelry, and glass art can be found in the gallery's extensive collection. They also do custom and conservation framing here. Hours are 10:00 A.M. to 5:00 P.M. Tuesday, Wednesday, and Friday; 10:00 A.M. to 7:00 P.M. Thursday; 10:00 A.M. to 4:00 P.M. Saturday; and 11:00 A.M. to 3:00 P.M. Sunday; closed Monday. Call (262) 567-8123.

Beverly Designs, LLC. 149 East Wisconsin Avenue, Oconomowoc. The shop offers an eclectic mixture of contemporary clothing and unique gifts for the person not afraid to be noticed. Wandering around this boutique is like experiencing an "art show an hour." Unusual objets d'art from local and national talent, as well as wearable art, adorn the store. They also have women's and children's clothing from a variety of designers. Hours are 10:00 A.M. to 5:00 P.M. Tuesday, Wednesday, and Saturday; 10:00 A.M. to 7:00 P.M. Thursday; 10:00 A.M. to 9:00 P.M. Friday; and 11:00 A.M. to 3:00 P.M. Sunday. Call (262) 567-3650 for more information.

WHERE TO EAT

Water Street Brewery Saloon & Grill. 3191 Golf Road, Delafield. Snuggle into a booth, enjoy the wintertime fireplace, and sip a refreshing beverage. Steaks, smoked baby-back pork ribs, monster sandwiches, and rotisserie chicken are on the menu. Carryout available, too. Hours are 11:00 A.M. to midnight daily. Call (262) 646-7878. $$; ☐

Prickly Pear. 621 Milwaukee Street, Delafield. Open Tuesday through Sunday, serving lunch from 11:00 A.M. to 2:00 P.M. and dinner from 5:00 to 10:00 P.M. Confirm reservations at (262) 646-8900. $$$; ☐

Marty's Pizza. 2580 Sun Valley Drive, Delafield (corner of I-94 and State Highway 83). Since 1957, Marty's has been serving up some of the best pizza west of Milwaukee. Try the five-footer if you think you can handle it. Hours are 11:00 A.M. to closing, daily. Call (262) 646-3327. $; ☐

Wholly Cow Frozen Custard. 637 Main Street, Delafield. Make a stop at the Wholly Cow for a refreshing cone during a day trip. Hours are 11:30 A.M. to 9:30 P.M. Monday through Saturday. Hours are seasonal, so you might want to call ahead in early spring or late autumn; (262) 646-2555. $; ☐

WHERE TO STAY

Country Pride Inn. 2412 Milwaukee Street, Delafield (exit 287 at I-94 and State Highway 83). Whirlpool suites; good rates. Call (262) 646-3300. $$; ☐

Holiday Inn Business Suites. 3030 Golf Road, Delafield. Okay, so it's a gimmick, but the freshly baked cookies at check-in are appreciated. Call (262) 646-7077. $$; ☐

JANESVILLE

The county seat of Rock County, Janesville, is only 41 miles south from Madison on I-90, making a good extension for a weekend that includes a day in the capital city area. Or you can drive the more scenic route via I-94 to State Highway 26 for a 71-mile jaunt southwest of Milwaukee. With the latter option, the motorist takes in several small towns along the route, such as Jefferson and Fort Atkinson (Southwest Day Trip 4).

Janesville was named in 1836 for early settler Henry Janes, after the Black Hawk War. The city was a farming hub for years. Gradually expanding its industrial base, the city is now one of Wisconsin's strongest economic centers. Even when it lost the hometown Parker Pen Company in the late 1990s to a corporate move out of state, Janesville kept its head up with other manufacturing and service industries.

Visitors now enjoy the city's restored and renovated historical sites. In fact, 20 percent of Wisconsin's structures listed on the National Register of Historic Places are found in Janesville. The city's 2,000 acres of parks have earned it the nickname of "Wisconsin's Park Place." The Rock River, which flows through the town, is also a draw for hikers and bikers who use its waterside paths.

For more tourism details contact the Janesville Area Convention & Visitors Bureau, 51 Jackson Street, Janesville, WI 53545;

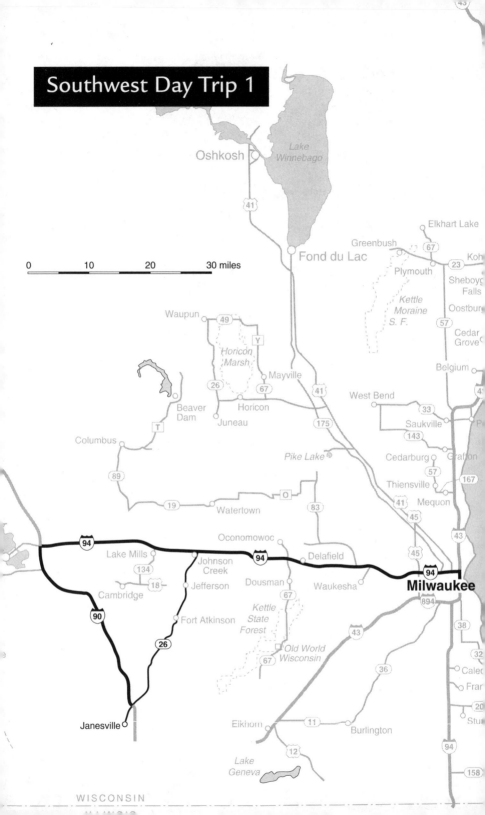

(608) 757-3171 or (800) 48-PARKS. The CVB Web site is www.janes villecvb.com. A visitor information center is open at the Palmer Park Pavilion from 9:00 A.M. to 5:00 P.M. daily from mid-May to mid-October.

WHERE TO GO

Country Furniture by Schuler. 533 North Main Street, Janesville. At Schuler's tables, chairs, and other furniture items are built with Old World craftsmanship, using the finest old pine boards from Midwest barns. Visitors are taken through the step-by-step process that goes into each piece. Tours are held Tuesday through Friday at 10:30 A.M. or at 1:00 P.M. (one tour per day) by appointment only. The entrance fee is $2.00 per person. The regular store hours are 10:00 A.M. to 7:00 P.M. Tuesday through Friday and 10:00 A.M. to 5:00 P.M. Saturday; closed Sunday and Monday. Call (608) 754-4052 or send a fax at (608) 754-7532.

Gray Brewing Company. 2424 West Court Street, Janesville. In this microbrewery it is possible to witness the production and enjoy the tasting of beers, root beer, and cream soda. Tours are available to groups of ten or more by appointment. Call (608) 752-3552.

General Motors Truck & Bus. 1000 Industrial Avenue, Janesville. The largest GM plant under one roof in the United States resumed its tours in January 2000 after a new line development. You can't miss the place. It is surrounded by parking lots packed with shiny new trucks and sporting vehicles assembled there. For opening hours call (608) 756-7681.

Ice Age Trail. The trail, part of a nationally designated hiking system, runs about 1,000 miles from the northwest to the southeast corner of the state, with a leg extending into south-central Wisconsin. The Janesville portion of the trail meanders from the north end of town on the west shore of the Rock River down to the southern part of town adjacent to the river and west toward U.S. Highway 14.

This 8-mile-long section rims a terminal moraine, a long pile of debris left by the retreating glaciers that shaped this region between 12,000 and 15,000 years ago. Volunteers are working to expand the route into the town of Milton, about 5 miles to the northeast, and east into adjacent Walworth County.

One of the main points of interest of the Janesville segment is the Rock River. At one time, the region was under an immense glacial meltwater. The river originates in part from the Horicon Marsh in north-central Wisconsin, which is one of nine Ice Age National Scientific Reserve units. Wear hiking boots because of the uneven surface of the trail. In some sections it is not mowed. The Ice Age Park and Trail Foundation, always eager to accept new people wanting to get involved in the building and maintaining of the trail, can be contacted at (800) 227-0046.

Lincoln-Tallman Restorations. 440 North Jackson Street, Janesville. Abraham Lincoln slept here, although he didn't leave behind his stovepipe hat or long black coat. He came to the city in 1859 on a speaking tour. On the invitation of William M. Tallman, a wealthy landowner with a keen interest in politics, Lincoln dropped by for some home cooking and a bed. No other private residence in Wisconsin can make the claim to have hosted the (eventual) sixteenth president of the United States. The 1855 Italian-style mansion complex comprises three buildings: the Wilson King Stone House, the Tallman Barn, and the Tallman House.

It is open 9:30 A.M. to 4:30 P.M. year-round on weekends from June through September. Tours start every half hour and last about an hour. From November 20 to December 31, holiday tours are offered every day. Other special events and displays are held throughout the year, including a spooky Halloween program. Tickets for the restorations can be purchased down the street at the Rock County Historical Society, where the tours start. Entrance fee; free for the members of the historical society. Closed all major holidays. Call (608) 752-4519 or (608) 752-4509.

Lusting Park Nature Trail. 17 North Franklin Street, Janesville. This ¼-mile section of the park offers outdoors accessibility to the physically challenged. Crushed limestone, a soil polymer stabilizer, and the absence of steep hills make it possible for individuals using wheelchairs, walkers, canes, or crutches to maneuver comfortably along the route. They can take in the twelve interpretative nature stations or picnic in the reserved areas. Leisure Services and the Wisconsin School of the Visually Handicapped provide portable tape recorders and audiocassettes so that the visually challenged can learn about the unique attractions of the site. The tapes describe the white oaks, some of which are up to 500 years old, as well as many other plants and the variety of wildlife.

Large groups can organize activities in the park pavilion by notifying Leisure Services and paying a reservation fee. The trail is open from 6:00 A.M. until 11:00 P.M. For more information call Leisure Services at (608) 755-3030, from 8:00 A.M. to 5:00 P.M. weekdays. Or ring the Wisconsin School for the Visually Handicapped at (608) 755-2950. Pets (with the exception of seeing-eye dogs) are not allowed from May 15 through September 15.

Miracle—the White Buffalo. Heider Farm, 2739 River Road, Janesville. Born on August 20, 1994, this calf figures importantly in the religious beliefs of many American Indians. According to tradition she will be forever a calf, never a cow. Miracle can be visited daily from 10:00 A.M. to 5:00 P.M. at the farm managed by Dave, Val, and Corey Heider. Days and hours open for viewing Miracle vary with the seasons and family commitments, so it is always advisable to call (608) 752-2224 or (608) 741-9632. You can fax (608) 756-9630 for an update on visiting hours.

To reach the farm take I-90 south to Avalon Road, exit 177. Go west about 4 miles to the Rock River; then turn right and proceed for another ¼ mile. Parking can be found just north of the farm. Because buffaloes are wild and unpredictable, the Heiders allow visitors to go only up to the fences. Keep an eye on the children because the fences are electrified. Miracle even has her own Web site (www.whitemiracle.com).

Rock Aqua Jays. Traxler Park (U.S. Highway 51 north), Janesville. The Rock Aqua Jays Water-Ski Team has consistently won national championships since its founding in 1961. The team program includes a jaw-dropping, five-person-high, twenty-three-skier pyramid, and other wet, wild, and wacky feats performed on the Rock River. Get there early to ensure a good seat. Shows are at 7:00 P.M. on Wednesday and Sunday from Memorial Day through July and at 6:30 P.M. from August through Labor Day. Dates vary for tournaments, such as the U.S. National Show Tournament, which are held at the team's Traxler Park site. There is no admission charge but donations are welcome. Call (800) 487-2757.

Rock County Historical Society's Helen Jeffris Wood Museum Center. 426 North Jackson Street, Janesville. The center is the primary place for digging deep into Janesville's history. The society provides frequently changing exhibits that re-create the lifestyle of the past. It also offers lectures, programs, a children's "hands-on" history, a museum gift shop, and meeting spaces for small groups. Admission fee. Open daily from 8:30 A.M. to 4:30 P.M. Closed all major holidays. Call (608) 756-4509 or (608) 741-9596.

Rotary Gardens. 1455 Palmer Drive, Janesville. The easiest access to this marvelous floral display is from exit 175-A on I-90 to State Highway 1. Palmer Drive is the first street on the left. English cottage, French, Italian, Japanese, sunken, and perennial plantings are among the international themes of the fifteen-acre site. It also includes a wildlife sanctuary, access to Wisconsin's Ice Age Trail, and a visitor center with a reference library and a gift shop. Horticultural training, plant sales, and seasonal walks are among the events held amid the wonderfully scented floral arrangements. This is just the place for a romantic stroll.

The gardens are open year-round during daylight hours. The gift shop and the Rath Environmental Center are open from 8:30 A.M. until 4:30 P.M. Monday through Friday, 10:00 A.M. until 6:00 P.M. holidays and weekends from May through October; and noon until 4:00 P.M. in November and December.

Admission is free, but donations are encouraged. Call (608) 752-3885, e-mail gardens@jvlnet.com, or visit the garden Web site at www.jvlnet.com/~gardens.

Wisconsin Wagon Company. 507 Laurel Avenue, Janesville. Constructing handcrafted wooden barrows, sleds, scooters, and the famous Coaster Wagon—built with good, old-fashioned classic design and superior quality—has been the mission of Wisconsin Wagon for the past twenty years. All this place needs are several hundred elves to be tap-tap-tapping away on the toys. Or maybe the "little people" are there after-hours, getting all the goodies ready for Christmas—or any other time when a kid (or grown-up) really needs a wagon. So, when on a tour of the plant, look closely. Tours are offered from 8:00 A.M. to 4:00 P.M. Monday, Tuesday, and Thursday, February 1 through December 15. Saturday tours are by appointment. *A hint:* Products can be bought directly in the plant. Call (608) 754-0026.

WHERE TO SHOP

When afflicted by a shop-'til-you-drop craving, Janesville offers everything from quaint antiques shops to standard brand-name goods offered by most modern national chains.

Here are some of the shops where antiques and craft fans can satisfy their desire to decorate their homes with a touch from the past.

Crafters Mall. 2561 Milton Avenue, Janesville. All that has shaped the items sold here are the 200 hands of their one hundred crafters. Check it out from 10:00 A.M. to 7:00 P.M. Monday through Friday, from 10:00 A.M. to 5:00 P.M. Saturday, and from noon to 5:00 P.M. Sunday. Call (608) 757-2527.

Carousel Consignments. 31 South Main Street, Janesville. Looking for a special collectible? Try at this store, from 9:30 A.M. to 5:30 P.M. Monday through Saturday. For more information call (608) 758-0553.

Foster Lee Antiques. 218 West Milwaukee Street, Janesville. All American, all furniture, all of the last century. Visit from 10:00 A.M. to 6:00 P.M. Wednesday. Call (608) 752-5188.

The General Antique Store. 8301 East Highway 14, Janesville. Besides a general line of antiques, this store offers old advertising items. Open from 1:00 to 5:00 P.M. daily. Call (608) 756-1812.

MacFarlane Pheasant Farm. 2821 South Highway 51, Janesville. The farm was established in 1929 and remains a family-owned business, selling more than five million pheasants since its founding. MacFarlane is one of the country's largest game-bird farms, located about 1 mile south of Janesville just before the Rock County Airport. The birds are penned away from the processing area and are not available for close-up viewing, but a retail outlet is on-site that sells dressed and smoked pheasant and pheasant breasts. Call (608) 757-7881 or (800) 345-8348

Oasis Cheese & Gift Shop. 3401 Milton Avenue (at the I-90 exit 171-A for easy-off and easy-on access), Janesville. If you are headed south, this shop might be your last best chance to buy Wisconsin cheese before crossing the Illinois border about 20 miles to the south. Along with a wide selection of dairy munchies, including those wonderful cheese curds (the fresher, the squeakier when chewed!), Oasis offers sausages, cranberry wine, maple syrup, and jelly beans. The store is open from 8:00 A.M. to 8:00 P.M. Monday through Thursday and 8:00 A.M. to 9:00 P.M. Friday through Sunday. Call (608) 752-9110.

Janesville Mall. 2500 Milton Avenue, Janesville. Janesville Mall is the largest enclosed regional shopping center in a five-county area. It features four department stores (Boston Store, JC Penney, Kohl's, and Sears.) The mall is open 10:00 A.M. to 9:00 P.M. Monday through Saturday and 11:00 A.M. to 6:00 P.M. Sunday. Check for variations in department stores' hours and for holiday times by calling (608) 752-2641. If you are cyber-literate, visit www.janesvillemall.com.

WHERE TO EAT

The Prime Quarter Steak House. 1900 Old Humes Road, Janesville. Steaks are grilled over flaming hickory charcoal for a smooth, smoky taste. Great with baked spuds. Casual dining. Call (608) 752-1881. $$; ☐

Hoffman House. 3431 Milton Avenue, Janesville. Nationally known for its slow-roasted, aged choice beef, this elegant restaurant also offers seafood and an excellent salad bar. The banquet room seats up to 400 people, and the sports bar is equipped with wide screens. Includes also a coffee shop. Open every day at 6:00 A.M. (except on Sunday, when it opens at 6:30 A.M.). Lunch is served from 11:30 A.M. to 1:30 P.M., dinner from 5:00 until 10:00 P.M. every day except Sunday (5:00 to 9:00 P.M.). Call (608) 756-2313. $$; ☐

Roherty's Restaurant & Irish Pub. 2121 Milton Avenue, Janesville. The oldest family-run restaurant in Janesville, established in 1903 by the great-grandparents of the current owner. Plenty to choose from, with about seventy dinner entrees, all-American with an Irish flare. Enjoy lunch and dinner in a homey but classy environment (there's always been great service) or enjoy the cozy Irish pub and its wide selection of beers. Hours vary, so call (608) 752-2393. $$; ☐

WHERE TO STAY

Baymont Inn. 616 Midland, Janesville, WI 53546. Pool, whirlpool, complimentary continental coffee, free local calls and meeting space. Call (608) 758-4545 or (800) 301-0200. $$; ☐

Holiday Inn. 3100 Wellington Place, Janesville. Kids under 18 stay free and they'll be sure to enjoy the indoor pool and whirlpool. Free local calls are handy. Restaurants are nearby. Call (608) 756-3100 or (800)-HOLIDAY. $$; ☐

Microtel Inn. 3121 Wellington Place, Janesville. The inn offers 24-hour coffee service for those who want to stay up for the night.

And free local phone calls, a perk that can't be beat. Plenty of restaurants are next door. Call (608) 752–3121 or (888) 771–7171. $$; ☐

Motel 6. 3907 Milton Avenue, Janesville. This 119-room motel lays out complimentary morning coffee from 7:00 to 10:00 A.M. Call (608) 756–1742 or (888) 466–8356. $$; ☐

Ramada Inn. 3431 Milton Avenue, Janesville. This is where to come for an indoor pool, whirlpool and exercise room, plus an on-site restaurant and lounge. A complimentary continental breakfast is available from Monday to Friday, but there are in-room coffeemakers for a late evening pick-me-up. Hair dryers, ironing boards, and irons available for something to do when watching the 25-inch television screen. Free HBO cable, too. Kids under 18 stay free with parents. $$–$$$; ☐

Scarlett House. 825 East Court Street, Janesville. Antique furnishings are abundant in this comfortable old Queen Anne B&B in the historical Court House Hill section of town. Call (608) 754–8000. $$; ☐

Christine's Victorian Rose Bed & Breakfast. 603 East Court Street, Janesville. This great old Queen Anne Victorian bed and breakfast offers a full breakfast . . . of course. Call (608) 758–3819. $$; ☐

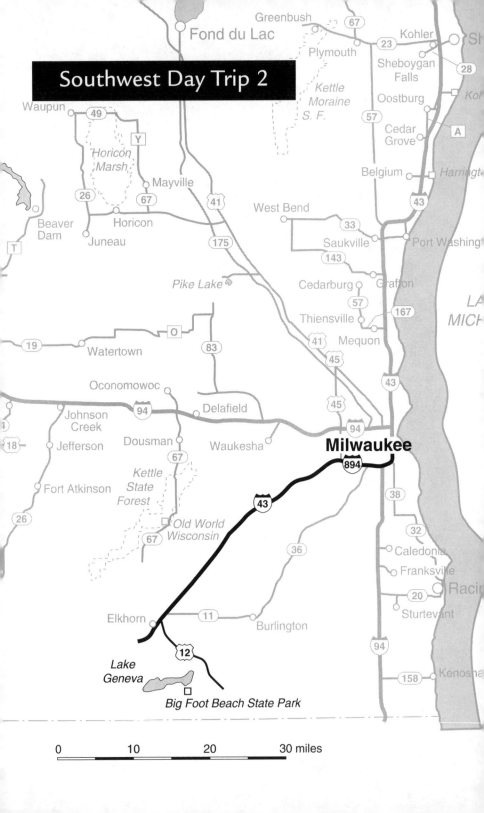

Southwest Day Trip 2

Greenbush
Fond du Lac
67
Kohler
23 Kohler
Plymouth
28
Sheboygan Falls
Waupun
49
Kettle Moraine S. F.
Oostburg
Y
57
Cedar Grove
A
Horicon Marsh
Belgium
Harringt
26
Mayville
41
West Bend
43
67
175
33
Horicon
Saukville
Port Washingt
Beaver Dam
Juneau
143
T
Pike Lake
Cedarburg
Grafton
57
Thiensville
167
LA MICH
19
Watertown
O
83
41
Mequon
45
45
Oconomowoc
94
Delafield
45
Johnson Creek
Dousman
Waukesha
94
Milwaukee
18
Jefferson
67
894
Fort Atkinson
Kettle State Forest
43
38
26
Old World Wisconsin
67
36
32
Caledonia
Franksville
Racir
20
Elkhorn
11
Burlington
Sturtevant
12
94
Lake Geneva
Big Foot Beach State Park
158
Kenosha

0   10   20   30 miles

SOUTHWEST DAY TRIP 2

Lake Geneva
Big Foot Beach State Park

Only forty-five minutes from General Billy Mitchell International Airport in Milwaukee and ninety minutes from Chicago's O'Hare International Airport, the Lake Geneva area of south-central Wisconsin's Walworth County has the best of all worlds. And "best" can be summed up in one word, repeated in a tourism mantra: location, location, location.

Native Americans from several nations knew this region generations before the first white settlers arrived to cut the forests and till the fields around Geneva Lake. They fished the waters, hunted its shoreline, and planted crops nearby. In addition to servicing the locals, the lake was a regular pit stop on the route of many other Indians as they hunted migrating large animals. A 26-mile walking trail around the lake, now used by hikers, was a well-known highway for those early tribes. The day-tripper can take an option of seven shorter walks, ranging from 2 to 3.5 miles each, developed by Walk, Talk and Gawk. WT&G maps and guides are available for purchase at area stores. Guided tours can be arranged by calling (262) 249–1445.

But even before the ancestors of today's Wisconsin native population lived here, the Oneota people of the Hopewell culture resided around the lake more than 1,000 years ago. They constructed effigy mounds in the shapes of animals and geometric symbols throughout the region, with some remaining hillocks still seen in Lake Geneva's Library Park. Much later, most of the tribes living in the region were forcibly removed to Kansas by the United States Army following the Black Hawk War of 1831 to 1832. Unfair treaties that followed in 1833 took the land that belonged to the

Potawatomis, the last remaining Indians who were eventually evicted in 1836.

Lake Geneva, at 5,262 acres, is the largest body of water in this part of Wisconsin aside from Lake Michigan. It is replenished by rainfall, as well as by dozens of streams and the springs that can be found on its western end. The lake bed remains from the Ice Age. It was carved out and filled barely 16,000 years ago, surrounded by rolling moraines, which are dumps of rock marking the perimeter of those long-ago sheets of ice. The lake's outlet is at the city of Lake Geneva, via the White River on the northeast rim. Its deepest section is about 135 feet, providing loads of room for the fish that now attract anglers. The lake is 7.6 miles long and 2.1 miles wide, making power- and sailboating a pleasure.

In addition to the city of Lake Geneva, other communities around the lake include Fontana, Williams Bay, and Como.

LAKE GENEVA

The earliest-known mention of whites seeing Lake Geneva was found in letters written by an army family traveling between Fort Dearborn (Chicago) and Fort Winnebago (Portage) in 1831. Government surveyor John Brink made his way to the lakeshore in 1835, naming it Geneva after his home in Geneva, New York. In 1836 Christopher Payne built the first log cabin on the lakeshore and constructed a mill. His homesite is marked with a boulder and plaque on Center Street north of the White River, which flows into the lake. The town was laid out in 1837, as more settlers arrived from New England and New York. As the community grew and more mills were erected, farmers brought their grain for processing from all around southern Wisconsin and northern Illinois. Tons of winter ice were also cut and sold to vendors in Chicago and Milwaukee, a practice that continued until World War II. Lake Geneva quickly became a boomtown.

Prior to the Civil War, Lake Geneva was also a primary stop in the Underground Railroad for escaping slaves from eastern Kentucky and southern Illinois. After the war wealthy Chicago families moved to the region and built vacation homes on the gentle hills overlooking the lake. The Chicago Fire of 1871 brought another influx of Windy City money. Cruising the lake today on the mailboat *Walworth II*, a visitor can see houses constructed by the chewing-gum Wrigleys, washing-machine Maytags, meatpacking Swifts, and other business magnates of that era. One even erected the reproduction of a Buddhist temple that had been exhibited at the 1893 Columbia Exposition. Purchase a copy of the *Walking Tour of Olde Lake Geneva* at the Lake Geneva Chamber of Commerce office at the lakefront. The booklet describes many of the homes and architectural styles found in town. Hours at the chamber are 9:00 A.M. to 5:00 P.M. weekdays and 10:00 A.M. to 4:00 P.M. Saturday and Sunday.

Downtown Lake Geneva retains its small-town, turn-of-the-century look, even with all the souvenir shops, which have been a staple here since the 1920s. Information personnel at the chamber can answer questions about what to see and do. Contact them at 201 Wrigley Drive, Lake Geneva, WI 53147. Call (262) 248-4416 or (800) 345-1020. Its Web site is www.lakegenevaw.com.

WHERE TO GO

Eddie Cash Show at the Belfry Music Theater. 7036 Grand Geneva Way, Lake Geneva. This Branson-style show club features Cash, a Lake Geneva singing staple since the 1960s. Showtimes vary. Call (262) 248-8144.

Lounge Entertainment. With all the resorts and nightclubs in the Lake Geneva area, there's no excuse not to have nighttime fun. Among the tops for tinkling tunes and smooth music, try the Mermaid Lounge at the Abbey in Fontana (262-275-6811), with a piano player Tuesday through Sunday. A DJ plays at the Abbey's Windjammer dance room Tuesday through Saturday from May to September. Live shows are held there on Friday and Saturday. A piano player plunks away in the Lobby Lounge at the Grand Geneva Resort & Spa (262-248-8811) Wednesday through Sunday. Lounge acts perform in the Newport Lounge in winter, summer, and fall. A DJ spins CDs nightly at Hogs & Kisses, 149 Broadway (262-248-7447). A pianist performs Monday through Saturday and at Sunday brunch at the Interlaken Resort & Country Spa in the Lake Bluff Dining Room, with a DJ there Monday through Saturday. Music from the '40s to the '90s rocks the Lake View Terrace at the Lake Lawn Resort in Delavan five nights a week (262-728-7950).

The Lookout Bar there offers live music and dancing, while singers perform in the Frontier Lounge six nights a week and singers entertain at the Timber Terrace on Saturday and Sunday afternoons, with a piano player for Sunday brunch. Entertainer Joy Smith performs regularly at the Mars Resort, overlooking Lake Como on State Highway 50 west. Call (262) 245–5689.

Lake Geneva Horse Park & Petting Zoo. Corner of State Highways 67 and 50, Lake Geneva. This great family attraction is open from May through October, opening at 11:00 A.M. daily. The zoo is closed Monday. An outdoor animal show is presented daily at 1:00 P.M. with an equestrian show at 2:00 P.M. (weather permitting) during the season. There are also horse-drawn carriage rides, pony rides, live animal shows, and a petting zoo. Admission. Call (262) 245–0770.

Yerkes Observatory. 373 West Geneva Street, Williams Bay. The world's largest refracting (lens) telescope gives a marvelous peek at the sky. The telescope is mounted on a 75-foot-diameter elevator floor, which raises and lowers the unit into place. The observatory was completed in 1897, as part of the University of Chicago's Department of Astronomy and Astrophysics and remains a major research center. Open Saturdays only, with tours at 10:00 A.M., 11:00 A.M., and noon. Tours present an overview of the observatory's history, as well as plenty of details about the heavens. Admission charged. Call (262) 245–5555.

Lake Geneva Museum. 818 West Geneva Street, Lake Geneva. Learn about the area history through a marvelous display of memorabilia and artifacts. Open from 1:00 to 5:00 P.M. Friday, Saturday, Sunday, and holidays May through October and also Monday and Thursday in summer.

Geneva Lake Cruise Line. Riviera Docks, Lake Geneva. Take a mailboat tour around the lake and watch the carriers leap from the boat to the dock to stuff the mailboxes. They then have to leap back aboard again. It's rare to see anyone take a dive, but all bets are on. The cruise line also offers dining tours, Sunday champagne-brunch excursions, and other boating adventures. Tours run seven days a week from late April through early November. Dress for the weather. Call (800) 558–5911.

Hiking. Get out of the car and go for a stroll. Take in some bird-watching for warblers while you are at it. The state's largest collection of this species is found here at the Duck Lake Nature Center, on the southern side of Lake Como. The center offers a 2-mile walkway through woods, pastures, and prairie land near the lake. For more hiking options Fontana Fen is a ten-acre conservation area on State Highway 67 between Fontana and Walworth, just west of St. Benedict's church. (A fen is a rare wetland prairie fed by underground springs.) And there's more. The Four Seasons Nature Preserve, part of the city of Lake Geneva park system, covers sixty-six acres, including forty acres of wetlands and twenty acres of prairie. Trails in the preserve have markers identifying the plants and animals found in the preserve.

Fishing. With water like this, bring your own boat or use the services of a pro guide. Tom Billing of Lake Geneva Fishing Guide Service (262-248-3905 or 262-791-0733) and the folks at Robert's Guide Service (262-763-2520) provide boats, tackle, and live bait. Remember that any fishing fan over age sixteen needs a Wisconsin license, which can be purchased at the Wal-Mart store, State Highway 50 west; (262) 248-2266. Also fun is winter fishing, a popular sport on the smooth lake surface even when the winds whip up the snow atop the ice. Be tough. Shanties can be rented, or you can just plunk down on an upturned bait bucket, auger a hole in the ice, and go to work.

Beaches. Loll on the sand under Wisconsin's summer sun. The stretch of beach on Wrigley Drive near the Riviera Pier is one of the best places to plop, open from 9:00 A.M. to 6:00 P.M. daily from Memorial Day through Labor Day. Admission charged for those age 6 and over, with season passes available. The facility has a bathhouse with shower and lifeguards on duty, so don't forget you came here to swim. Food (but no glass) and flotation devices are allowed. Police your blanket area and pick up your rubble when it's time to depart. Call (262) 248-4416. Other beaches in the area are on Fontana Boulevard, Fontana (262-275-6136); the Williams Bay beach on Geneva Street, Williams Bay (262-245-2700); and Big Foot Beach State Park on State Highway 120 south (262-248-2528). Nearby Delavan Lake, about 5 miles northwest of Lake Geneva on State Highway 50, also has beach access; however, no lifeguards are on duty at the locale. Call (262) 728-3471.

Boating. There are several municipal launch sites in the Lake Geneva area where boats can be launched for a fee. For details contact Delavan Township Park (262-728-3471), the City of Lake Geneva pier (262-248-3673), or the Village of Williams Bay ramp (262-245-2700). Boat rentals are also available at area resorts and marinas.

Golfing. In addition to the links at the Grand Geneva Resort and Spa, Lake Lawn Resort, and Geneva National Resort, other courses include the Evergreen Golf Club, considered one of the top ten courses in the state (262-723-5722 or 800-868-8618); George Williams Golf Course, established in 1902 (262-245-7000); and Hillmoor Golf Club (262-248-4570). For the munchkin set Paradise Golf Park, 511 Wells Street, offers eighteen holes of mini-golf. For hours call (262) 248-3456.

WHERE TO SHOP

Geneva Village Shops. 777 Geneva Street (corner of Geneva and Broad Streets), Lake Geneva. Nine shops in this historic landmark building offer a range of retail items. Call the shops for hours: Geneva Artists and Gallery, stained glass (262-248-9078); Kathleen's Bears 'n Things, collectibles (262-248-9958); CoCoa's, pastries (262-348-0508); Rosemary's Courtyard Garden, plants (262-248-4689); Sacred Sisters, sterling silver (262-248-8289); and Wild Rubies, fashion accessories (262-248-8289).

Aerial Stunt Kites. 121 Wrigley Drive, Lake Geneva. Wind socks, kites, toys, wind chimes, lawn dice, and loads of other outdoor gizmos line the shelves and dangle from the ceiling. Hours are 10:00 A.M. to 5:00 P.M. daily. Call (262) 249-0631.

Dockside Surf & Swim, Ltd. 235 Broad Street, Lake Geneva. No need to panic if you forgot your suit. Dockside has swimwear for the family. Open year-round from 10:00 A.M. to 5:00 P.M. daily. Call (262) 248-8135.

WHERE TO EAT

Anthony's Steakhouse. State Highway 50 west, Lake Geneva. The carnivore crowd loves Anthony's for its steaks. But if fish is your forte, fresh seafood is an alternative. Open 4:00 to 10:00 P.M. Monday through Saturday for dinner. Sunday dinner presented from May through October. Call (262) 248-1818. $$$; □

Cactus Club. 430 Broad Street, Lake Geneva. Richly flavored Native American, Spanish, and Mexican dishes are prepared here. Great margaritas. Open from 10:30 A.M. to 2:00 A.M. seven days a week; food is served until midnight. Call (262) 248-1999. $$; ☐

Popeye's on Lake Geneva. 811 Wrigley Drive, Lake Geneva. Casual dining with burgers and fries, but also award-winning soups and homemade apple pie. All summer, Popeye's outdoor grill broils chicken, pork, and lamb. Fantastic lake view. From June through Labor Day, hours are 11:00 A.M. to 10:00 P.M. Sunday through Thursday, and 11:00 A.M. to 11:00 P.M. Friday and Saturday; from October through April hours are 11:30 A.M. to 8:30 P.M. Sunday through Thursday, and 11:30 A.M. to 9:30 P.M. Friday and Saturday; hours in May are 11:00 A.M. to 9:00 P.M. Sunday through Thursday, and 11:00 A.M. to 10:00 P.M. Friday and Saturday. Call (262) 248-4381. $$; ☐

Speedo's Harborside Cafe. 100 Broad Street, Lake Geneva. You get a range of foods, from breakfast omelets to luncheon burgers to supper steaks, plus carryout. Hours are 6:30 A.M. to 10:00 P.M. daily. Call (262) 248-3835. $$; ☐

The Original Chicago Pizza Co. 150 Center Street, Lake Geneva. Thin- or thick-crusted pizza offered for all types of pizza fans. Dine in, carryout, or delivery. Hours are 10:30 A.M. to 11:30 P.M. Call (262) 248-8544. $$; ☐

Champs Sports Bar & Grill. 747 Main Street, Lake Geneva. For ace pub grub, especially chicken, try Champs. The place also has a DJ for dancing, plus an outdoor beer garden for summer hoopla. Hours are 11:00 A.M. to 2:00 A.M. daily, with food served until midnight. Call (262) 248-6008. $; ☐

Red Geranium. State Highway 50 east, Lake Geneva. Reservations are recommended for this popular dining spot. Lunch hours are 11:30 A.M. to 2:30 P.M. Monday through Saturday, with dinner from 5:00 to 9:30 P.M. Monday through Sunday. Sunday brunch is from 11:00 A.M. to 3:00 P.M. Call (262) 248-3637. $$$; ☐

WHERE TO STAY

Abbey Resorts. The Abbey on Lake Geneva, the Interlaken Resort and Inns of Geneva National in Lake Geneva, plus the Fontana Spa offer golfing, lake activities, dining, exercise facilities, spas, and a host of other upscale amenities. Call (800) 643-6382 for details or reservations at any of these resorts. $$$; ☐

Strawberry Hill Bed & Breakfast. 1071 Jenkins Drive, Fontana. Innkeepers Christi and Fred Moritz keep a neat, shipshape home. Call (262) 275-5998 or tap into its Web site at www.genevaonline. com/-strbryhl. $$-$$$

Golden Oaks Mansion. 421 Baker Street, Lake Geneva. This grand old house recalls the grand old days of high living on the lake. Call (262) 248-9711 or use the Web site at www.oaksinn.com. $$$; ☐

T.C. Smith Historic Inn. 834 Dodge Street, Lake Geneva. The mansion was built in 1845 and is a National Historic Landmark. Eight spacious rooms with whirlpool and fireplace suites make for a fantastic getaway. A courtyard on the grounds features a garden, fish pool, and gazebo. Call (262) 248-1097. The Web site is tcsmithinn.com. $$$; ☐

The Watersedge of Lake Geneva. W4232 West End Road, Lake Geneva. Gangster Bugsy Moran used to vacation in this quiet hideaway in the 1930s, taking a break from bank robbery and general mayhem. The Watersedge is still just as quiet today, even without such clientele. There are five rooms on the property, which also has a private dock. Call (262) 245-9845. $$$; ☐

Duffy's Pub & Cottages. W4086 Lakeshore Drive, Como. A collegial place that serves up a good pint of Guinness stout in its bar, Duffy's also has cabins with full cooking facilities. Call (262) 248-7100. $$; ☐

Pederson Victorian Bed & Breakfast. 1782 State Highway 120 north (3 miles north of Lake Geneva). This Queen Anne–style home has four guest rooms. Vegetarian breakfasts, crisp, line-dried linens, and organic coffee are also offered. No pets, no smoking, and no whirlpools here—just clean, quiet comfort. Call (262) 248-9110. $$-$$$

BIG FOOT BEACH STATE PARK

Big Foot Beach State Park, named after a long-ago Potawatomi leader, is located on State Highway 120 south, only a fifteen-minute drive from downtown Lake Geneva. Sprawling over 272 acres, the park offers camping, 5 miles of hiking trails, swimming, and cross-country skiing opportunities. Years after the Native Americans were forcibly removed from the area, the Maytag family came into possession of the property. Their home was razed in 1957, and subsequently the park was developed. It is the only state park within a city boundary in Wisconsin.

Open twenty-four hours. Lifeguards are on duty during weekends only July 4 through Labor Day. Beach admission is free, but autos need state park stickers. Call (262) 248-2528.

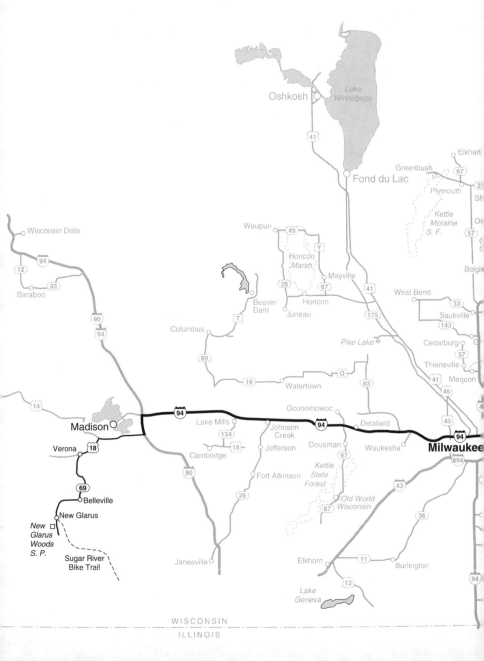

Southwest Day Trip 3

0   10   20   30 miles

Green Bay

De Pere

Oshkosh

Lake Winnebago

41

Fond du Lac

Elkhart

Greenbush   67

Plymouth

Sh

Kettle Moraine S. F.

57

Waupun   49

Belgi

Wisconsin Dells

94

Horicon Marsh

Y

12

33

Mayville

West Bend   33

Baraboo

26   67

Saukville   143

90
94

Beaver Dam

Horicon

Juneau   175

Pike Lake

Cedarburg   57

T

Columbus

Thiensville

89

O

41   45   Mequon

19   Watertown   83

45

14

Oconomowoc

94

Madison

Lake Mills   94   Delafield   45

134

Johnson Creek   94   Milwaukee

Verona   18

18   Jefferson   Dousman   Waukesha   894

Cambridge   67

69

90   Kettle State Forest   43

Belleville

26   Fort Atkinson

New Glarus

Old World Wisconsin   36

New Glarus Woods S. P.   67

Sugar River Bike Trail

Janesville   Elkhorn   11   Burlington

94

Lake Geneva   12

WISCONSIN

ILLINOIS

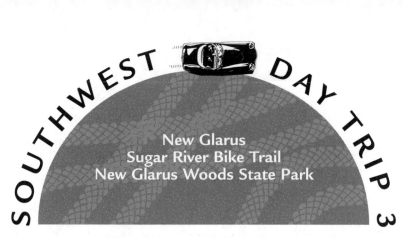

Green County reminds the traveler of the verdant green hills and meadows of Switzerland. Not only present-day visitors but also early settlers got that same impression. South-central Wisconsin could have been picked up and carried here directly from Europe. Expansive oak and maple woodlands, wide meadows (watch for cows), and slowly flowing rivers and clear trout streams create their own natural story. Even the area's villages and crossroads communities seem to have sprung from the earth. There's always a naturalness in the air. It is seen in spring's first dazzling array of jack-in-the pulpits, summer's cicada-sounded hikes, autumn's dry-leaf perfuming, or even winter's gray, storm-tossed skies. This part of the state is soothing.

Green County is only about 25 miles south of Madison (a thirty-minute drive) and about a two-hour drive from Milwaukee. From Milwaukee, take I–94 west to Madison. Pick up I–90 on the capital's eastern edge and drive south to join the Beltline exit, which goes around the southern rim of the city. Look for the U.S. 18/151 off-ramp, which will be on the right side as you drive west. Stay on the four-lane 18/151 to State Highway 69 in Verona (the town is 5 miles west of Madison). Drive south on 69 through Paoli and Bellville. New Glarus is the next small town. The white steeples of its churches can be seen for miles.

NEW GLARUS

With Green County's natural look straight from a European geography textbook, it was only natural that some of the first pioneers were from the alpine canton, or county, of Glarus, Switzerland. In 1845 economic times were tough, so the Glarus Emigration Society scouted out territories in the Midwestern United States where they thought some of their members would like to homestead. Two of the society's agents took $2,600 in cash in order to buy property. The landscape they discovered seemed a perfect match: ergo, New Glarus was born. And the men got a great deal, paying only $1.25 an acre.

The community's rich Swiss tradition is evident everywhere, from the chalet-style architecture downtown to the geranium-crammed flower boxes and fluttering red Swiss flags with their white crosses. Festivals, folklore, and food keep the Swiss heritage alive and vibrant.

The community remains an agricultural hub. The pastures, dotted with Holsteins, jerseys, and guernsey cattle, ensure fantastic fodder for the munching bovine set. As a result, excellent dairies are scattered along the side roads throughout the county. Cheese making is king here. Smooth and tasty Swiss, Gruyère, and butterkäse are among the many varieties of cheese that can be purchased from the area display coolers.

Milwaukee day-trippers love driving down to New Glarus for the day, for a lunch of schnitzel, meatballs, Roesti potatoes, or fondue. That leaves plenty of time to take in the Swiss Historical Village and squeeze in some shopping for locally made sausage. Hmmm, the perfume of New Glarus mettwurst, landjaeger, or kalberwurst can't be beaten even by the most delectable of high-fashion scents. Naturally, one must have a pilsner from the New Glarus Brewery to wash it all down. What's great is that no one is ever more than a block from a great restaurant in New Glarus. In summer wise travelers augment their stay with a local theater production of *Heidi* or *Wilhelm Tell*.

For more details on New Glarus, contact the New Glarus Tourism and Chamber of Commerce information center, Box 713, New Glarus, WI 53574-0713; (608) 527-2095 or (800) 527-6838. Visit the chamber's Web site at www.swisstown.com. Some of the promotion material produced by the city and hometown attractions is also printed in German, to accommodate the many European visitors who flock to New Glarus throughout the year. A great number of the locals speak fluent German, who often say *"wilkommen,"* instead of the more pedestrian "hello."

For Green County visitor details, log on to www.greencounty.org. Or contact the Green County Welcome Center, 2108 Seventh Avenue, Monroe, WI 53566; (608) 325-4636 or (888) 222-9111.

WHERE TO GO

Chalet of the Golden Fleece. 618 Second Avenue, New Glarus. An eclectic display of artifacts greets the day-tripper here. Edwin Barlow, who originated the Wilhelm Tell folk drama in New Glarus, built the chalet as his home in 1937. True to his wishes, the building looks like a Bernese mountain house. It even has rocks and logs on the roof to keep the slate from blowing off in high winds, a true Swiss construction earmark. A world traveler, Barlow collected almost everything: from statuary to dolls. As a result of his inquisitive acquiring, included in the exhibition is a King Louis XVI watch, Etruscan earrings, sixteenth-century Bolivian gourd jewelry cases, antique pewter, quilts, and sixteenth-century furniture. Admission. Hours are 10:00 A.M. to 4:30 P.M. May 1 through October 31. Call (608) 527-2614.

New Glarus Brewing Company. Green County Highway West/State Highway 69, New Glarus. Watch how beer is brewed, drop by the gift shop, and then sip some of the wares. The brewery makes Apple Ale, Spotted Cow, Uff-Da-Bock, Staghorn, Solstice Weiss, Wisconsin Belgian Red, and other labels. Guided tours are at 1:00, 2:00, 3:00, and 4:00 P.M. Saturday. Self-guided tours are offered Monday through Friday between noon and 4:30 P.M. Call for reservations, especially in summer, because space can be limited. Call (608) 527-5850 for details.

Volksvest. Tell Shooting Park, ½-mile north of New Glarus on Green County Highway O. Each year New Glarus recalls its roots by celebrating Swiss Independence Day on the first Sunday in August. The nation was considered to be born on August 1, 1291. On that day—objecting to high taxes levied by the Hapsburg Empire, which was ruling Switzerland at the time—the residents of Uri, Schwyz, and Unterwalden in Switzerland gathered in a meadow overlooking Lake Luzern. There they drew up a pact of mutual help and support for one another, which is considered to be the first declaration of Swiss independence.

The program includes Swiss flag throwing, accordion music, and a lively concert by the New Glarus *Kinderchor*, where the kids sing in fluent German, as well as in English. The New Clarus *Maennerchor*, a men's choral group, is the Volksvest sponsoring organization. Admission is charged. Volksvest runs from 1:00 to 4:00 P.M. with dancing from 4:00 to 6:00 P.M. In case of rain the festival is presented in the local elementary-school gym.

Wilhelm Tell Festival. Tell Grounds, 1 mile east of New Glarus on Green County Highway W. Held on Labor Day weekend since 1938, the Tell Festival is presented by local actors re-creating the legendary Wilhelm Tell story about a rebellious Swiss mountaineer. The lively production, complete with historic costume, was written by German playwright Friedrich Schiller. All the performers are local residents, members of the Wilhelm Tell Community Guild. Even goats, cows, and horses have "roles" in the piece. Admission. Entertainment begins at 1:00 P.M. each day, with the drama starting at 1:30 P.M. in English on Saturday and Monday, with a German production on Sunday. If it rains, tickets may be exchanged or refunded. After the play the town sponsors an Alpine Festival in the high-school auditorium, a costume parade, and an Outdoor Art Fair. Naturally there is lots of yodeling, alphorn blowing, and polka dancing throughout the entire weekend. Call (608) 527-2095 or (800) 527-6836.

Octoberfest. Village Park. You can't go wrong with a day trip through southern Wisconsin in autumn. New Glarus capitalizes on the harvest season with its Octoberfest program, usually held on Columbus Day weekend in early October. A harvest parade on the festival's Saturday wends its way through downtown. A bake sale, craft demonstrations, and historical displays are presented at the New Glarus town hall, 1 block north of the park. Visitors who have had their fill of yodeling for a day can take in the Bluegrass Bash on Friday evening. Call the New Glarus Visitor Information office for particulars; (608) 527-2095 or (800) 527-6836.

Tastes and Treasures. Downtown New Glarus. Local merchants offer hot summer bargains on the downtown sidewalks at this annual mid-July celebration. But the best part of the weekend is the New Glarus Lions Club chicken barbecue at the Lions Pavilion in the Village Park. In addition to the chicken offered on Friday evening (beginning at 5:00 P.M.), restaurants put samples of their wares out on street-side tables from 11:00 A.M. to 4:00 P.M. on Saturday. This

isn't your typical fast-food spread, either. Swiss pizza, crème brûlée, and roasted-garlic mashed potatoes elevate the tastes to new heights. Yodeling? Ya betcha. Call (608) 527-2095 or (800) 527-6836.

WHERE TO SHOP

Roughing It. 130 Fifth Avenue, New Glarus. Furniture, pottery, dinnerware, and artwork found here give a rustic, log-cabin feel to a home. Some of the items are made by local artists and craftspersons. Hours are 9:00 A.M. to 5:00 P.M. Monday through Saturday and 10:00 A.M. to 5:00 P.M. Sunday. The shop is closed on holidays. Call (608) 527-4438.

Roberts European Imports. 102 Fifth Avenue, New Glarus. Roberts specializes in gift items from Europe, making it one of the best places in the area for cowbells, Swiss army knives, chimes, and German and Norwegian greeting cards. Hours are 9:00 A.M. to 9:00 P.M. weekdays and 8:00 A.M. to 5:00 P.M. Saturday and Sunday. Call (608) 527-2517. Order a free catalog by calling (800) 968-2517. The shop Web site is www.shopswiss.com.

WHERE TO EAT

Ott Haus Pub & Grill. 406 Second Street, New Glarus. Some of the best pub grub in New Glarus is here: homemade pizza, subs, burritos, and hamburgers. Hours are 10:00 A.M. to 2:00 A.M. Monday through Thursday, 10:00 A.M. to 2:30 P.M. Friday and Saturday, and 11:00 A.M. to 6:00 P.M. Sunday. Call (608) 527-2218. $; ☐

Deininger's Restaurant. 119 Fifth Avenue, New Glarus. Deininger's is home of chef Roland's Famous Apple Pancake, a delectable treat that has only a few (ya, sure) calories. The restaurant is in a restored Victorian home, with a comfortably wide porch tailor-made for sprawling. Daily lunch hours are 11:00 A.M. to 2:30 P.M.; Thursday, Friday, and Saturday dinners are offered from 5:00 to 8:30 P.M., with Sunday and Monday dinner hours from 4:00 to 7:30 P.M. Call (608) 527-2012. $$$; ☐

Flannery's Wilhelm Tell Restaurant. 114 Second Street, New Glarus. To satisfy cravings for Swiss-style sausage, try the locally made delights presented here by owners Mike and Ruth Flannery. Don't worry about the Irish name. Mike, who was born in New Glarus, is half Swiss. So if schnitzels and fondue are not your style, there's always prime rib. The restaurant is 5 blocks out of the downtown area. Hours are 5:00 to 9:00 P.M. Tuesday through Thursday and 5:00 to 10:00 P.M. Friday and Saturday. Closed Sunday and Monday. Call (608) 527–2618. $$; ☐

WHERE TO STAY

Chalet Landhouse Inn. 801 State Highway 69, New Glarus. The hotel looks as if it should be back in Switzerland's Glarus, with its chalet-style image and plethora of flowers. Some of the rooms have private balconies, whirlpool baths, and sitting areas. The hotel's restaurant offers a great Sunday brunch. Call (608) 527–5234 or use the Web site at www.chalelandhaus.com. $$–$$$; ☐

New Glarus Hotel. 100 Sixth Avenue, New Glarus. The hotel's original building was constructed in 1853 and was greatly expanded over the past generations. The hotel, located in the heart of downtown, serves cold and frothy beer in the Chalet Bar. Call (608) 527–5244. $$–$$$; ☐

Hoch Haus B&B. 218 Second Street, New Glarus. The turn-of-the-nineteenth-century house is located in the heart of New Glarus, a short walk from all the community's attractions. Off-street parking and bike storage are bonuses. Call (608) 527–4019. $$; ☐

SUGAR RIVER BIKE TRAIL

The Sugar River Bike Trail runs 23 miles (39 kilometers) from New Glarus to Brodhead, built on an old Milwaukee Road railroad right-of-way. Its bridges cross the Little Sugar and Sugar Rivers. New Glarus's old depot is home to the trail headquarters, containing rest rooms, an information booth, and bike rentals. The first leg of the trip is a 6-mile run to Monticello, which has several pristine parks alongside a beautiful little lake. A restored railroad station along the trail has rest rooms and doubles as a youth hostel. Albany, "Pearl of the Sugar River," is another 7 miles down the pathway. More than one hundred years ago, the village was a national producer of pearl buttons, using the river's mussels. Pedal parallel to the river, which has a picture-perfect dam and rough waterway for memorable photos.

Beyond Albany the Little Sugar and Sugar Rivers converge as they flow through the fertile black-earth farmland. It's fun to bike across the river, through a covered bridge on the slow way to Brodhead. There are numerous restaurants and shops in Brodhead, which features a fantastic downtown square replete with benches and a small shelter. A trail pass, valid on all state park trails, is required from April 1 to October 31. Contact the Sugar River Trail, Box 781, New Glarus, WI 53574 or call (608) 527-2334.

WHERE TO STAY

Oak Hill Manor. 401 East Main Street, Albany (15 miles southeast of New Glarus on State Highway 39). Located midway on the Sugar River Trail, Oak Hill Manor makes for a comfortable stopover. Call (608) 862-1400 or use the Web site at www.oakhillmanor.com. $$

NEW GLARUS WOODS STATE PARK

New Glarus Woods sprawls over 350 acres of beech, maple, oak, and hickory forest, plus reclaimed prairie growth and some farmland. A large picnic site, with grills and tables, is perfect for a day-tripper stop. The park is bisected by Green County Highway NN, used as early as 1832 by oxcarts hauling goods to the lead mines along the Mississippi River. Militia soldiers tramped along here around the same time on their way to Madison to join federal troops pursuing Sac war chief Black Hawk. The Native American leader was merely trying to lead his people away from encroaching white settlement, but in the fervor of the times, his flight became a full-blown military mission to (it was believed) end the Indian "problem" on the Wisconsin frontier.

Hikers have a wide range of paths from which to choose. The Basswood Nature Trail is barely a half mile long, leading from the picnic area through an oak and maple grove to the north of Green County Highway NN. Look for the thirty interpretive signs along the way that describe the flora of the park. The Chattermark Trail is another half-miler, linking with the Basswood. Other short trails meander through the woods around the campground.

For longer hikes the North Loop of the Havenridge Natural Trail will take about ninety minutes to stroll. A carpet of black snakeroot, merrybells, enchanter's nightshade, and other plants spread amid the tree roots. This is a bird-watcher's paradise, with cardinals, nuthatches, chickadees, and larger birds whistling and calling from the branches. About halfway along the trail is a bench overlooking a valley where New Glarus can be seen in the distance. In summer a brilliantly yellow field of goldenrod, with scattered explosions of purple coneflowers, races down the bluff to a pasture and on to the town.

Havenwood's South Loop starts south of Highway NN, with a gravel path soon narrowing to a dirt trail, so wear strong shoes or hiking boots. Some magnificent shagbark hickory can be spotted along the trek. Watch for dive-bombing red-winged blackbirds guarding their spring and summer nests when walking through a meadow along the way. Parts of this loop are framed by giant red sumac, which tower over the hiker's head by autumn to make a wonderful autumnal arch of color.

The park office is open 8:00 A.M. to 8:00 P.M. weekdays and 8:00 A.M. to 11:00 P.M. weekends from April through October. There are thirty-one individual campsites in the park, plus a group campsite. Call the park superintendent at (608) 527-2335.

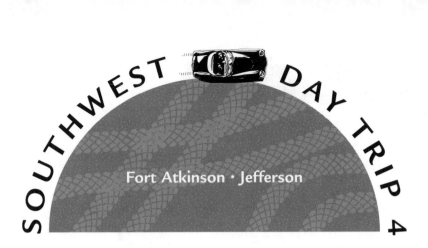

Jefferson County is an hour's drive from Milwaukee, proudly proclaiming that it lies along Wisconsin's Main Street: I-94. The county emphasizes that it is a year-round outdoor-lover's paradise, with fishing, hiking, cross-country skiing, and snowmobiling opportunities. One prime vacation draw is Lake Koshkonong, Wisconsin's second-largest lake, which covers 10,089 acres in southwestern Jefferson County. The lake has long been a prime draw for day-trippers seeking some exciting water action. The Rock River, which also flows through the county, provides additional recreational opportunities for those who enjoy canoeing.

Cycling is another favorite activity in Jefferson County, which is traversed by the Glacial Drumlin State Bicycle Trail. This is a 53-mile route between Waukesha on the east and Dane County's Cottage Grove on the west. Between the Glacial Drumlin and the county's many side roads, opportunities for pedaling are extensive. A free bike map is available from the University of Wisconsin Extension office (920-674-7295), the Jefferson County Parks Department (920-674-6260), or the Jefferson County Tourism Council (920-674-8880). The map indicates which high-traffic roads to avoid and suggests safe recreational trails.

The county also has several quality campgrounds for those wishing to commune with the stars after a day trip. Haki Dehair is host at the Bark River Campground, 2340 West Hanson Road, in Jefferson (262-593-2421); and Burt and Kim Kincannon preside over Pilgrim's Campground, W271 Jefferson County Highway C, Fort Atkinson (920-563-8122 or 800-742-1697). Jellystone Park is

tucked into the woods at N5551 Wishing Well Lane, Fort Atkinson; (920) 563-5714.

But there's more to Jefferson County than rambling the outback; a vibrant arts scene waits to be sampled. The Council for the Performing Arts, 305 South Main Street, Jefferson, coordinates shows in several county communities. The council makes access to the arts really easy. Listen to an Irish band, take in a classical guitarist, enjoy a puppet show, and chuckle along with nationally known comedians. Box office hours are 8:00 A.M. to 4:30 P.M. Monday through Friday. Call (920) 674-2179. The Web site is www.councilfortheperformingarts.org. Performances are held at the Performing Arts Center, 700 West Milwaukee Street, Jefferson; and at the Fort Atkinson High School Auditorium, 925 Lexington Boulevard, Fort Atkinson; and the Watertown High School Auditorium, 825 Endeavor Drive, Watertown.

FORT ATKINSON

Founded in 1836, Fort Atkinson was actually the site of a fort during Wisconsin's early pioneer days. A replica of the fort hosts several buckskinner and other historical activities throughout the year. With that protective base on the strategic Rock River, the town's economy quickly prospered. In the heart of Wisconsin's richest pastureland, it wasn't long before it became a focal point for the dairy industry. Fort Atkinson remains an urban island surrounded by Holsteins, jerseys, and other cattle that not only moo but produce great milk. But don't let the rural image fool you. *Money Magazine* has called Fort Atkinson "One of America's Hottest Little Hometowns."

It is a busy community, with festivals, ice-cream socials, concerts, bike rides, holiday programs, and tons of other activities that provide a friendly sense of small-town permanence. For additional details on the city, contact the chamber of commerce, 244 North Main Street, Fort Atkinson, WI 53538. Call (920) 563-3210 or (888) SEE-FORT. The chamber's Web site is fortchamber.com. Hours are 8:00 A.M. to 4:30 P.M. weekdays.

WHERE TO GO

The Fireside Restaurant & Playhouse. 1131 Janesville Avenue (Business Highway 26 south), Fort Atkinson. Wisconsin's very own "Broadway" playhouse features musicals and revues with nationally known performers. Shows have included *Brigadoon, On Golden Pond, A Closer Walk with Patsy Cline,* and *Once Upon a Mattress.* Luncheon matinees are held Wednesday through Saturday, with a buffet offered on Thursday night. Menu dining and theater packages are available on Friday and Saturday night, with a Sunday brunch. A large gift shop offers a range of items from Fenton glassware to Boyd's Bears. For show times and production schedules, call (920) 563–9505 or (800) 477–9505. The Fireside Web site is www.firesidetheatre.com.

Hoard Historical Museum/National Dairy Shrine Visitor's Center. 407 Merchants Avenue, Fort Atkinson. Frank Hoard, the youngest son of Governor W. D. Hoard and president of the Hoard Printing Company, donated the complex to the city for use as a museum in 1956. The historical museum, housed in a Gothic Revival home, has an extensive collection of Native American artifacts, mounted birds, quilts, and dolls. One display elaborates on Wisconsin's role in the Civil War. The National Dairy Shrine is a memorial to the country's dairy farmers, with a dairy industry multimedia show, a research library, and an exhibit of farm tools. Check out the dog-powered butter churn and learn the history of ice cream while you are there. The Dwight Foster House, a restoration of the first frame house built in Fort Atkinson, is also on the grounds. Assembled with pegs instead of nails, the old home retains its dignity and charm. The structure was constructed in 1841 at a cost of $2,000. Summer hours (Memorial Day through Labor Day) are 9:30 A.M. to 4:30 P.M. Tuesday through Saturday and 11:00 A.M. to 3:00 P.M. Sunday. Closed Monday. Winter hours are 9:30 A.M. to 3:30 P.M. Tuesday through Saturday. Free admission, but donations are welcome. The sites are supported by the Fort Atkinson Historical Society. Call (920) 563–7769.

Cafe Carpe. 18 South Water Street, Fort Atkinson. Folk music at its best can be heard at the Carpe, a favorite for touring national acts, as well as many local and regional performers. Its restaurant has a range of great grub, with gourmet pizza as a top choice. For hours and performance times, call (920) 563–9391.

Merchants Avenue Historic District. Stroll the streets of old-time Fort Atkinson. Bounded by Milwaukee Avenue East on the north and Whitewater Avenue on the south, the town's historic district contains more than a dozen interesting old properties, some of which are on the state and national historic registers. Italianate, Queen Anne, French Second Empire, Greek Revival, Gothic Revival, and other architectural styles can be identified. A map of the district and description of the impressive yellow-brick and clapboard homes can be secured from the Fort Atkinson Chamber of Commerce.

WHERE TO SHOP

Antiques Exchange Mall. 232 South Main Street, Fort Atkinson. The mall, which is open daily from 10:00 A.M. to 5:00 P.M., features loads of antique furniture, clothing, toys, and other items. Call (920) 674–1400.

The Velveteen Rabbit Bookstore. 20 East Sherman Avenue, Fort Atkinson. Adult books, literature for children and young adults, parenting and teacher resources, books on tape, cassettes and cards, and journals and calendars are available. Hours are 10:00 A.M. to 5:00 P.M. weekdays and 10:00 A.M. to 2:00 P.M. Saturday. Call (920) 568–9940.

Gallery on the Main. 121 North Main Street, Fort Atkinson. A determined day-tripper can find an eclectic mix of art and crafts by Wisconsin artists here. Displays change regularly, emphasizing watercolors, jewelry, prints, or art glass and other media at any given time. Hours are 10:00 A.M. to 5:30 P.M. Tuesday through Friday, 10:00 A.M. to 8:00 P.M. Thursday, and 9:00 A.M. to 1:00 P.M. Saturday. Call (920) 563–9959.

Light Shine. N1895 U.S. Highway 12 east, Fort Atkinson. Light Shine has a little something for everyone, from a Christmas-gift house to a garden center, plus a tearoom where light (of course) lunches are served. Hours are 10:00 A.M. to 5:00 P.M. Tuesday through Friday and 9:00 A.M. to 5:00 P.M. Saturday. Closed Sunday and Monday. Call (920) 563–5128.

The Nasco Store. 901 Janesville Avenue (south side of Fort Atkinson on Business Highway 26). If you can't find it here, they probably don't make it. Farm and ranch equipment, saddles, blankets, liniment, stable supplies, nutritional aids, arts and crafts, science tools, puzzles, and even dissection materials are peddled. More than 50,000 stocked items of all kinds line the shelves and overflow the bins. Nasco has to be seen to be believed. Open from 8:00 A.M. to 5:30 P.M. Monday through Saturday. Call (920) 568–5600.

WHERE TO EAT

Canton Restaurant. 120 North Main Street, Fort Atkinson. You won't stay hungry long with the Canton's ample portions. For hours call (920) 563–7268. $$; ☐

Tuckers Too. 300 Washington Street, Fort Atkinson. Sip a cuppa your favorite joe and chat with friends. Tuckers is a homey place, perfect for relaxing after a day of driving. Hours vary. Call (920) 568–9330. $; ☐

Club 26. N898 State Highway 26, Fort Atkinson. Full range of menu items. For hours call (920) 563–9301. $$; ☐

Stagecoach Inn. 11946 North State Road (Highway 26), Fort Atkinson. This is a great spot for getting away into the nineteenth century. Good food, too. Call (920) 563–6511. $$$; ☐

WHERE TO STAY

Lamp Post Inn. 408 South Main Street, Fort Atkinson. Innkeepers Debbie and Mike Rusch emphasize that you'll "come a stranger and leave a friend." This is a pleasant B&B, perfect for a hideaway when the getaway mood chimes. Call (920) 563–6561 for rates and information.

La Grange Bed & Breakfast. 1050 East Street, Fort Atkinson. Lounge in comfort . . . after all you are taking a day away from home. Call (920) 563–1421. Cash or check only. $$

Best Western Courtyard Inn. 1225 Janesville Avenue, Fort Atkinson. The inn is adjacent to the Fireside, which makes it easily accessible after an evening theater performance. Hop up early the next A.M. and head back home. Call (920) 563–6444. $$; ☐

JEFFERSON

The first white settlers arrived in the Jefferson area in December 1836, when several families trekked overland from Milwaukee and set up housekeeping along the banks of the Crawfish and Rock Rivers. Over the next few years, more and more folks arrived to claim homesteads. A two-story hotel was built in 1839 to accommodate the newcomers until they were able to build their own homes. On April 13, 1857, the village of Jefferson was incorporated and town officers elected. The village of 3,000 was named a city in 1878.

Jefferson is the county seat of Jefferson County, retaining much of the old-time charm that it had when there was a horse-watering tank in the middle of Main Street. The community is 6 miles south of I-94 between Madison and Milwaukee, at the intersection of U.S. Highway 18 and State Highway 26. I-90 is 20 miles southwest of the city. Feeding into Jefferson are Jefferson County Highways J, K, N, and W.

It has several excellent parks, perfect for day-tripper picnics. Oakridge Park is a six-and-a-half-acre property named for its cluster of oaks on the highest point in the city. The park hosts a Family Aquatic Center (920-563-7799) with pool, 120-foot water slide, volleyball court, picnic sites, and warming shelter. Rotary/Waterfront Park incorporates one and three-tenths acres downtown, with space for festivals, arts fairs, and concerts. The thirty-five acres of Tensfelt Park include picnic space and a children's play area along the river. Riverfront Park incorporates nineteen acres with ball fields, lighted tennis and basketball courts, park shelters, and restroom facilities. Stoppebach Park, at six and a half acres, is adjacent to the Meadow Springs golf course and is located in a residential neighborhood. It includes shelters, bathrooms, and tennis and volleyball courts.

WHERE TO GO

Car Shows. Two large car shows, both of which started in the early 1970s, are held yearly at the Jefferson County Fairgrounds on U.S. Highway 18. Showgrounds open at 6:00 A.M., with more than a thousand cars offered for sale, plus antique car displays and a swap meet.

Jefferson Speedway. Situated halfway between Jefferson and Cambridge on U.S. Highway 18. Every Saturday night during the season, rip roarin' racing action features late model, sportsman, and hobby stock classes. Gates open at 3:00 P.M. with time trials at 5:00 P.M. Racing starts at 7:00 P.M. On Sunday the Jefferson Speedway hosts a Bargain Fair from 6:30 A.M. to 2:00 P.M., with free admission and parking. Call (920) 674–4445 or (920) 648–2705.

Meadow Springs Country Club. 424 South Sanborn Avenue, Jefferson. The public is welcome to use the eighteen-hole course, one of the best in south-central Wisconsin. Special prices are available for early-bird golf, from opening to 10:00 A.M. Monday through Friday, or for Twilight Golf every day after 4:00 P.M. Lunch and dinner are served daily in the clubhouse, along with a Friday-night fish fry. Call (920) 674–6858. The Web site is www.madisongolf.com.

WHERE TO SHOP

The Jones Store. Adjacent to the Jones Dairy Farm meat plant, 1 block off State Highway 26 across from Jones Park. Get your favorite sausages and other premium meat products here. For hours call (920) 563–2963.

WHERE TO EAT

Armstrong's Hamburger Stand and Ice Cream Parlor. 200 East Racine Street. A real institution here, Armstrong's serves up some of the best burgers in the Badger State from its little two-person stand, open only from March to the end of October. So get there early, eat lots and be sure to ask for the fried onions. Sit on benches outside or eat 'em while strolling around town. Then come back for more. Hours are 10:30 A.M. to 9:30 P.M. Sunday through Thursday, 10:30 A.M. to 10:30 P.M. Friday and Saturday. Call (920) 674–3637. $

d. b. Puffins. 221 South Main Street, Jefferson. Good home cooking of comfort food, with pie to walk across fire for . . . and then devour. Hearty American fare served from 6:00 A.M. to 2:00 P.M., Monday through Saturday, 7:00 A.M. to 2:00 P.M. Sunday. Call (920) 674–6273. $$; ☐

El Chaparral. 135 South Main Street, Jefferson. This is the place to satisfy a salsa craving, with food that can do a hat dance whenever the place starts hopping. Hours are 10:00 A.M. to 2:30 A.M. Monday, Tuesday, Thursday, and Friday; 9:30 A.M. to 9:00 P.M. Sunday. Closed Wednesday. Call (920)723–0972 or (920) 674–6040. $$; ☐

Golden Wok. 1509 State Highway 26, Jefferson. Won ton soup, egg rolls, and a wide range of other Chinese selections are on the menu. Hours are 10:30 A.M. to 10:00 P.M. Monday through Thursday;

10:30 A.M. to 11:00 P.M. Friday and Saturday; noon to 10:00 P.M. Sunday. Call (920) 674-4848. $$; ☐

Ken's Towne Inn. 124 West Rockwell Street, Jefferson. Owner Ramona Brockman makes her own soups and fries up grand burgers and steak sandwiches. She has fries to die for. Hours are 8:00 A.M. to bar time every day of the week. Food is served 11:00 A.M. to 10:00 P.M. Call (920) 674-2547. $$; ☐

Riverfront II Family Restaurant. 149 Collins Road, Jefferson. Ah, the specials every day. Get your beef tips or chicken stuffed with rice. Finish with pretty darn good pie. Hours are 5:30 A.M. to 9:00 P.M. Monday through Friday and 6:00 A.M. to 9:00 P.M. Saturday and Sunday. Call (920) 674-4296. $$; ☐

WHERE TO STAY

Hilltop Motel. 200 East Truman Street, Jefferson. The tree-shaded Hilltop has twenty-eight units, each with direct-dial phones and complimentary cable television. Call (920) 674-4610. $; ☐

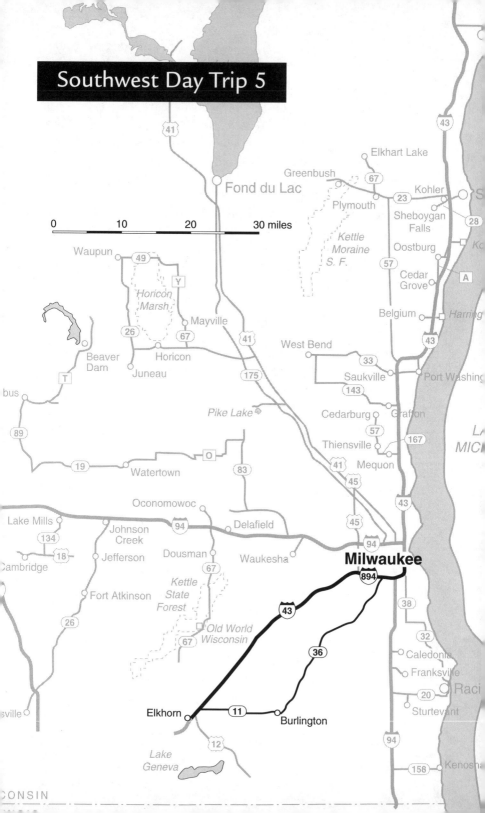

Southwest Day Trip 5

Burlington · Elkhorn

BURLINGTON

No chocolate fanatic can possibly skip a visit to Burlington, home of Nestle Chocolate Company, USA. A day trip here is especially fun in the middle of May, when the annual Chocolate Festival revs up. Believe it or not, you'll find more chocolate than you can eat. And this amount of chocolate is also amazing to see. Among the displays are a 1,600-pound chocolate Nestle Crunch Bar, a 2,756-pound chocolate chip, or a half-ton chocolate dinosaur. If you think chocolate, then the festival is for you.

But you'll also have to somehow work off the poundage earned by the choco-munching. Burlington is an action place, with plenty of opportunities to swim, boat, fish, hike, or cycle. And, if you prefer to stay on shore, there are plenty of picnic areas and also a bike trail that begins in Burlington's Riverside Park and follows the Fox River heading north, on a railroad bed.

Lemuel Smith arrived in the Burlington area during a frosty December 1835, probably wishing he had a cup of hot chocolate to fend off the cold. He scouted the area for homesites and headed back to warmer climes. In 1836 his brother, Moses, and William Whiting arrived to build homesteads. These two Yankees from the stern and rockbound East Coast were lured by the promise of rich farmland. They staked their claim by carving their initials in a tree where the Burlington Standard Press building now stands. Smith called the area Foxville.

Smith and Whiting were followed by other settlers, who built a sawmill and gristmill that served Milwaukee, Racine, and Kenosha. A woolen mill was also constructed, turning out the first cloth made in the Wisconsin territory. Burlington subsequently became a hub for the wool trade prior to the Civil War. The Burlington Blanket Company made horse blankets and switched to producing felt lining for automobile trunks when the motorized age edged out the horse and buggy. During World War II the company went on to make ammunition belts.

The Wisconsin Condensed Milk Company was launched in the 1870s, the first in the country. The milk was shipped all over the country and found international markets, as well. After a series of owners, the company was purchased by the Nestle company in the 1920s, which operated a plant in the city until the 1950s, when it shuttered the plant. In the mid-1960s Nestle returned and began producing chocolate, concentrating on candy bars.

Burlington has always been proud of its heritage, becoming a city in 1900. It established a historic district in 1999, which ensures keeping the old-time charm of its downtown buildings. The community can also brag that it was an important stop on the Underground Railway in the 1850s. The city's State Street was originally called Liberty Street because a local doctor who lived there once housed escaping slaves.

Burlington is easily reached from Milwaukee by taking either State Highway 36 south or I-94 to Highway 45 to I-43 to State Highway 11 west. The ride takes about an hour.

WHERE TO GO

Canoeing on Fox River. 31423 Bridge Drive (north of Waterford), Burlington. Follow State Highway 164 to the Grebe First Stop Union 76 gas station and turn left onto North Lake Drive. Fox River Landing is on the left, directly across the river. Whether you go 7, 11, or 17 miles, all that scenic paddling is sure to be relaxing. Bring your camera. Jim and Yvonne DeCleene will take care of the rest, including a complete outfit, if you need it. After the ride enjoy a picnic on the grounds of the Fox River Landing. Call (262) 662-5690 or (262) 614-1270.

Biking and Walking along Fox River. The Burlington Trail, which meanders through Saller Woods, starts at the east end of

Congress Street. So if canoeing is not for you, the river's tranquility can still be enjoyed. The trail is part of a 100-mile-long hiking and biking pathway established in 1970 through Racine County. The usual safety suggestions apply: Wear a helmet and brightly colored clothing; check that your bike's brakes, headlights, taillights, and reflectors are working properly; respect traffic laws and signs; and bring a reliable lock if you are planning on leaving your two-wheeler unattended anywhere along the route.

Kane's Circle Coach and Carriage, Inc. 27535 Ketterhagen Road, Burlington. Hitch a ride on a hay wagon, on a sleigh, or on a stagecoach. Also a great idea for parties or special events. Call to reserve at (262) 534-2771.

Bong State Recreation Area. 26313 Burlington Road (6 miles east of Burlington on State Highway 142, 1 mile west of State Highway 75). Originally slated to be a U.S. Air Force base—named after Richard Bon, a Wisconsin-born World War II flying ace—this 4,515-acre park has become one of Wisconsin's largest recreational areas. Only 6 percent of Bong, which includes a web of easily hiked trails, is for recreational use. The other 4,235 acres are reserved for fish-and-game management studies. Bong is subsequently known as one of the best places in the state for bird-watching. All trails begin and end at the parking lot east of Molinaro Visitor Center. If you love the outdoors but are tired of just picnicking, camping, and horseback riding, Bong Recreation Area has plenty of other outdoor opportunities. This area allows for dog sledding, dog training/trailing, falconry, hot-air ballooning, hunting, trapping, all-terrain/dirt bike riding, and much more. Bong Recreation Area also offers ski trails both north and south of State Highway 142. They are color coded according to their length, starting at 1.7 miles and going all the way up to 8.3 miles. The area is famous for its gusty winds, so dress accordingly. It is also recommended to stay in the spaces designed and maintained by park staff for each activity. Also, keep in mind that personnel do not monitor ice conditions in winter, so skate only on the pond east of the visitor center. A small windbreak with barbecue grill is there for day-trippers' use. A Wisconsin State Park sticker for your car is required: Stop in the recreation area or in the Molinaro Visitor Center, or self-register when park offices are closed. Call (262) 878-5600 or (262) 652-0377.

Historic Walking Tour. Burlington. Tour up to 3 miles of 1800s buildings and surroundings. The chamber of commerce has a booklet to guide you through this beautiful walk, which takes you all the way to the scenic lakefront park.

The Historical Society Museum. 232 North Perkins Boulevard, Burlington. A special display is in the restored Whitman School, an 1840s schoolhouse with original furnishings. The museum and the school are open from 1:00 to 4:00 P.M. Sunday or by appointment. Call (262) 767-2884.

Malt House Theatre. 109 North Main Street, Burlington. The Haylofters, the oldest community theater group in Wisconsin, was organized in 1932. The troupe performs at the Malt House Theatre in May, July, and October. Broadway musicals, children's theater, classical drama, and melodrama are always popular. The theater building used to be the malt house (hence the name) of the Finke-Uhen brewery. The Haylofters purchased the property in the 1950s and renovated it into a compact, viewer-friendly ninety-nine-seat theater. Call (262) 763-9873.

Spinning Top Exploration Museum. 533 Milwaukee Avenue, Burlington. Two hours of fun for children (and sure, older folks, too) age five years and older can be in a guided tour. The museum displays 2,000 toys, along with videos and hands-on entertainment. Admission. Reservations are required.

The gift shop is open 1:00 to 6:00 P.M. Tuesday and Wednesday and 10:00 A.M. to 2:00 P.M. Saturday; guided tours by appointment. Call (262) 763-3946 or (262) 728-5623.

Burlington Area Chamber of Commerce. 112 East Chestnut Street, Burlington. Call (262) 763-6044.

WHERE TO SHOP

Delights. 133 East Chestnut Street, Burlington. Sip some gourmet coffee accompanied by fine chocolate. Then take some goodies home to satisfy future cravings. Open 9:30 A.M. to 6:00 P.M. Monday through Friday and 9:30 A.M. to 5:00 P.M. Saturday. Call (262) 763-9448.

Schuette-Daniels. 425 North Pine Street, Burlington. Elegant leather furniture. Open 9:00 A.M. to 5:00 P.M. Monday through Saturday, noon to 4:00 P.M. on Sunday. Call (262) 763-3542.

WHERE TO EAT

B. J. Wentker's Triangle Tavern and Grill. 230 Milwaukee Avenue (State Highway 36), Burlington. Locals have given the thumbs up for dining here. Original appetizers; sandwiches for every taste; salads with chicken, crawfish, or duck; wraps; and soups, including the award-winning Elk and Black Bean Chili. Also carryout (orders received by 11:00 A.M. are ready by noon). Call (262) 767-1514. Orders can also be faxed to (262) 767-1557. $$; □

WHERE TO STAY

Beachview Motel & Lounge. 30427 Durand Avenue, Burlington. Call (262) 763-8802 between 6:00 and 10:00 A.M. $

Hillcrest Inn & Carriage House. 540 Storle Avenue, Burlington. Lots of quiet in a historic setting. Call (262) 763-4706 or (800) 313-9030 or visit the Web site (www.thehillcrestinn.com). $$-$$$

Meadowlark Acres. N5146 North Road, Burlington. If you prefer camping with amenities, Meadowlark has rest rooms and shower facilities. Call (262) 763-7200. Open May 1. Cash or check only. $

ELKHORN

From Burlington you can drive to Elkhorn (45 miles southwest of Milwaukee). The Walworth County seat is a mere 10 miles west of Burlington on State Highway 11. Brothers Milo and Daniel Bradley and LeGrand Rockwell were the first white settlers to lay claim on land here. They were impressed by the woods and rich soil, figuring this was the place they wanted to call home. The city name came from Army surveyor Samuel Phoenix, who found a set of elk antlers stuck in a tree and subsequently figured that was as good a handle as any for the new village. Fourteen people lived in the vicinity in 1837, a number that grew to 539 when the community held its first town meeting in 1846. When the town was platted a couple of years earlier, the farsighted Elkhornians had marked out space for a school and a jail, in addition to the residential lots. Land for a city hall and firehouse was purchased in 1884. Over the years curbs and gutters were added to the streets, buildings were given numbers, and a library was established with 200 donated books.

Folks here like to preserve and protect images from that past. For instance, the city bandshell was dismantled in the town square and relocated in Sunset Park in 1963 to make room for the new Walworth County Courthouse. The bandshell, originally constructed in 1926, is only one of two of its kind in the country. It is constructed with narrow wooden slats rather than larger boards. In 1996 the structure was restored and spruced up and now hosts the Elkhorn Band Concert series, held on Friday evenings from June through August. Business buildings throughout the downtown have been renovated, and numerous homes in town have been rejuvenated to their original 1800s splendor, demonstrating the citizens' concern for keeping up a quality impression.

Elkhorn is also known as the "Christmas Card City." In 1952 the *March of Time* television program selected the community as a backdrop for one of its shows because of its small-town feel and elaborate decorations. In 1958 a Ford Motor Company artist painted holiday scenes around the town to illustrate an article for its magazine, *The Ford Times*. Several of the paintings became well-known Christmas cards. Five of the six original pictures by artist Cecile Johnson are now displayed in the Elkhorn City Hall.

WHERE TO GO

Walworth County Fair. State Highway 11 east (Court Street), Elkhorn. This is a real blue-ribbon fair, considered by devoted fairgoers as one of the best in the country. It was first held in 1851 a block southwest of the current Courthouse Park and was moved to Delavan for a year in 1853. The fair returned to Elkhorn in 1854 and has remained here every year since then. The original fairgrounds encompassed six acres. Today the grounds cover ninety acres owned by the Walworth County Agricultural Society. There's plenty of room for chickens, ducks, cows, horses, tractors, plows, and people who want to have a "fairly" good time. The fair is held for six days around Labor Day weekend, attracting several hundred thousand persons. Tickets are needed at the gate, but there is free grandstand admission for the big-name entertainment. Free parking is a plus. Especially fun are the harness-racing events and the demo derby. The fairgrounds also hosts other events throughout the year. Call (262) 723-3228.

Webster House Museum. Corner of Washington and Rockwell Streets, Elkhorn. The house was the home of Jospeh Philbrick Webster, songwriter of "In the Sweet Bye and Bye" and hundreds of other pop tunes of two generations ago. A Music Room showcases Elkhorn's many other contributions to the musical world, with several companies in town manufacturing band instruments since the early 1900s. In fact, the French horn, indicating the "o" in Elkhorn, is another reminder of that heritage. Historical information on Elkhorn and Civil War artifacts are displayed in the Webster House, as well. Open 1:00 to 5:00 P.M. Wednesday through Saturday, or by appointment. Call (262) 723-5788.

Special Events. Elkhorn's central square, called Courthouse Park, is home to arts-and-crafts fairs, a Christmas holiday program, and the Festival of Summer in August. Other city events include the Fit for Life Marathon, the Rotary Corn and Brat Days, Maxwell Street Days, a classic-car show, and a volleyball tournament. For details contact the Elkhorn Chamber of Commerce, 114 West Court Street, Elkhorn, 53121. Call (262) 723-5788 or use the Web site, elkchamber@elkhorn-wi.org.

WHERE TO SHOP

Sawdust & Stitches. 13 South Wisconsin Street, Elkhorn. For your quilting and woodcraft hobbies. Classes are also available. Hours are 10:00 A.M. to 5:30 P.M. weekdays and 10:00 A.M. to 4:00 P.M. Saturday. Call (262) 723-1213.

Powell's Antique Shop. 14 West Geneva Street, Elkhorn. Owners Howard and Lois Powell can help find the perfect antique home accessory or furnishing, or know where to get them. Open 10:00 A.M. to 4:30 P.M. Wednesday through Sunday. Closed Monday and Tuesday. Call (262) 723-2952.

WHERE TO EAT

Luke's on Market Street. 117 West Market Street, Elkhorn. Dine in or carry out a sandwich for your trip. Luke's features hot dogs, grilled chicken, brats, burgers, and wonderful homemade Italian beef and meatballs. Hours are 10:00 A.M. to 10:00 P.M. Monday through Saturday and 11:00 A.M. to 9:00 P.M. Sunday. Call (262) 723-4676. $; ☐

CJ's Kountry Inn. Corner of U.S. Highway 12 and State Highway 67 and Walworth County Highway ES, Elkhorn. Wednesday specials include barbecued ribs, with a superb Friday fish fry. Danger, danger . . . whole pies are made to order, so don't say we didn't warn you about calories. Hours are 4:30 A.M. to 1:30 P.M. Monday through Sunday. Call (262) 742-3480. $; ☐

Annie's Burger Town. 645 North Lincoln Street, Elkhorn. Burgers, natch, of all styles, shapes, and toppings. Hours are 11:00 A.M. to 10:00 P.M. Monday through Sunday, depending on weather. Call (262) 723-3250. $; ☐

Honey Creek Cafe. 18 South Wisconsin Street, Elkhorn. Soup, sandwiches, and coffee in a cozy little place with friendly service. Hours are 9:00 A.M. to 3:00 P.M. Monday through Friday. Closed weekends. Call (262) 723-8234. $; ☐

Moy's Restaurant. 3 North Wisconsin Street (historic Lorraine Hotel), Elkhorn. Hours are 5:00 A.M. to 9:30 P.M. Monday through Thursday, 5:00 A.M. to 10:30 P.M. Friday, 4:00 A.M. to 10:30 P.M. Saturday, and 4:00 A.M. to 9:00 P.M. Sunday. Call (262) 723-3993. $$; ☐

Someplace Else Restaurant. 1 West Walworth, Elkhorn. Home cooking, daily specials. Hmmm, good. Hours are 11:00 A.M. to 9:00 P.M. Closed Sunday. Call (262) 723-3111. $$; ☐

Sperino's Little Italy. 720 North Wisconsin Street, Elkhorn. Delicate pasta, lotsa meatballs, and mellow wine make for a fine dining experience. Sperino's opened in Elkhorn in 1967. Hours are 4:00 to 9:00 P.M. Tuesday through Thursday, 4:00 to 10:00 P.M. Friday and Saturday, and 3:00 to 9:00 P.M. Sunday; closed Monday. Carry-outs available from 11:00 A.M. Call (262) 723-2222. $$; ☐

Sugar Creek Inn. N7073 U.S. Highway 12 north, Elkhorn. Hours are from 7:00 A.M. to 2:30 P.M. daily and from 5:00 to 9:00 P.M. for dinner Friday and Saturday only. Call (262) 742-3866. $$; ☐

The Jury Room. 39 North Wisconsin Street, Elkhorn. Casual atmosphere for Mexican food and pizza. Hours are 2:00 P.M. to midnight Monday through Thursday and 2:00 P.M. to 2:00 A.M. Friday and Saturday. If the flag is flying outside on Sunday afternoons during football games, that means the place is open. Call (262) 723-8021. $

WHERE TO STAY

Ye Olde Manor House. N7622 U.S. Highway 12, Elkhorn. Call (262) 742-2450. $$; ☐

Americinn of Elkhorn. 210 East Commerce Court, Elkhorn. Indoor pool, sauna, lobby with fireplace, whirlpool suites. Call (262) 723-7799 or (800) 634-3444. $$; ☐

The Thomas Motel. 840 North Wisconsin, Elkhorn. Folks call this "your vacation home away from home." Okay. Call (262) 723-2955. $$; ☐

Crossroads Motel. N6476 State Highway 12/67 at Walworth County Highway ES, Elkhorn. Indoor pool provides a refreshing respite after a day-trip tour or golf, cross-country skiing, or snow-mobiling nearby during the appropriate season. $$; ☐

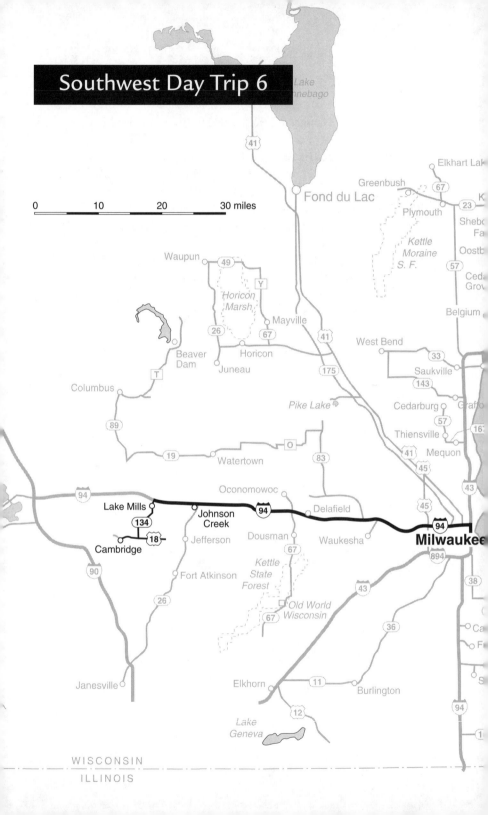

SOUTHWEST DAY TRIP 6

Johnson Creek
Lake Mills · Cambridge

Driving west from Milwaukee along I-94, the day-tripper has a straight shot toward adventure. The 77-mile corridor to Madison offers many side jaunts, making for a one- to two-day excursion. Several communities along the northern edge of Jefferson County, about an hour from Milwaukee, can serve up a tasty dish of outdoor fun, shopping potential, and historical attractions. There's no chance you'll go wrong anywhere along the way.

JOHNSON CREEK

The first stop on today's expedition is Johnson Creek, at one time merely a crossroads along the freeway where it intersects with State Highway 26. Where it once had only a couple of restaurants, a motel, and a truck stop to service the traveler, it is now the home of the Johnson Creek Outlet Center and an industrial park. The local motto has been upscaled to read, "The Crossroads with a Future." The village is bordered on the west by the Rock River and the highway intersection on the east. The village of Johnson Creek was incorporated in 1836, when Timothy Johnson and Charles Goodhue jointly claimed the land where the village now stands. After constructing the log cabins, they built a dam and a sawmill.

Until 1873 the village was known as Belleville, although the name Johnson Creek was the post office name. In 1868 the name was officially changed to Johnson's Creek to memorialize that first settler (the possessive was gradually phased out over the years).

Located in a productive farming district, Johnson Creek became the state's largest supplier of eggs, butter, and milk in the early 1900s. It remains primarily a farm community, but encroaching developments such as the outlet center have nibbled away at the landscape.

WHERE TO GO

Neat Repeats. 540 Village Walk Lane, Johnson Creek. This is a quality resale shop, where many items are sold on consignment. Look for toys, baby accessories, and clothing. Hours are 9:00 A.M. to 8:00 P.M. Monday through Thursday, 9:30 A.M. to 6:00 P.M. Friday, and 9:30 A.M. to 5:00 P.M. Saturday. Closed Sunday. Call (920) 699–4020.

WHERE TO SHOP

Johnson Creek Outlet Center. State Highway 26. At present visitors come to shop 'til they drop at the outlet complex, high on a hill on the north side of the freeway. From I-94, take exit 267 to State Highway 26. The usual selection of brand-name discounts are offered here, with 60 outlet stores presenting everything from luggage to blue jeans. Call (920) 699–4111. Hours are 10:00 A.M. to 9:00 P.M. Monday through Saturday and 11:00 A.M. to 6:00 P.M. Sunday.

WHERE TO STAY

Days Inn. Located on I-94 at State Highway 27, Johnson Creek. Clean, convenient chain property. Call (920) 699–8000. $$; ☐

LAKE MILLS

Next along I-94, Lake Mills is a tidy little community along the shore of Rock Lake. The cool green waters offer fine fishing, swimming, sailing, and waterskiing opportunities. And don't let winter scare you off. There's always ice fishing for perch, blue gill, and crappies, plus skating on the lake surface. A Glacial Drumlin bike-path trailhead is located in the city, where a dedicated cyclist can pedal up for miles through the nearby farmlands and woodlots.

Downtown Lake Mills has many historical old buildings, such as the L. D. Fargo Library. Many buildings border the Commons Park, set in the middle of Lake Mills, which makes for an easy stroll. Farmers' markets, Friday-night band concerts in summer, and an ice rink in winter ensure that there is a lot going on in the heart of the pleasant community. A drive from Milwaukee takes about seventy minutes. For details on the community, contact the Lake Mills Area Chamber of Commerce, 200C Water Street, Lake Mills, WI 53551-0125. Call (920) 648-3585.

WHERE TO GO

Aztalan State Park. Three miles east of town on Jefferson County Highway B. The park's main office is at 1213 South Main Street, and there is no resident ranger on-site. The 172-acre Aztalan has a reconstructed stockade and burial mounds of a prehistoric culture dating from A.D. 1200. A picnic site is at the bottom of a hill in the park near a creek, where these ancient people used to fish. The Aztalan residents also were apparently great traders because numerous shells, precious metals, and tools not indigenous to the region have been found here. Admission is free, but a state park sticker is required for parking. A museum near the park entrance is open daily from May through October. For museum hours, call (920) 648-4632. Donations are requested. The museum complex includes several refurbished log cabins and displays artifacts depicting Lake Mills and Native American history. Ask about the "lost pyramids" of Rock Lake when visiting the museum. The park's open terrain and its gentle slopes also make it a grand cross-country spot for winter sports lovers. Skiing is allowed between 6:00 A.M. and 10:00 P.M. Call (920) 648-8774.

WHERE TO SHOP

Dutch Design. N5706 Jefferson County Highway S, Lake Mills. This one-room schoolhouse has been transformed into a garden center with potted plants, digging aids, seeds, and other items essential for anyone nursing a green thumb. The shop is closed in February; call because days and hours change seasonally; (920) 648-8234.

Old Mills Market. 109 North Main Street, Lake Mills. The antiques lover will have a field day here. Hours are 10:00 A.M. to 5:00 P.M. daily. Call (920) 648-3030.

WHERE TO EAT

Cafe on the Park. 131 North Main Street, Lake Mills. Located in the heart of town, the cafe serves up a good range of comfort foods and swell coffee. Hours are 5:00 A.M. to 7:00 P.M. Monday through Friday and 5:00 A.M. to 2:00 P.M. Saturday and Sunday. Call (920) 648-2915. $; ☐

Lake Oasis Truck Stop. I-94 and State Highway 89, Lake Mills. This is where the truckers eat, so you know it has to be good. Open twenty-four hours a day, seven days a week. Call (920) 648-3408 or (920) 648-3409. $; ☐

Sportsman's Pub on the Park. 129 North Main Street, Lake Mills. Ten beer taps make sure no one is thirsty. Burgers and pizza available until midnight. Regulation-size pool table and five television sets are constantly busy. Hunting and fishing information available. Hours are 8:00 A.M. to bar closing time, usually 2:00 A.M. daily. Call (920) 648-5061. $

TT's Timeout, 107 South Main Street, Lake Mills. Good pub grub. Hours are 9:00 A.M. to closing weekdays and 10:00 A.M. to closing Saturday and Sunday. Call (920) 648-3013. $

WHERE TO STAY

Fargo Mansion Inn. 406 Mulberry Street, Lake Mills. Enoch Fargo, a distant relative of the stagecoach family, built this old home at the turn of the nineteenth century. It was the town's social center at one time, with its huge kitchen and walk-in freezer. Fargo, who was quite a builder, even installed the state's first cement sidewalk. The graceful walk leads up to his home. The building was listed on the National Register of Historic Places in 1982 and was made into a guest house in 1986. It has five comfortable bedrooms on the second floor, reached by a sweeping staircase. Another set of suites is on the top floor. The inn has tandem bikes for summertime cycling. Call (920) 648-3654. $$-$$$; ☐

Lake Country Inn. I-94 and State Highway 89, Lake Mills. Whirl-pool suites and econo rooms are available. Call (920) 648-3800. $$; ☐

CAMBRIDGE

From Lake Mills drive south on Jefferson County Highway A through the Lake Mills Wildlife area. You'll pick up U.S. Highway 18, a drive of about thirty minutes, even if you stop for a bit to watch the great blue herons in the wetlands. Turn west on U.S. Highway 18 to Cambridge. The historic old town's main street bills itself as "right out of a Norman Rockwell painting." It is now a craft and art haven, with numerous artists setting up shop in the old, renovated build-ings.

Although most visitors flock here to peruse the shop offerings, a day-tripper can also bike along the Glacial Drumlin Trail or moun-tain-bike and cross-country ski at CamRock County Park, tucked along Jefferson County Highway B between Cambridge and Rock-dale (608-246-3896). Koskonong Creek, a favorite with canoeists, runs through town. You can also just loaf a pleasant summer after-noon away in West Side Park. Or bring your skates and use the lighted rink there in winter. The Cambridge Chamber of Commerce is located at 105 South Spring Street, Cambridge, WI 53523. Call (608) 423-3780. Hours are 9:00 A.M. to 5:00 P.M. weekdays. The office is also open on festival weekends, but call to confirm.

WHERE TO SHOP

Rowe Pottery Works. 217 West Main Street, Cambridge. Glazed pottery tableware and gifts are the signature items at Rowe. During the holiday season the store sells collectible plates and limited-edition ornaments. Hours are 9:00 A.M. to 5:00 P.M. Monday through Saturday and 11:00 A.M. to 5:00 P.M. Sunday. Call (608) 423-3935 or use the Web site at www.rowepottery.com.

Front Pew. 109 North Spring Street, Cambridge. The "mall" is actually in a restored century-plus-old church. Two floors of antiques and collectibles are waiting to find another happy home. Owner Nancy Barth knows where to get interesting items. Bring a big pocketbook. Hours are 11:00 A.M. to 5:30 P.M. Monday through Friday, 10:00 A.M. to 5:30 P.M. Saturday, and noon to 4:00 P.M. Sunday, year-round. Call (608) 423-9952.

The Little Flower Shop. 209 River Street, Cambridge. Located 1 block north of downtown Cambridge, the shop is in the historic Cambridge Creamery building. Fenton art glass, porcelain dolls, concrete statuary, and wonderfully scented flowers make this a one-stop gift mecca. There is a Christmas room for shoppers who can't wait for the holidays. Hours are 8:30 A.M. to 5:30 P.M. weekdays and 7:30 A.M. to 4:00 P.M. Saturday. Usually closed Sunday except for weekends leading up to Christmas. Call (608) 423-7127.

Katy's Corner. 130 West Main Street, Cambridge. For sugar-free candy, gourmet foods, and a huge wine selection, drop by Katy's Corner. The store also sells Scandinavian gifts and tableware. Open daily from 9:00 A.M. to 5:00 P.M. Call (608) 423-3277 or use the Web site at www.katyscorner.com.

The Voyagers Jewelry Design. 212 West Main Street, Cambridge. Located in a stone house built in 1851, the gem store offers loose diamonds and other stones that can be made into rings, bracelets, and other ornamental wear. The folks here can also restring necklaces if a day-tripper has an emergency en route. Hours are 10:00 A.M to 7:00 P.M. Tuesday and Wednesday, 10:00 A.M. to 4:00 P.M. Thursday, 10:00 A.M. to 5:00 P.M. Friday, and 10:00 A.M. to 5:00 P.M. Saturday. Call (608) 423-4446.

WHERE TO EAT

Cambridge Country Inn & Pub. 206 West Main Street, Cambridge. Located in downtown Cambridge, this cozy inn has great steaks and seafood. Hours are 10:30 A.M. to 8:00 P.M. Sunday through Thursday and 8:00 A.M. to 9:00 P.M. Friday and Saturday. Call (608) 423-3275. $$; ☐

Cardinal Ridge. W9292 U.S. Highway 18, Cambridge. Steaks, chops, and seafoods, plus loads of specials make this a popular local restaurant. Hours are 5:00 to 9:00 P.M. Tuesday through Thursday and 5:00 to 10:00 P.M. Friday and Saturday. Call (608) 423-3956. $$$; ☐

Ten thousand years ago, the glaciers crunched across Wisconsin and flattened the landscape. The towering ice sheets, like a giant bulldozer, filled in low spots and dumped a trail of rubble when they finally retreated, as if they were teenagers heading to bed. As soon as the weather warmed, humans moved in. Archaeologists have found artifacts in this stretch of Wisconsin landscape that date from 6000 B.C. The first white settlers didn't show up until the 1830s.

A drive here is a fascinating trip for scenery, historical attractions, and plain old getaway fun. There are hiking, biking, camping, skiing, swimming, boating, fishing, hunting, snowmobiling, and other outdoor recreational opportunities. For a more sedentary trip, take in autumn's vibrant colorama or simply roll down your car windows and enjoy the fresh air during a long summer-afternoon drive.

OLD WORLD WISCONSIN

Old World Wisconsin is the place for history lovers, who will enjoy stepping back a century to experience the sights and sounds of Wisconsin's pioneer heritage. The site can also be enjoyed by those who might not be all that caught up in history but who just want a day in the sun, with a bit of a stroll added in for good measure.

The complex is located at S203 W37890 State Highway 67, 1½ miles south of the hamlet of Eagle, a village platted after early pioneers spotted an eagle in the area. It is easily reached by following the signs. The acreage is 35 miles from Milwaukee and 55 miles from

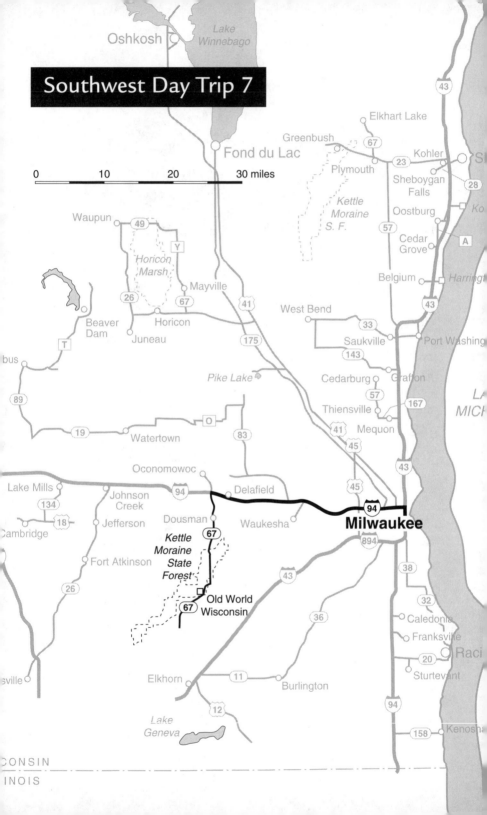

Southwest Day Trip 7

0   10   20   30 miles

Oshkosh
Lake Winnebago
Fond du Lac
Elkhart Lake
Greenbush
67
Kohler
Plymouth
23
Sheboygan Falls
28
Kettle Moraine S. F.
Oostburg
57
Cedar Grove
A
Waupun
49
Y
Horicon Marsh
26
67
Mayville
41
Belgium
Harring
West Bend
43
Beaver Dam
Horicon
33
Juneau
T
175
Saukville
Port Washing
143
bus
Pike Lake
Cedarburg
Grafton
89
57
167
19
O
83
Thiensville
LA
MICH
Watertown
41
Mequon
45
Oconomowoc
45
43
Lake Mills
94
Delafield
45
134
Johnson Creek
Dousman
94
18
Jefferson
67
Waukesha
Milwaukee
ambridge
Kettle Moraine State Forest
894
Fort Atkinson
43
38
26
Old World Wisconsin
67
36
32
Caledonia
Franksville
Raci
Elkhorn
11
20
sville
Burlington
Sturtevant
12
94
Lake Geneva
158
Kenosha
CONSIN
INOIS

Madison, making it easy to go back several generations in time even on a half-day drive.

There are sixty-five buildings of historic importance scattered around the 576 acres of Old World; many of the structures are featured in farmsteads of German, Polish, Scandinavian, and Yankee heritage. Knowledgeable guides are dressed in the appropriate period and ethnic costumes, each talking as a character who might have lived on one of the farms or worked in the shops. The look is so complete that even the animal breeds are historically correct. Strawberries, dill, kohlrabi, cucumbers, and other appropriate vegetables are planted in the gardens. Autumn crops of hay, wheat, corn, and rye are harvested by hand or by steam-powered threshers, depending on the date of the respective farmsite.

The oldest building is a Norwegian log cabin dating from 1848. A seven-building Finnish farm depicts the decade of 1910 to 1920. The buildings were collected from around the state and rebuilt at Old World.

A crossroads village of the 1870s demonstrates a small community's important social and business element of the nineteenth century. The three-story Four Mile House, a former stagecoach inn, now is a "rooming house." There are also blacksmith and wagon-maker's shops, as well as a town hall and church. The staff go about their daily chores as if they lived there. They prepare meals, take care of livestock and crops, and generally act as the original homesteaders would have.

The living-history museum, which opened in 1976, is operated by the State Historical Society of Wisconsin. In 1985 it was given a prestigious Phoenix Award for historic preservation by the Society of American Travel Writers.

In addition to its regular tours, Old World offers special events coinciding with the appropriate season. Among them Independence Day is marked with rousing speeches and Civil War music concerts. Plenty of red, white, and blue bunting drapes across the Harmony Town Hall, built in 1876 in the Town of Harmony, Rock County. Choral concerts and a Christmas program enliven St. Peter's Church during the holidays. The old Catholic church, one of Milwaukee's first, was constructed around 1839.

Cross-country skiing is great fun on the hills and ridges of Old World, with skiing available from 9:00 A.M. to 5:00 P.M. Friday through Sunday, weather permitting. Sometimes a farmhouse is open where skiers can stop for hot cider and cookies.

Admission is charged. Hours at Old World are 10:00 A.M. to 4:00 P.M. weekdays and 10:00 A.M. to 5:00 P.M. weekends in May, June, September, and October. Hours are 10:00 A.M. to 5:00 P.M. daily, July through August.

Three buildings—the Clausing Barn, built in 1897; the Lueskow House (1850); and the Ramsey Barn (1841)—are used as a visitor center. Take a look at the exhibits, the orientation program, and the gift shop. You can buy hot sandwiches, soft drinks, and snacks in the Clausing Barn.

Horse-drawn and tractor-pulled wagons take visitors around the grounds, with pickups scattered near the larger farms. Guests are free to hop on and off the wagons if they don't wish to walk the entire 2½-mile route. A tour of the complex takes from three to six hours, depending on how long you want to stay and talk with the interpreters or look around all the buildings. Benches are provided along the way for tired strollers. Rest rooms and pit toilets are available.

WHERE TO GO

Finnish Area. The Rankinen House, built in 1892, is restored to its 1897 look, after a kitchen wing was added. The Kortesmaa outhouse is the only such structure preserved at Old World Wisconsin. Other buildings include a granary, barns, and a sauna. The latter, built in 1909, was integral to helping the Finns make it through the Wisconsin winters. They took a steam bath and then went outside to roll in the snow.

Danish Area. The Pederson House was constructed in 1872 in the Polk County Town of Luck. The queen of Denmark dedicated this house at Old World when she visited in 1976. The Jensen barn, also in the Danish area, dates from 1890.

Norwegian Area. The Raspberry School, from 1896, is a popular attraction. It was used until 1914 by Norwegian and Swedish families who lived along Lake Superior's Raspberry Bay. The Sorbergshaben barn is one of the more interesting structures, with corn cribs along two of its sides and a drive-through for farm wagons in the middle of the building.

Germanic Area. The Koepsell House, built in 1858 with a typical half-timbered look, is on the National Register of Historic Places. The nearby Schulz House was constructed in 1856 and is another traditional half-timbered structure. Mud and straw served as caulking between the beams and side timbers that make up the walls.

WHERE TO STAY

Eagle Centre House. W370 S9590 State Highway 67, Eagle. Eagle Centre is a replica of an 1846 Greek-Revival–style stagecoach inn. The antiques are authentic, however, so the entire package comes together well. All five guest rooms have private baths. Although there is central heating, the two wood-burning stoves on the main floor add a helpful, cozy element during winter. Innkeepers are Riene Wells Herriges and Dean Herriges. Call (262) 363–4700 or check the Web site at www.eagle-house.com. $$; ☐

KETTLE MORAINE STATE FOREST, SOUTHERN UNIT

The forest is about an hour's drive southwest of Milwaukee via I–94 and State Highway 67, among other routes, so just check a map. The city of Oconomowoc is to the north of the freeway, whereas the woods are several miles to the south. The forest blankets 18,000 acres in chunks of Jefferson, Waukesha, and Walworth Counties and surrounds Old World Wisconsin. It is one of the few places in the state to find rare pasqueflowers, which bloom only in mid-April. There are three major recreational areas inside the forest: Whitewater Lake, Ottawa Lake, and Pinewoods, for a total of 265 campsites. The Kettle Moraine Forest has 27 miles of bridal paths, along with a horse campground with sixty sites, so you don't need to leave ol' Dobbin home when you day-trip here. There are more than 34 miles of hiking along the Scuppernong and McMiller trail system. The paths are looped for easy access and exit.

While hiking, you'll find interesting geological formations such as the Stone Elephant, a huge boulder dumped in the forest by the retreating glaciers. The stone is 39 feet in diameter. There are many other interesting geological locales around the area, as well. On State Highway 67, 3 miles north of the intersection with State Highway 59, is an ancient glacial lake bed that was once 40 feet deep. A giant kettle, a depression in the ground formed when earth-covered ice melted and fell inward, can be spotted on County Highway H, not quite a mile north of the intersection with U.S. Highway 12. La Grange Lake, near the marked Ice Age Trail where it crosses U.S. Highway 12, is a shallow pool surrounded by marshland. Bird-watchers assert this is one of the best places in the region to see green-back herons, spotted sandpipers, and American woodcocks.

Seeds that had been dormant for more than a century are springing to life in the forest's Scuppernong River Habitat, after controlled burns and removal of buckthorn shrubbery and trees have cleared the land. The acreage, especially near County Highway K and Wilton Road, subsequently explodes with wildflowers. The landscape now looks much like it did during the pre-pioneer days. Since 1999, about 1,500 acres have been cleared, allowing brilliant new life to be enjoyed. The site is roughly between Ottawa Lake south to State Highway 59. In the summer, look for the rare purple blazing star and the brilliant yellow of compass plants prairie dock.

The trail headquarters is open year-round from 7:45 A.M. to 4:30 P.M. weekdays and from 8:00 A.M. to 4:30 P.M. Saturday and Sunday. Visitors must leave the campgrounds and other forest sites by 11:00 P.M. The campgrounds reopen at 6:00 A.M. A state park sticker is required for entry to the forest and a trail pass is needed for biking on designated pathways. For more details contact the superinten-dent, Kettle Moraine State Forest, Southern Unit, S91 W39091, State Highway 59, Eagle, WI 533119; (262) 594–6200.

WHERE TO GO

John Muir Biking-Hiking Trail. There are several excellent loops in this section of the Kettle Moraine along County Highway H. Look for the parking area that allows access to the 2-mile-long Red Loop that meanders through fields and clumps of hardwoods, pine, and sweet-smelling spruce. The Orange Loop is a steep, narrow 4.8-mile trek that takes hikers into a bog. The Green Loop is even more picturesque, snaking along for 7.4 miles through some of the most

diverse portions of the Kettle Moraine. This is a great place to find pasqueflower showing off its spectacular spring displays. The 4-mile path edges through prairielands, with scattered pine stands. It wriggles in and out of hardwood plantations and through a bog. The trail's blue loop is the most extensive, covering 10 miles through mature hardwood forests. If hiking, watch out for the mountain bikers who love this stretch. In the spring, jack-in-the-pulpits nod and bob in the season's soft breeze.

Emma F. Carlin Biking and Hiking Trails. The trail takes walkers and cyclists along a razorback ridge overlooking a glacial outwash sand plain. Some of the trails are along abandoned logging routes. The trail system is on Waukesha County Highway Z, 1 mile south of State Highway 59. Park in the lot off Z and walk toward the trailhead, which is marked by a large map carved on a wooden sign. There are steep slopes along the path, particularly on the Red Loop. This is a great stretch in autumn, when the oaks and maples are ablaze with orange and red.

Nordic Ski and Hiking Trails. There is a variety of trail types along this route, from the simple to the more strenuous. After the first steeply wooded hill, a panorama of meadowland sweeps off to the horizon. The system is on Walworth County Highway H, about 2 miles south of Bluff Road. The main trails are 6 miles south of the village of Palmyra. Rest rooms are open at the trailhead.

Ice Age Trail. The trail is part of the 1,000-mile-long stretch of hiking paths reaching across Wisconsin's midsection, following the perimeter of the retreating glaciers. Park in the gravel lot, where both the Ice Age Trail and the Horse Trail cross U.S. Highway 12. The lot is on the north side of the road near Sweno Road. Be sure to look for the orange and yellow markers indicating the trail. The system is about 3½ miles west of Whitewater.

Scuppernong Springs Nature Trail. This region was a well-used campsite for several Native American nations centuries ago. Plentiful food overflowed the marshes, woods, and prairies. Where the original wetland once stretched for more than 20 miles, it now consists of only a few square miles surrounded by creeping subdivisions and large home lots. The trail is across Waukesha County Highway ZZ, reached from the Ottawa Lake Recreational Area about 1 mile west of State Highway 67. *A hint:* Watch out for poison ivy. Other than that, you should have a fine time strolling along the smooth, easily traversed path. An elevated boardwalk now stands where an earth dam at one time blocked the Scuppernong River to create a fish pond. At the turn of the last century, trout were raised here. A few crumbling walls and building foundations are all that remain of this once thriving business that peddled fish in Milwaukee and Chicago.

East Troy Electric Railroad Museum. East Troy. Located about 20 miles south of the main Kettle Moraine Forest, the museum is open from Memorial Day to mid-October. In the past the electric railroad was a major interurban transportation line linking this part of the state with Milwaukee. The museum now operates a 10-mile run through woods and along prairieland to a small lake and back. Visitors to the museum in downtown East Troy can also look over the repair sheds and poke around displays of old trolley memorabilia. Because it is so close to the Kettle Moraine, a visit to the trolley museum is a quick add-on for any day trip to the region. Admission charged. Hours are irregular, so call (262) 642–3263 for details.

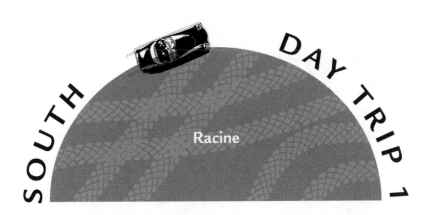

RACINE

Racine County is Milwaukee County's closest neighbor on the south. In fact, downtown Milwaukee and downtown Racine are merely 26 miles apart. Although there are still open spaces between communities, interurban sprawl is slowly chipping away at the farmland that formerly separated them. Milwaukee's southern suburbs of West Milwaukee, St. Francis, Cudahy, South Milwaukee, and Oak Creek are now part of the Greater Milwaukee spread. There are several roadways linking the counties. I-94 is the quickest (look for the several Racine off-ramps, with the major exit being State Highway 20 east).

Or take State Highway 32 out of South Milwaukee (closest to Lake Michigan), which leads directly to Racine. State Highway 38 (closest to I-94) is picked up near Gen. Billy Mitchell International Airport on Milwaukee's South Side and continues south to Five Mile Road, where it runs east to State Highway 32. If you keep going south on Racine County H, which starts at Five Mile Road where State Highway 38 turns, you drive through the villages of Caledonia and Franksville. County H will connect with State Highway 11 at Sturtevant, which also runs east into Racine. This all becomes clear by simply looking at a map.

For information about the area, contact the Racine County Convention & Visitors Bureau, 345 Main Street, Racine, WI 53403. Call (262) 634-3293 or (800) C-RACINE (272-2463). The bureau's Web site is www.racine.org.

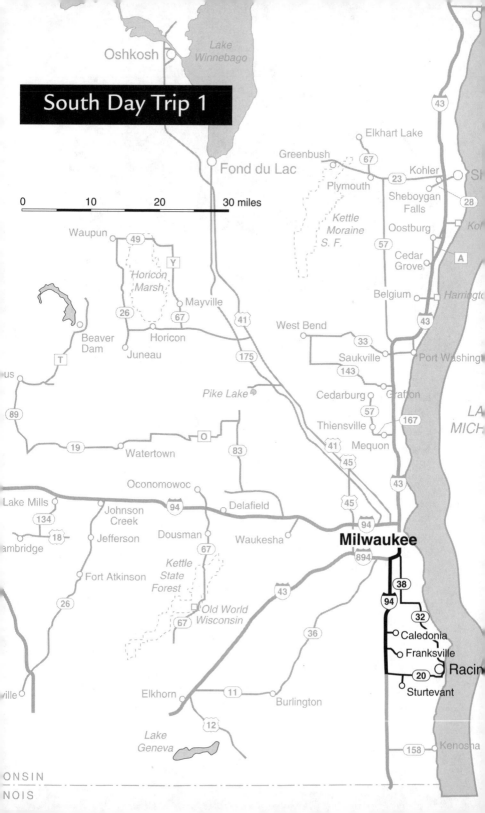

The first threshing machine, the first horseless carriage, the first powdered milk, and the first official woman minister have all one thing in common: Racine. The town fathers and mothers like to proclaim that their city is tops in "innovation, invention, and ingenuity."

From the past century on, Racine has had the distinction of being the birthplace of where many household products and engineering marvels were first made and where milestone events took place. The city is the home of internationally recognized firms such as Johnson Wax, Hamilton Beach, Andis, and J. I. Case.

The wealth of its most famous citizens was poured into Racine's elegant homes and the refined, tree-shaded streets, especially in the historic downtown. Hand-carved wood and leaded windows even mark the business district, with explosions of seasonal floral displays adding a touch of class at almost every street corner.

Racine's shops can satisfy every taste, the restaurants every palate, the entertainments every age.

The city, on the banks of the Root River and the shore of Lake Michigan, is the county seat of Racine County. Gilbert Knapp, a Great Lakes freighter captain, founded the original settlement in 1834. It was incorporated in 1848, the year Wisconsin became the Union's thirtieth state. Because of its prime location on the water and proximity to both Milwaukee and Chicago, Racine quickly grew into a major commercial center. From the beginning it had a strong industrial base, one complemented by a rich inland agricultural scene. Lake freighters, highways, and railroads linked Racine to the wider world. Tractors, furniture, farm machinery, household wax, clothing, and electrical products poured out of its factories.

The city has rebounded from a Rust Belt slump in the 1970s and early 1980s, when several of its principal companies closed or moved elsewhere. Presently, the recovered Racine has a bright, bustling downtown scene, with an emphasis on the arts and culture. It is a city proud of its ethnic mix, history, and recreational opportunities—and that's not a chamber of commerce promotional pitch. Racine is a community that has kept its spirit alive.

WHERE TO GO

Fishing on the Lake. For day-trippers seeking the quiet that only the water and a rod can provide, several professional fishing charter captains sail out of Racine harbor. For contacts call Fishing Charters of Racine (262-633-6113 or 800-475-6113), Gateway Sport Fishing Charter (262-637-8822), Brian Eggert (262-573-1975), Jim Mueller (708-981-1426), or Bob O'Brien (262-554-7912). While no one can ever guarantee a catch, odds are excellent that several giant German brown trout or lake salmon will be in the ship cooler by the end of a half-day or full-day boating excursion.

Case Tractor Plant. East of the crossing of Sheridan Road and Durand Avenue, Racine. J. I. Case Corporation offers one-and-a-half-to two-hour tours of its sprawling main plant, its foundry, and its transmission assembly facility. Choose one of the tours and learn the secrets of how a tractor is built. Enthusiastic retired employees who really know the inside and outside operations of Case lead the expeditions to the world of clanging metal presses, roaring furnaces, and pounding machinery. There are a few requirements for visitors: must be age fourteen or older, must be able to do a lot of walking, but, for safety reasons, no high heels or open-toe shoes.

Case is Wisconsin's oldest manufacturer, starting operations in 1844 as a threshing-machine company. It built its first combine in 1923, and numerous other farm implements and heavy equipment followed. The firm's original offices at 700 State Street, in a magnificent old building across from its current world headquarters, were modeled after the Boston Public Library.

Tours of the Case plants, which must be scheduled in advance, are offered from 9:00 A.M. to 1:00 P.M. Monday through Friday, year-round, unless the factory is closed for some reason. Call (262) 636-7818.

Racine Heritage Museum. 701 South Main Street, Racine. It's hard to imagine that at one time the world lived without all the numerous inventions born in Racine. Featured here are steam-powered vehicles, electric motors, food mixers, marine transmissions, malted milk, and dozens of other devices and products that make it easier to function in the modern world. The building, in a magnificent Renaissance Revival style, was built in 1902 as the city's public library, with money donated by industrialist Andrew Carnegie. Admission is free. Open from 9:00 A.M. to 5:00 P.M. Tuesday to Friday and from 1:00 to 5:00 P.M. Saturday and Sunday. Call (262) 636-3926.

Oak Clearing Farm & Museum. 704 Oak Clearing Drive (exit I-45 north of Union Grove), Yorkville. When the land was purchased in 1988, new owner Gerald Karwowski promised the Callendar family (who had lived on the property since 1844) that it would be preserved. Karwowski stayed true to his word. He began collecting artifacts of the county's past and exhibiting them on-site, renovating the main house and keeping the barns and other outbuildings intact. On the tree-shaded grounds, Karwowski now displays hundreds of artifacts ranging from antique tractors to an entire blacksmith shop. He also has a bottle shop with hundreds of blue and brown glass soda bottles, as well as milk bottles. Karwowski even set up a Wall of Fame with a lineup of Hamilton Beach blenders and mixers, showcasing products made by this famous company. Admission to Oak Clearing is free. Open May through October on Sunday from noon to 5:00 P.M. or by appointment. Call (262) 878-1688.

The Racine Theater Guild. 2519 Northwestern Avenue, Racine. Theater fans consider the guild's shows as among the best in community theater performances. Eight plays annually. Call (262) 633-4218.

The Charles A. Wustum Museum of Fine Arts. 2519 Northwestern Avenue, Racine. The museum is a true learning experience, with classes (both for children and adults), tours, and lectures. More than 2,500 works are displayed, with an emphasis on twentieth-century American artists. Also enjoy the beautiful gardens around the building and don't forget to check out its art purchase and rental opportunities. Admission and parking are free. Open from 11:00 A.M. to 9:00 P.M. Monday and Thursday, 1:00 to 5:00 P.M. Sunday, and all other days from 11:00 A.M. to 5:00 P.M. Call (262) 636-9177.

Racine Zoological Gardens. 2131 North Main Street, Racine. For a great natural symphonic rendition, listen to the animals growl, roar, bark, and whoop. Open daily except Christmas Day. Summer hours (Memorial Day through Labor Day) are 9:00 A.M. to 8:00 P.M. From September to May the zoo is open from 9:00 A.M. to 4:00 P.M. Call (414) 636-9189.

SC Johnson Administration Building. At the crossing of Fourteenth and Franklin Streets, Racine. The building, designed by Frank Lloyd Wright, hosts the headquarters of SC Johnson, A Family Company. Thirty-minute tours are offered on Friday at 11:00 A.M. and 1:15 P.M. Reservations are required for the walk-through, so call (262) 260-2154.

The Golden Rondelle Theater is also located on the administration building grounds. The slightly flattened, egg-shaped structure was originally an exhibition building used at the 1964 New York World's Fair. When the fair closed, the theater was moved to its current location. The Golden Rondelle features two films every Friday: *On the Wing* and *Living Planet*. *On the Wing* was prepared in cooperation with the National Aerospace Museum, showing different environments and climates through the lens of a camera fixed on the tail of a large commercial airplane. *Living Planet* focuses on the flight of birds and of man. For showtimes call (262) 260-2154.

Wingspread. Wingspread, also designed by Frank Lloyd Wright, and at one time a residence for the Johnson family, is now a conference center for the Johnson Foundation. The 14,000-square-foot prairie-style mansion is located on a thirty-acre estate. When programs are not in session, Wingspread is open to the public. Tour the building at leisure or wander around the nature trails. Since the conference schedule varies, opening hours also change, but they will always be from Monday through Friday between 9:00 A.M. and 4:00 P.M. Call (262) 681-3353.

River Bend Nature Center. 3600 North Green Bay Road, Racine. Eighty acres of woods and waters northwest of Racine offer a different look at the world throughout the year: in spring, wildflowers blooming; in fall, a harvest festival. Summer hiking is a popular getaway. In winter visitors enjoy cross-country skiing. Educational programs are geared for children between age four and thirteen. Kids ages seven and older can also enjoy canoe trips organized by the center. For program times and hours of operation, call (262) 639-0930.

Modine-Benstead Observatory. Racine County Highway A and Sixty-third Drive, Racine. Take another close look . . . at the galaxy. Stargazers love these specs: 16-inch Cassegrain-Newtonian reflecting telescope with a 6-inch refractor telescope on the same mounting for both direct visual observing and photography, a 14-inch Schmidt-Cassegrain, and a 12.5-inch Newtonian telescope. The instruments are available to the public for sky-watching every clear Thursday evening from June to September. Viewing starts at dusk and continues until 11:00 P.M. The facility is operated by the Racine Astronomical Society. Call (262) 878-2774.

Racine County Parks. Variety is the answer when asking about what there is to see and do in Racine County parks. Each has its own personality and attractions. A map showing locations can be secured from the Racine County Park and Recreation Department, 14200 Washington Avenue, Sturtevant, WI, 53177-1253; (262) 886-8440. Quarry Lake Park is on the site of an abandoned quarry, now an eighteen-acre lake. The clear water is fantastic for scuba diving, swimming, and fishing. The park offers an air-conditioned beach house with changing rooms, lockers, concessions, showers, and rest rooms. Colonel Heg Memorial Park, the county's first, is named after a noted Civil War hero who hailed from Racine County. On-site is a museum relating to the history of Norwegian settlers in the vicinity and an 1837 log cabin to explore. Each June, Heg Park hosts a Heritage Days celebration.

Sanders Park features a marked nature trail that wends its way through thirty acres of state-designated scientific area with numerous examples of presettlement vegetation. More than ninety species of wildflowers ensure a perfumed palette that delights the eye and sniffer. There are also the requisite picnic tables, baseball diamond, horseshoe court, and kids' playground. For a wonderful view of Lake Michigan, Cliffside Park offers one of the best vistas along this stretch of shoreline. It also has a ninety-two-site campground, many with both water and electricity. For travelers with RVs, a sanitary station is available for use.

The county also has a great network of cycling opportunities, both urban and rural. A signed 100-mile route circles the entire county, with city streets and country lanes making for an enjoyable jaunt. Along the route you will find the Tichigan Wildlife Refuge, the Root and Lower Fox Rivers, and even the corporate headquarters of Johnson Wax. Included are 17 miles of off-road bike challenges via the North Shore Trail, the Waterford-Windlake Trail, and others. The trails are made of crushed limestone.

WHERE TO SHOP

Racine Antique Mall. 310 Main Street, Racine. This is the place to find exclusive pieces of furniture, art glass, pottery, jewelry, and much more from around the world. Open from 11:00 A.M. to 5:00 P.M. Tuesday through Saturday. For more information call (262) 633-9229.

Riley's Sweet Shop. 3308 Washington Avenue, Racine. Riley's presents an interesting mix of candy and Irish imports, for a whimsical bit of charm. Call (262) 637-9100 for hours.

Nelson's Variety Stores. 3223 Washington Avenue (262-633-3912) and 4636 Douglas Avenue (262-639-0170), Racine. These stores have the same charm as an old-time dime store, where a shopper can purchase anything from an eraser to socks. The North Store on Douglas is the more modern of the two outlets, located on U.S. Highway 32 between Three- and Four-Mile Roads.

Holiday Manor. 2367 Twenty-seventh Street (exit Racine County Highway G and I-94 and turn south on West Frontage Road; the exit is 1 mile south of Seven Mile Road). A year-round Christmas store where a wide variety of collectibles, ornaments, and holiday gifts can be purchased even in the heat of mid-August. But, what the heck. Get a running start on the Frosty the Snowman season. Look for brand names such as Fontanini, Colonial Village, Charming Tails, Old World Christmas, and David Frykman. Call (262) 835-9010 for hours.

Kringles are Racine's "sweet heritage," as the local bakers like to say. The recipe came to the city in the late-nineteenth century, when a large contingent of Danes moved here. The bakeries that sprang up to cater to the hungry Scandinavians still use family baking secrets handed down over several generations. A Danish kringle is certainly one of earth's culinary delights. For the uninitiated the oval pastries offer a thin, buttery crust filled with an almond paste, nuts, or fruit. Here are three of the best bakeries:

O&H Danish Bakery. 4006 Durand Avenue (262-554-1311) and 1841 Douglas Avenue (262-637-8895), Racine. Hours are 5:30 A.M. to 6:00 P.M. weekdays and 5:30 A.M. to 5:00 P.M. Saturday. Orders can also be shipped. A store featuring European gourmet foods and coffee is also at the Durand Avenue site. Call (800) 227-6665. Or use the bakery Web site at www.ohdanishbakery.com.

Larsen Bakery. 3311 Washington Avenue, Racine. Weekday hours are 6:00 A.M. to 6:00 P.M., with Saturday hours from 6:00 A.M. to 5:00 P.M. Closed Sunday. Call (262) 633-4298. Larsen's can also ship internationally.

Lehmann's Bakery. 2210 Sixteenth Street, Racine. The *Racine Journal Times* says that Lehmann's has the "dough that made Racine famous." In addition to marvelous kringles, the shop offers pies, muffins, buns, bagels, sandwiches, tortes, wedding cakes, and specialty breads. Hours are 5:30 A.M. to 5:30 P.M. Monday through Saturday. Call (262) 632-4636. Check the Lehmann Web site at www.lehmanns.com. Lehmann's West Store, State Highway 31 and Newman Road, also serves cold custard cones in addition to its bakery items. Hours are 6:30 A.M. to 6:00 P.M. daily. Call (262) 633-3302.

7-Mile Fair. I-94 and Seven Mile Road. The "granddaddy of all outdoor markets" is open from 5:00 A.M. to 5:00 P.M. Saturdays and Sundays, April through October. The determined shopper can find all sorts of treasures, from wrenches to antique cabinets, vegetables, plates, tires, medals, clothing, radios, and nails. Be prepared to walk, walk, and walk. The fair is about a twenty-minute drive south of downtown Milwaukee. Call (262) 835-2177.

WHERE TO EAT

Kewpee. 520 West Wisconsin Avenue, Racine. Undeniably, Racine's best hamburgers can be had here. Smoothly delicious, especially topped with raw onion, tomato, and lettuce. Okay, okay. Make it a cheeseburger, too. Hours are 7:00 A.M. to 6:00 P.M. weekdays and 7:00 A.M. to 5:00 P.M. Saturday. Call (262) 634-9601. $

Yardarm Bar & Grill. 920 Erie Street, Racine. Racine is hamburger nuts. Food critic Dennis Getto of the *Milwaukee Journal-Sentinel* says the Yardarm has "the best hamburgers in the state." Sure enough, they are supergood. But so are the apple-smoked ribs and the Friday fish fry. Not bad imported beer and wine list, either. Hours are 11:00 A.M. to 10:00 P.M. Sunday and Monday, 11:00 A.M. to midnight Wednesday and Thursday, and 11:00 A.M. to 2:00 A.M. Friday and Saturday. Carryouts available. Call (262) 633-8270. $$; ☐

Hobnob. 277 South Sheridan Road, Racine. For a casual, but still elegant, night out, try the Hobnob restaurant and cocktail lounge. Some of the best seafood in the Racine area is served, along with prime Angus beef cuts. It also has full bar service and an excellent wine list. Some folks visit only for the homemade desserts of the month. Hours are 5:30 to 9:00 P.M. Monday through Friday and 5:00 to 10:00 P.M. Saturday and Sunday. The restaurant is closed Christmas Eve and Christmas Day, the Fourth of July, and Super Bowl Sunday. Call (262) 552-8008. $$$; ☐

Apple Holler. 5006 South Sylvania Avenue, Sturtevant (exit 337 off I-94). Live music revue, strawberry and pumpkin picking, kids' activities, gift shop, bakery, and weekend pony and Hogan rides, plus horse-drawn sleigh rides in winter make Apple Holler an all-around stop. And the restaurant serves up lip-smackin' goodies, as well, especially the chicken. Hours are 7:30 A.M. to 9:00 P.M. daily. Closed Christmas Eve and Christmas Day. Call (262) 886–8500. $$; ☐

The Summit. 6825 Washington Avenue, Racine. Candlelight dining for those romantic day trips . . . or evening getaways. Although the steaks, lobster, chops, and seafood are worth several stars, the Summit also serves up fantastic baked potatoes. Gents should probably wear a sport coat. And, please no, nay, never wear a baseball cap while eating here or anywhere for that matter. Hours are 4:30 to 10:00 P.M. Friday; 5:00 to 10:00 P.M. Saturday; 10:00 A.M. to 1:30 P.M. for brunch and 4:00 to 8:00 P.M. for dinner on Sunday; and 5:00 to 9:00 P.M. Monday through Thursday. Call (262) 886–9866. $$$; ☐

Wells Brothers Italian Restaurant. 2148 Mead Street, Racine. Racine's oldest family-run restaurant has been operating for three generations, winning numerous awards. The national publication *Pizza Today* called Wells Brothers one of the Top Ten Independents in the country. Catering to families, the restaurant even has a children's menu. Lunch hours are 11:00 A.M. to 3:00 P.M., and dinner hours are 3:00 to 9:00 P.M. Tuesday through Saturday. On Monday the restaurant closes at 3:00 P.M. Sunday hours are 4:00 to 8:00 P.M. Call (262) 632–4408. $$; ☐

WHERE TO STAY

Comfort Inn. 1154 Prairie Drive, Mount Pleasant. About 1 mile west of Racine, it offers continental breakfasts and nonsmoking rooms. Places to eat are close by. Call (800) 221–2222 or (262) 886–6055. $$; ☐

Lochnaiar Inn. 1121 Lake Avenue, Racine. The inn is a renovated three-story English Tudor home on a bluff overlooking Lake Michigan, for one of the best views in the city. Rooms have private baths, with some offering whirlpool tubs. Suites with fireplaces are also available. Call (262) 633–3300. $$–$$$

The Mansards On-the-Lake. 827 Lake Avenue, Racine. Each suite in this Empire-style home has its own bath, parlor, and fully equipped kitchen with a microwave. You can prepare your own continental breakfast. The facility is nonsmoking. Call (262) 632–1135. $$–$$$; ☐

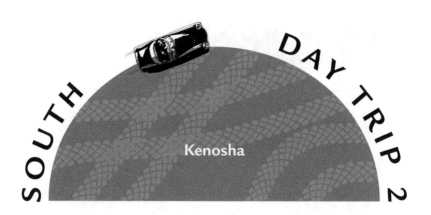

KENOSHA

Kenosha, voted the "Second Best City to Raise a Family" by *Readers Digest* magazine, has been one of Wisconsin's best-kept secrets. Nestled tightly against the shores of Lake Michigan, Kenosha lies between Milwaukee (36 miles to the north) and Chicago (55 miles to the south). Because of its location, Kenosha has become a bedroom neighborhood for both cities, and its many attractions reflect the rapidly growing community.

First known as Pike Creek, Kenosha was established in 1835. Farmers from New England came in droves to work the fertile land just beyond the lake plain. But the community quickly became known as a "harbor city," exporting wheat and importing lumber and other goods from cities around the Great Lakes. Changing its name to Southport in 1836, and incorporated as the county seat in 1850, the city finally settled on its current name.

Kenosha is now in the midst of a complete makeover. New pubs, galleries, arts centers, and restaurants are making their way back into the downtown area. The community's many festivals, as well as its famous charter fishing, also makes Kenosha a great destination. An easy drive on I-94 south, it takes just thirty minutes from Milwaukee. A more scenic route, however, winds along the lakefront, starting in the South Milwaukee area from State Highway 794 to State Highway 62. Turning into State Highway 32 just south of Oak Creek, the road follows the shoreline, allowing the day-tripper to visit some of the smaller communities on the way

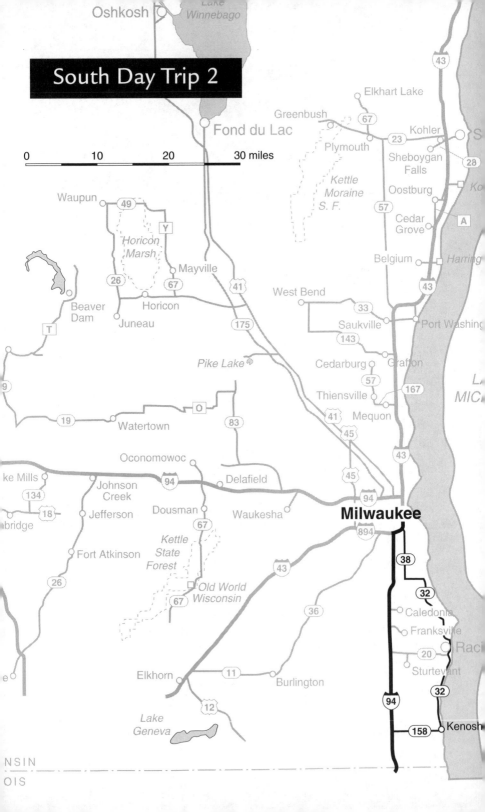

South Day Trip 2

down to Kenosha. A fun way to see the city is via the Kenosha Lakeshore Trolley, which can be rented for special events. Call (862) 652-9986.

Contact the Kenosha Area Convention and Visitors Bureau at (800) 654-7309 or visit its Web site at www.kenoshacvb.com. The bureau is located at 812 Fifty-sixth Street. Hours are 8:00 A.M. to 4:30 P.M. Monday through Friday. The office is closed on holidays and December 23, 24, 30, and 31.

WHERE TO GO

Kenosha Public Museum. 5500 First Avenue, Kenosha. Capture Mammoth Mania at the museum by checking out the big woolies that once roamed this part of southern Wisconsin. The skeletons and assorted bones of several of the great, furry prehistoric beasts are displayed here, giving an in-depth look into Kenosha's distant wild and really wooly past. More than 65,000 other artifacts are also in the museum's large collection of historical objects. The building design, according to the designers, is an "architectural metaphor" of a glacier cutting through the Wisconsin landscape. In fact, the lobby exposes a glacial till wall as it cuts through the stone building. A two-story atrium opens over part of the museum interior, with an overlook offering a marvelous vista of Lake Michigan. In addition to the natural-history displays, fine art is also presented in a wonderful array of painting, sculpture, and craftwork. There's also a good gift shop, with plenty of knickknacks for kid purchases, as well as more major objects for the adult crowd. Call (262) 653-4140.

Kenosha Military Museum. Located on I-94 and State Highway 165, Kenosha. Kids recall driving past this museum on their way down to Chicago and gawking at the tanks and guns on the front lawn, assuming that someone was really scared of their neighbors. The museum is certainly not worried about an invasion from across the street, however, with its sixteenth anniversary celebrated in August 2002. The museum specializes in authentic military aircraft and vehicles from World War I through Desert Storm. Hours are 9:00 A.M. to 5:00 P.M. Monday through Saturday from Memorial Day through Labor Day; open the rest of the year 9:00 A.M. to 5:00 P.M. Wednesday through Saturday and 10:00 A.M. to 5:00 P.M. Sunday. Admission charged. For more information call (262)-857-7933.

Mike Bjorn's Museum Store. 5614 Sixth Avenue, Kenosha. If you are in the mood for a night on the town but have forgotten where you put your tuxedo, Mike Bjorn's store is a perfect place to pick up a spare. Even Clark Gable on Oscar night would be hard-pressed not to walk away with some cool duds. Although the tuxedos are interesting and the men's clothing selection is great, it is actually Bjorn's taste in decorating that draws people into his emporium. The walls are lined with masked mannequins and plastic penguins (which he bought by the truckload). Hanging over the entrance is a display of Egyptian wares straight from the Nile. Shake it, King Tut! The eclectic mix makes for a great shopping experience. Store hours are 10:00 A.M. to 5:30 P.M. weekdays and 10:00 A.M. to 1:00 P.M. Saturday. For more information call (262) 857-7933.

Seebeck Gallery. 5801 Sixth Avenue, Kenosha. John and Victoria Seebeck have one of the best selections of local and regional artists' work in the area. The Seebecks carry the rich oil paintings by Jan Seer, the vibrant watercolors of Bruce Hustad, intricate glasswork from Wes Hunting, and the beautiful pottery of Jeff Shawhan. They also sell jewelry and other "unique gifts." Seebeck's is a must-stop while gallery hopping downtown. Store hours are 10:00 A.M. to 5:30 P.M. Monday through Friday and 10:00 A.M. to 4:00 P.M. Saturday. For more information call (262) 942-8888.

Lemon Street Gallery. 4601 Sheridan Road, Kenosha. Owned and operated by more than seventeen local artists, this gallery is the only co-op of its kind in the area. Named after the original street outside this turn-of-the-twentieth-century building, the gallery features different artists once a month. One of the trendiest art sites in Kenosha, the eclectic media mix makes for a great stopping point to view up-and-coming work. The hours are 11:00 A.M. to 5:00 P.M. Wednesday, Thursday, and Saturday; 11:00 A.M. to 9:00 P.M. Friday; and 1:00 to 4:00 P.M. Sunday. Call (262) 605-4745 for more information.

Kenosha Charter Boat Association. If gallery hopping isn't your cup of tea, then perhaps going out on one of Kenosha's many charter fishing boats is more to your liking. What better way to visit the area than watching your fishing pole bend under the weight of a monster brown trout at the end of the line. Famous for its fantastic fishing, this area of Lake Michigan has been known to give up a few of its granddaddy fish to the persistent angler. If you don't already have a favorite captain, call the association to hook up with some of the best guides on the lake. The fishing season falls between April and October. Contact the association for more information at (800) 522-6699.

Palumbo Civil War Museum. 2001 Alford Drive (Carthage College), Kenosha. Presenting one of the state's largest private collections of Civil War artifacts, this museum features hundreds of items dating from the bloody 1860s. Memorabilia includes artwork, photographs, uniforms, weapons, currency, and personal papers. This esteemed museum is one of the many jewels of the Kenosha area, open from 1:00 to 4:00 P.M. Monday through Friday, September through May. Saturday visits are by appointment only. From June through August the museum is open only by appointment. For more information contact the museum at (262) 551-8500.

Anderson Arts Center. 121 Sixty-sixth Street, Kenosha. Donated to the Kemper Center by the Anderson family in 1990, this 1931 mansion houses work from local artists, as well as youth artworks from the area schools. The center has more than thirty rooms where it hosts lectures, conventions, juried art exhibits, and a series of Christmas events. Gallery hours are 1:00 to 4:00 P.M. Tuesday through Saturday. Contact the center at (262) 653-0481. More information can be gathered on the Web at www.kempercenter.com.

Kenosha Symphony Orchestra. 4917 Sixty-eighth Street, Kenosha. Fine art is not the only thing Kenosha touts to the cultural folks. The city symphony, which celebrated its sixtieth season in 1999, has hosted a variety of national and international musicians. Past guest performers have included clarinetist Eddie Daniels, pianists Ursula Oppins and Santiago Rodrigues, and violinist Rachel Barton. Bizet, Beethoven, Mozart, Stravinsky, Tchaikovsky, and Ravel have all made comfortable homes here in Kenosha. Contact the symphony at (262) 654-9080 for more information.

Dairyland Greyhound Park. 5522 104th Avenue (I-94 and State Highway 158). Stopping here doesn't mean a road trip has actually "gone to the dogs." But watching the greyhounds galloping around this modern track can be fun. The facility is open seven days a week, year-round. Gamblers can also watch other horse and dog track action from around the United States via simulcast television. VIP and clubhouse reservations make for an add-on win for this type of getaway day trip. Call (262) 657-8200 or (800) 233-3357.

LakeView Rec Plex. 9900 Terwall Terrace, Prairie Springs Park. This comprehensive athletic facility has an indoor water park and athletic fieldhouse for basketball, soccer, and volleyball. A one-sixth-mile jogging track, plus fitness center, programs, and classes are available for the out-of-shape and the buff. The Plex is also the kick-off point for several regional marathons. It's located along State Highway 165 and County Highway H in the village of Pleasant Prairie. Hours are 4:30 A.M. to 10:00 P.M. weekdays; 6:00 A.M. to 8:00 P.M. Saturday; and 9:00 A.M. to 6:00 P.M. Sunday. Call (262) 947-0437.

University of Wisconsin-Parkside. The university not only teaches the masses the basics of science and literature but also has a fantastic performance space. Arts Alive, a performance series that brings in internationally acclaimed dance, music, and theater, has its home here in the Communication Arts Theater. UW-Parkside also offers its Accent on Enrichment, featuring professional touring groups and Broadway favorites. The university's Department of Dramatic Arts also highlights its young thespians here. Contact the theater at (262) 595-2345.

WHERE TO SHOP

The Original Outlet Mall. 7700 120th Avenue off I-94, Kenosha. If shopping is your bag, then this is the place. With more than a hundred outlet stores, ranging from furniture to clothes, this is a shop-o-holic's dream. For a complete rundown of outlets, call (262) 857-7961. The hours are 10:00 A.M. to 9:00 P.M. Monday through Saturday and 11:00 A.M. to 6:00 P.M. Sunday.

Tenuta's. 3203 Fifty-second Street (State Highway 158). A Kenosha fixture since 1950, Tenuta's offers the best Italian deli and food store this side of Rome. You want tortellini? You got it. You need a roast beef and chedder foot-long sandwich? You got that, too! And then there is mostaccioli, linguine, polenta, stuffed green peppers, pasta faggioli, and stewed Italian green beans. Hmmm. Canned and boxed foodstuffs overflow the counters, along with fresh bread, cheese, and a wine stock that usually offers a two-for-one price. Tenuta's also knows how to treat the cigar smoker and whiskey drinkers in the family, with its selection of great smokes and mellow beverages also for sale. In the summer sit outside under the umbrellas and chow down on Italian sausage sandwiches, homemade pasta salad, and oodles of other goodies. Call (262) 657–9001. Here's a road tip. Purchase a pound of meatballs, slices of cheese, a container of giant green Italian olives, and maybe a chocolate-covered cannoli or two. Plus a bottled root beer. You can't beat this lunch while on the way to the next stop on your day-trip outing to Kenosha. Just be careful of dripping sauce while driving.

WHERE TO EAT

Hob Nob Restaurant and Lounge. 277 South Sheridan Road, Kenosha. After a night at the symphony, stop into the Hob Nob. Boasting the area's most extensive seafood selection, this restaurant offers white-tablecloth service as well as a full wine and bar menu. Established in 1954, this is one of Kenosha's best. The view is great, overlooking Lake Michigan. Call (262) 552–8008 for hours and more information. $$$

Brewmasters Restaurant and Pub. Two locations: 4017 Eightieth Street (262-694-9050) and 1170 Twenty-second Avenue (262-552-2805). Reminiscent of an English pub, Brewmasters claims to be the first brewpub in the Midwest. Offering steaks, barbecued ribs, and seafood, as well as a variety of homemade beers, the restaurant also has daily food specials and seasonal brews. Their hours are 11:00 A.M. to midnight, seven days a week. $$; ☐

Boathouse Pub and Eatery. 4917 Seventh Avenue, Kenosha. With a beautiful view of Lake Michigan, this is a great place to go after a night of theater or when just beginning a night on the town. The menu offers seafood, sandwiches, and Jamaican Grills, plus impressive specials. The Boathouse also provides courtesy customer docking for boats up to 50 feet in length. Live entertainment on Wednesday, Thursday, and Saturday. Hours are 11:00 A.M. till closing, seven days a week. $$; ☐

The Brat Stop. Northwest corner of the intersection of I-94 and State Highway 50, Kenosha. Home of the "World Famous Bratwurst Sandwich," this is a beer-and-brat oasis. It has a huge selection of imported and domestic beers, as well as a cheese shop. This place couldn't get anymore Wisconsin, especially with its seventy televisions tuned to the Packer games for gridiron overload. Hours are 8:00 A.M. to midnight, seven days a week. $

House of Gerhard. 3927 Seventy-fifth Street, Kenosha. If you want a little taste of Germany while you are visiting all the eateries in Kenosha, head on down to this culinary Teutonic Eden. Menu items, such as beef rouladen and wienerschnitzel, flow from the kitchen like a good German beer from the tap. Contact them at (262) 694–5212. Hours are 11:30 A.M. to 2:30 P.M. and 4:30 P.M. to closing Monday through Friday, and 4:30 P.M. to closing on Saturday. $$; ☐

Little Europe at Timber Ridge. I–94 and State Highway 50, Kenosha. If German cuisine isn't hitting the hunger spot, then how about a little Bohemian food? Try Eastern European staples such as Hungarian goulash, pierogies, chicken paprikash, and kolacky—they might just do the trick. The restaurant also has a full deli, so you can take a little taste of Bohemia with you. The number to call for great food is (262) 857–9073. Hours are 11:00 A.M. to 9:00 P.M. Wednesday through Saturday and 9:00 A.M. to 9:00 P.M. Sunday. $$; ☐

Mangia Trattoria. 5717 Sheridan Road, Kenosha. A little slice of Italy in Wisconsin, the scent of rosemary, garlic, and the smoke from the wood-burning oven remind the diner of a warm night along the Mediterranean Sea. This is a comfortably snug place to hunker in and enjoy great food over witty conversation and a bit o' bubbly. Call (262) 652–4285 for more information about specials. Lunch hours are 11:30 A.M. to 2:00 P.M. Monday through Friday. Dinner hours are 5:00 to 9:00 P.M. Monday through Thursday, 5:00 to 10:00 P.M. Friday and Saturday, and 4:00 to 9:00 P.M. Sunday. $$$; ☐

WHERE TO STAY

Park Ridge Inn. 6121 Seventy-fifth Street, Kenosha. Touted as Kenosha's most centrally located motel, this is a great place to stay after a night on the town. Call (262) 694–2510 or (888) 897–2288 for more information. $$; ☐

Best Western Executive Inn. 7220 122nd Avenue, Kenosha. If you want to spoil yourself, this is the place. More than 155 deluxe rooms are available, with suites including Jacuzzis and outdoor terraces, as well as an indoor swimming pool. Call (262) 857–7699 or (800) 438–3932 for more information. $$$; ☐

Holiday Inn Express Harborside. 5125 Sixth Avenue (downtown), Kenosha. A great place to wake up to a view of Lake Michigan. The facilities include a whirlpool, a game room, and an indoor pool.

A complimentary continental breakfast is offered daily. Call (262) 658-3281 or (800) 465-4329 for more information. $$$; ☐

Country Inn & Suites. 7011 122nd Avenue, Kenosha. After eating in all the great restaurants in Kenosha, you may want to spend some time here to rest and recuperate. In addition to comfortable beds, the hotel also has an exercise room. If you just want to kick back, it also provides premium movie channels and cable television. Call (262) 857-3680 for more information. $$; ☐

Appendix A: State Parks and Forests Information

A vehicle admission sticker is necessary for all motor vehicles stopping in state parks. Motorists can purchase a ticket either at the park or through the state Department of Natural Resources. One-hour stickers are available at most state parks and forests.

State park entry fee: $5.00 for a daily pass and $20.00 for the year. Fees for out-of-staters are $10.00 for a day pass and $30.00 for an annual sticker.

Camping fees: Fees for residents are $7.00 to $10.00 per night; for nonresidents, $9.00 to $12.00. Sites with electricity are $3.00 per night extra. Recreation fee of $9.50.

State Trail Pass: A trail pass is necessary for all persons age sixteen or older who are biking, horseback riding, or cross-country skiing on designated trails. An annual trail pass costs $10.00; a daily pass is $3.00

For information on Wisconsin State Parks, forests, and trails, or to request campground reservation forms, contact the parks directly, or call or write:

Wisconsin Department of Natural Resources
Bureau of Parks and Recreation
Box 7921
Madison, WI 53707-7921
(608) 266-2621
e-mail: wiparks@dnr.state.wi.us
Web site: www.dnr.state.wi.us

STATE PARKS AND FORESTS KEY

BC	Bicycling	NC	Nature center
BR	Boat ramp	P	Picnicking
C	Canoeing	PL	Playground
CC	Cross-country skiing	S	Swimming
E	Electrical hookup	SH	Showers
F	Fishing	SK	Skiing
G	Golfing nearby	SN	Snowmobiling
HB	Horseback riding	SR	Sewer hookup
L	Laundry	W	Water hookup
N	Naturalist on duty		

The following state parks and state forests are within a day-tripper's excursion from Milwaukee.

NORTH

Kohler-Andrae State Park. This 1,000-acre park is on the shore of Lake Michigan, with wooded campsites and 2 miles of beach. Fee. Write 1020 Beach Park Lane, Sheboygan, WI 53081; (920) 451–4080. BC, CC, E, F, G, HB, NC, P, PL, S, SH, SN.

Harrington Beach State Park. Walk for a mile along the rolling waters of Lake Michigan. Fee. Write 531 County Highway D, Belgium, WI 53004; (262) 285–3015. BC, P, PL, S, SN.

Point Beach State Forest. The forest's 6-mile-long beach is one of the best along Lake Michigan. Fee. Write 9400 County Highway O, Two Rivers, WI 54241; (920) 794–7480. BC, CC, G, P, PL.

NORTHWEST

Kettle Moraine State Forest, Northern Unit. More than 29,000 acres are open to the public for outdoor recreational opportunities, with 133 miles of trails. Ice Age Visitor Center open daily. Fee. Write N1765 County Highway G, Campbellsport, WI 53010; (920) 626–2116 Monday through Friday, (920) 533–8322 weekends. BC, CC, F, G, HB, P, S, SH, SN.

Pike Lake-Kettle Moraine State Forest. Tour the 1,350-foot glacial ridge overlooking the state forest. C, CC, F, G, P, SH, SN, W.

SOUTH

Kettle Moraine State Forest, Southern Unit. This 21,000-acre parcel of glacial hills and lakes has hiking, biking, and skiing opportunities. Fee. Write S91 W39091 State Highway 59, Eagle, WI 53119; (262) 594–6200. BC, CC, F, G, HB, P, S, SH, SN.

Bong Recreational Area. Encompassing 4,515 acres of open space, it is available for all types of multiuse recreational opportunities. Fee. Write 26313 Burlington Road, Kansasville, WI 53139; (262) 652–0377. BC, CC, F, G, N, NC, P, PL.

SOUTHWEST

Big Foot Beach State Park. Tucked away on the shore of Lake Geneva, the park has wooded campsites, a sand beach, and picnic areas. Fee. Write 1452 County Highway H, Lake Geneva, WI 53147; (262) 248–2528. BC, CC, F, G, P, PL, S, SH, SN.

Browntown-Cadiz Springs State Recreational Area. Two spring-fed lakes and a 600-acre wildlife refuge are open for fishing and other recreational experiences. Day use only. Fee. Write N3150 State Highway 81, Monroe, WI 53566; (608) 966–3777 in summer, (608) 325–4844 in winter. BC, CC, F.

New Glarus Woods State Park. Located adjacent to the Sugar River Bike Trail, there are numerous hiking and cycling opportunities in the vicinity. Fee. Write Box 256, Monroe, WI 53566-0256; (608) 527–2355 in summer; (608) 527–2335 year-round. BC, CC, F, G, P, PL, S, SH, SN.

WEST

Lapham Peak-Kettle Moraine State Forest. Climb a 45-foot-high observation tower atop the highest peak in Waukesha County. Enclosed shelter. Fee. Write W329 N846 County Highway C, Delafield, WI 53018; (262) 646–3025. BC, CC, G.

Blue Mound State Park. This is the only state park with a swimming pool. Perched on the highest point in southern Wisconsin, the park presents magnificent views in all directions. Fee. Write 4350 Mounds Park Road, Box 98, Blue Mounds, WI 53517; (608) 437–5711. BC, CC, F, G, P, PL, S, SH, SN, SR, W.

Governor Dodge State Park. Steep hills, two lakes, and a waterfall provide the scenery. Great opportunities for hiking. Fee. Write 4175 State Road 23, Dodgeville, WI 53533; (608) 935–2315. BC, C, CC, F, G, HB, P, PL, S, SH, SN, SR, W.

Tower Hill State Park. Visit the park's restored shot tower and historic area. Excellent hiking along the bluffs near the Wisconsin River. Open mid-April through October. Fee. Write 5808 County Highway C, Spring Green, WI 53588; (608) 588–2116. C, P, S.

Appendix B:
Festivals and Celebrations

Here is a sample of the numerous events that take place in Wisconsin all through the year. Since dates and times of the events are subject to change, please refer to the telephone number(s) provided with each entry, the local convention and visitors bureau, or the state division of tourism (see Introduction) for updated information and more opportunities for fun and entertainment.

JANUARY

WEST

WISCONSIN DELLS: Flake Out Festival. Late January. Entertaining for everybody, this annual event features kite flying, snowman making, ice skating, horse-drawn sleigh rides, fireworks, and a lot more. Come on Saturday evening to see the glowing hot-air balloons. (800) 223–3557.

NORTH

GREEN BAY: Hiking and Bird-watching. Early January. Meander the trails at the Bay Beach Wildlife Sanctuary. (920) 391–3671.

SOUTHWEST

FORT ATKINSON: SnowFORT. Late January. This is a family game night with fort-building contests and an indoor hobby extravaganza where enthusiasts can purchase materials for quilts, train sets, woodworking, and other crafts. Held at the Fort Atkinson High School commons, 925 Lexington Boulevard. Call (920) 563–3210.

BURLINGTON: Chilly Chocolate Days. Last weekend in January. Meander through the booths at the city craft fair and save time to sample the chili and chocolate goodies. Held at the Burlington High School. Call (262) 763-6044.

FEBRUARY

SOUTHWEST

NORTH FREEDOM: Snow Train. Second half of February. An authentic steam train will take you on a special tour across the snow. Dinner is available both in coach and first class. Make sure you have your camera if taking the tour at night. Reservations are recommended. Mid-Continent Railway Museum. (800) 930-1385.

NORTH

MANITOWOC: Valentine Victorian Tea. Early February. Sip in classic style at the Manitowoc Historical Society. Call (920) 684-4445.

NORTHWEST

GREEN BAY: Night Cross-Country Skiing. Mid-February, depending on snow conditions. Schuss the slopes under the moonlight at the Bay Beach Wildlife Sanctuary from 6:30 to 8:00 P.M. Reservations required. Call (920) 391-3671.

MARCH

SOUTH

RACINE: Sugarin' Off Pancake Sundays. All-you-can-eat pancake breakfasts with real maple sugar are held each weekend at the River Bend Nature Center. Tour the sugarbush groves to see how maple syrup is tapped. For hours call (920) 639-0930.

NORTHWEST

APPLETON: Adopt a Bucket. Beginning and second half of March. Maple syrup by the bucket. Watch it being made or help yourself to it. At Gordon Bubolz Nature Preserve, they will show you how to do it. Afterward, dribble abundantly on ice cream. 4815 North Lyndell Drive. (920) 731-6041.

NEW LONDON: St. Patrick's Day Parade & Irish Fest. One of the largest celebrations of Irish heritage in Wisconsin: more than one hundred units, including seven bands for lots of music, concessions, and an Irish market. Of course, the town renames itself as "New Dublin" for the day. The parade steps off at 1:00 P.M. at the corner of North Water and Shawano Streets, but other Gaelic-themed events start as early as 11:00 A.M. and go on until 7:00 P.M. (920) 982-5822.

MILWAUKEE: St. Patrick's Day Parade. Always on St. Patrick's Day, except when it falls on a Saturday or on a Sunday (call for the exact date). The parade starts at noon in front of Wisconsn Avenue and Fourth Street and it features an ever-increasing number of units, currently about one hundred. A party follows, held at the Irish Cultural and Heritage Center, 2133 West Wisconsin Avenue; (414) 345-8800 or (414) 276-6696.

NORTH

TWO RIVERS: Lions Club Smelt Fry. Late March. Held at the Two Rivers Community House. The members of the benevolent association provide tasty dinners of these tiny lake fish, with all the side trimmings of fries, pies, and extras. Hours are 4:30 to 9:00 P.M. Call (920) 794-1222.

APRIL

NORTHWEST

CHILTON: Spring Bird Camps. Usually the first Saturday of April. Held at the Kaytee Avian Education Center from 9:30 A.M. to noon. Call (800) 669-9580.

SOUTHWEST

BURLINGTON: Annual State Yo-Yo Competition. April. Held at the Spinning Top Museum, 533 Milwaukee Avenue. Take part in classes, look over the exhibits, and talk with yo-yo experts to learn the latest techniques. Call (262) 763-3946.

MAY

NORTHWEST

MISHICOT: Villagewide Rummage Sale. Mid-May weekend. Everywhere you turn are bargains in basements, garages, and parks. Call (920) 755-2525.

    OSHKOSH: Festival of Spring. Mid-May. Tour the gardens of the Paine Art Center & Arboretum, 1410 Algoma Boulevard. Call (920) 235-6903, ext. 27.

SOUTHWEST

BURLINGTON: Street Dance. Mid-May. Dancing begins at 6:00 and runs to 11:00 P.M. Call the Burlington Chamber of Commerce, (262) 763-6044.

    BURLINGTON: Jaycees Annual Brat Day and Hydroplane Races. Held on Memorial Day in Echo Park. Admission. Call the Burlington Chamber of Commerce, (262) 763-6044.

    ELKHORN and BURLINGTON: Memorial Day Parades. Held on Memorial Day. Call the Elkhorn Chamber of Commerce, (262) 723-5788.

SOUTH

RACINE: Sixth Street Artwalk. Late May. Local artists show their wares in downtown businesses, with galleries hosting evening receptions. Hours are 10:00 A.M. to 9:00 P.M. Call (262) 639-3995.

    KENOSHA: Fly In/Drive In Pancake Breakfast. 8:00 A.M. to noon, usually the third Sunday in May. Eat on the fly! Kenosha

Regional Airport 9420 52nd Street, Kenosha 53144. Call (262) 658-2025.

JUNE

SOUTHWEST

NEW GLARUS: Swiss Polkafest. Twirl away an early June weekend to the tunes of German and Swiss polka music. Led by major performers such as the Mike Austin Band, Verne Meisner, and other bandleaders, dancers hop and skip their way around the big-top show tent. Things jump from early Saturday afternoon until 1:00 A.M. and from early Sunday until 10:00 P.M. For details on Polkafest write Box 713, New Glarus, WI 53574-0713 or call (608) 527-2095 or (800) 527-6838.

NEW GLARUS: Heidi Festival. June. The story of Heidi, the Swiss girl who goes to live with her grandfather in the Alps, has been a New Glarus tradition since the early 1960s. Performances in the New Glarus High School are held at 7:30 P.M. Friday, 10:00 A.M. and 1:30 P.M. Saturday, and 1:30 P.M. Sunday during the Heidi Festival. Swiss music, dance, and a parade round out the festivities. For details, times, and ticket prices, call (608) 527-6838.

CAMBRIDGE: Pottery Festival. Early June. Tour the Rowe Pottery Works and check out the art galleries and gift shops around town.

ELKHORN: Antique and Flea Markets. Late June. Walworth County fairgrounds. Call NL Productions, (262) 723-3651.

WEST BEND: Farmers' Market. Held downtown from 7:30 A.M. to 11:00 A.M. every Saturday from June through October. Call (262) 338-3909.

SOUTH

KENOSHA: Good Old Summertime Art Fair. Civic Center Park. Held between 10:00 A.M. and 4:00 P.M. on the first weekend in June. More than ninety artists show their creative side. Sponsored by the Kenosha Art Association. Call (262) 654-0065.

FRANKSVILLE: Franksville Kraut Festival. End of June at Memorial Park. Look for carnival rides, bingo, craft booths, live music, and games. Admission. Call (262) 639-4088.

JULY

SOUTHWEST

FONTANA: Fireworks on the Beach. Fourth of July. Call the Geneva Lake West Chamber of Commerce, (262) 275-9300.

BURLINGTON: Garden Tour. Tours showcasing home gardens run from 11:00 A.M. to 5:00 P.M. every even-numbered year. Call the Burlington Area Garden Club at (262) 767-0913.

NORTH

MANITOWOC: German Fest. Held in mid-July. Learn more about the area's German heritage at this oompah-heavy festival at Pinecrest Historical Village, 3 miles west of I-43 (exit 152) on Manitowoc County Highway JJ. Call (920) 684-4445.

NORTHWEST

OSHKOSH: EAA AirVenture. Thousands of visitors and planes make Oshkosh the busiest airport in the world on the last week of July. Activities are held around the community, with the bulk of exhibits and displays on the EAA Air Adventure Museum grounds, 3000 Poberezny Drive. Call (920) 303-0013.

OSHKOSH: Public Museum Art Fair. Early July. Held at the Oshkosh Museum, 1331 Algoma Boulevard. The exhibition features top painters and sculptors. Call (920) 424-4731. The Faire on the Green is held at the Paine Art Center on the same weekend. The Paine is at 1410 Algoma Boulevard. Call (920) 235-6903.

SOUTH

BRISTOL: Bristol Progress Days. Early July. Held from 8:00 A.M. to 10:00 P.M. in Hanson Park. Call (262) 857-2740.

RACINE: Salmon-O-Rama. Mid-July in Racine's Festival Park. The world's largest freshwater fishing event draws contestants from around the world. Concerts, kids' area, auctions, and exhibits round out the fun. Call (262) 884-6400.

AUGUST

SOUTH

RACINE: Armenian Fest. Usually held on the first weekend in August. Sample a wide range of Armenian foods. Be sure not to miss the pastries. Hours are 11:00 A.M. to 4:00 P.M. Call (262) 639-0531.

WILMOT: Kenosha County Fair. Mid-August. Check out the pigs, the tractors, and all the other fun at the fair. Take I-94 to Kenosha County Highway C to Kenosha County Highway W. Call (262) 862-6121.

NORTH

ALGOMA: Shanty Days Fishing Contest. Early August. Try for the big ones on the pier or from your boat. Call (920) 487-2433.

MANITOWOC: Indo-Chinese New Year Celebration. Mid-August at Silver Creek Park. Numerous Hmong families emigrated to Wisconsin after the Vietnam War. Their colorful New Year's program brings the East to the West. Call (920) 684-1228.

WEST BEND: Maxwell Street Days. First weekend in August. Held on downtown streets. Merchants offer plenty of bargains from 7:00 A.M. to 7:00 P.M. Call (262) 338-3909.

WEST BEND: Germanfest. Held the last weekend in August from 10:00 A.M. to 11:00 P.M. Friday, 7:30 A.M. to 11:30 P.M. Saturday, and 11:00 A.M. to 8:30 P.M. Sunday. German music, dancing, and foods enliven the downtown. Call (262) 338-3909.

SOUTHWEST

BURLINGTON: Franciscan Harvest Festival. Mid-August, from 9:00 A.M. to 5:00 P.M. at the St. Francis Retreat Center in Burlington. Car show, food, arts and crafts, music, and games. Call (262) 763-3600.

LAKE GENEVA: Maxwell Street Days. Late August. Loads of bargains can be had by strolling down the streets of town. Call (262) 248-4416.

SEPTEMBER

SOUTH

RACINE: Tour of Historic Places. Last weekend in September. Tour the city's historic homes. Noon to 5:00 P.M. Call (262) 634-5748.

SOUTHWEST

EAGLE: Civil War Encampment. Labor Day weekend. The grounds of Old World Wisconsin turn back 150 years to memorialize the War Between the States. Observe camp life, listen to period music, and sample foods. Call (262) 594-6300.

ELKHORN: Walworth County Fair. Since 1849, farmers have proudly shown off their produce and animals to the city folk each autumn. Displays, music, dancing—all the works. Call (262) 723-3228.

NEW GLARUS: Wilhelm Tell Festival. Held on Labor Day weekend since 1938, more than 200 local volunteers present the Friedrich Schiller tale of legendary Wilhelm Tell. Overnight camping is allowed on the Tell Grounds, with storytelling and treats. An Alpine music festival, outdoor art fair, book sale, ethnic fashion show, cast reunion picnic, and street dance round out the activities. Call the New Glarus Information Center at (800) 527-6838 or visit the Web site at www.newglarus-wi.com.

WISCONSIN DELLS WEST: Polish Fest. Held at Riverview Park and waterworld, this annual celebration of all things Polish brings alive music, culture, and art. Call (800) 659-6065.

NORTH

GERMANTOWN: Hunsrucker Oktoberfest. Held in late September in the Historical Park. German food and music. Admission charged. Hours are noon to 9:00 P.M. Call (262) 628-3170.

NORTHWEST

APPLETON: Octoberfest. Late September. More than one hundred food booths sponsored by area charities, plus music, crafts, and apple bake-off contribute to autumn fun. Downtown. 9:00 A.M. to 6:00 P.M. Call (920) 734-3377.

NORTH

DE PERE: Fall Fest. Late September. Family event with children's games, antique car show, bands, and food. Held on St. Norbert College campus from 10:00 A.M. to 4:00 P.M. (920) 337-3181.

FOND DU LAC: Frostbite Sailboat Race. Late September. This 15-mile race across Lake Winnebago is open to all cruising sailboats. A continental breakfast is provided for racers. Trophies awarded. Lakeside Park. Call (800) 937-9123.

OCTOBER

SOUTHWEST

DELAVAN: Oktoberfest. Early October. Celebrate autumn with music, dancing, food, and refreshing beverages at Lake Lawn Resort. Call (262) 728-7950.

LAKE GENEVA: Oktoberfest. Early October. Food, crafts, music, and children's activities make for excitement in downtown Lake Geneva, from 10:00 A.M. to 5:00 P.M. Call (262) 248-4416.

NORTH

TWO RIVERS: Applefest. Early October at the Two Rivers Community House, from 9:00 A.M. to 4:00 P.M. The area's apple growers lay out the best of their fruit in bulk, as well as butter and jelly. Call the Two Rivers Visitor Information Center, (920) 793-2490 or (888) 857-3529; www.ci.two-rivers.wi.us.

CEDARBURG: Arts Weekend. Early October. Take a gallery walk of Cedarburg's leading art showcases. Held from 3:00 to 9:00 P.M. Friday and from 10:00 A.M. to 5:00 P.M. Saturday and Sunday. Call the Cedarburg Visitors Bureau, (262) 377–9620 or (800) 237–2874; www.cedarburg.org.

WEST

MADISON: Isthmus Jazz Festival. First weekend in October. The nation's top jazz bands and soloists appear at the Madison Civic Center from 7:00 to 11:00 P.M. Friday and from noon to 5:00 P.M., with show at 8:00 P.M., Saturday. Call (608) 266–6550.

OCONOMOWOC: Country Craftfest. Early October. Juried arts-and-crafts fair, along with indoor and outdoor sales booths, shows off a wide range of regional talent. More than sixty exhibits show their wares at the First Congregational Church from 9:00 A.M. to 4:00 P.M. (262) 567–4461.

HARTFORD: Polkafest. Mid-October. Live music sets feet a' flyin' around the dance floor at the Chandelier Ballroom, 150 Jefferson Avenue, from 5:00 P.M. to midnight Friday, 1:00 P.M. to midnight Saturday, and 11:00 A.M. to 6:00 P.M. Sunday. Call (262) 673–7800.

EAGLE: Autumn on the Farms. Mid-October. Historic re-creation of harvest time at Old World Wisconsin from 10:00 A.M. to 5:00 P.M. Call (262) 594–6300.

NORTHWEST

PLYMOUTH: Heritage & Arts Festival. Late September. The city marks its heritage with music, art shows, and walking tours of historic homes from 9:00 A.M. to 4:00 P.M. Call the Plymouth Chamber of Commerce, (920) 893–0079.

GREENBUSH: Civil War Weekend. Early October. One of the largest Civil War reenactments in the Midwest takes place on the grounds of the Old Wade House historical site from 9:00 A.M. to 5:00 P.M. Saturday and Sunday. Call (800) 937–9123.

GREENBUSH: Pumpkinfest. Third Saturday in October. Festival arts and crafts, with a pumpkin pancake breakfast. Held from 8:00 A.M. to 4:00 P.M. Call (920) 755–3411.

NOVEMBER

NORTH

MANITOWOC: Maritime Holiday Open House. Late November. Celebrate Wisconsin's maritime heritage at the Wisconsin Maritime Museum, 75 Maritime Drive. Hours are 7:00 to 9:00 P.M. Call (920) 684-0218.

DE PERE: Celebration of Lights. Late November. Downtown De Pere holds its annual holiday program with lights and displays showcased through the end of December. Call (920) 338-0000.

GREEN BAY: Garden of Lights. Weekends from the end of November until Christmas. The Green Bay Botanical Garden offers walking and wagon tours around the property decorated for the holidays. Sponsored by the Wisconsin Public Service Corporation. Call (920) 490-9457.

GREEN BAY: Walk the Wild Lights. November 24. Holiday festival featuring lights and music amid the animal compounds, until Christmas. Call (920) 434-7841.

SOUTH

RACINE: Festival of Trees. Mid-November. More than eighty decorated trees bring the holiday season alive with glitter and light in Racine's Festival Hall. Live entertainment. Call (262) 634-6002.

SOUTHWEST

DELAVAN: Tree-Lighting Ceremony. Late November. Tower Park. Call (262) 728-5095.

JEFFERSON: Fall Harvest Dinner and Bake Sale. Early November. Immanuel United Methodist Church, 201 East Racine Street. Dinner, featuring hot ham, potatoes, cranberry pie, and other delicacies, from 4:00 to 7:00 P.M. Call (920) 674-4511.

FORT ATKINSON: Blackhawk Artists Art Show and Sale. Mid-November. Held annually at the Hoard Historical Museum, 407 Merchants Avenue. Call (920) 563-7769.

WEST

WATERTOWN: Christmas in the Octagon House. Last weekend in November, from 1:00 to 4:00 P.M. Tour this old home, hear the choral groups caroling, and purchase some craft items. Call (920) 261–6320 or (920) 261–2796.

DECEMBER

NORTH

MANITOWOC: Downtown Walkabout. First Saturday in December. Stroll the streets of historic downtown Manitowoc. Call (920) 684–4450.

DE PERE: Santa House and Carriage Rides. Early December. Keep the kids excited by bringing them to the White Pillars Museum, for programs hosted by the De Pere Historical Society. Hours are 5:00 to 8:00 P.M. Call (920) 336–3877.

GREEN BAY: Spirit of Christmas Past. Weekends leading up to Christmas. Heritage Hill State Historical Park comes alive with the lights and sounds of an old-time Christmas. Call (920) 448–5150 or (800) 721–5150.

SOUTHWEST

CAMBRIDGE: Cambridge Country Christmas. First weekend in December. Tree lighting, arrival of Santa, caroling, hot apple cider, and roasted chestnuts. Call (608) 423–3780.

FORT ATKINSON: Community-wide Holiday Parade. First weekend in December. Special holiday activities throughout town. Call (920) 563–3210.

JEFFERSON: Chili and Wild Game Cookoff & Holiday Music Jam. Held in early December at Jefferson County Fair Park. For details call (920) 674–5782.

WHITEWATER: Winterfest. Held in early December, with a Christmas parade, decorating contest, teen dance, breakfast with Santa. Call (262) 473–4005.

BURLINGTON: Christmas at the Top Museum. December 26 and 27. Spinning Top Museum, 533 Milwaukee Avenue. Reservations required. Call (262) 763-3946.

BURLINGTON: Burlington Liars Club. Held on the last day of the year, the club selects the Championship Lie. To submit a tall tale, or become a lifetime member send $1.00 with entry to the Burlington Liars Club, c/o John Soeth, 179 Beth Court, Burlington, WI 53105. You will receive a membership card.

WEST

LAKE MILLS: Lake Mills Classic Christmas. First weekend in December. Fargo Mansion opens with an arts-and-crafts show. Also a tour of homes, music in the park, and Santa. Plus horse-drawn wagon rides, 11:00 A.M. to noon. Call (920) 648-3585.